THE FELON'S TRACK

General Shields

Dedication.

TO

GENERAL JAMES SHIELDS

UNITED STATES SENATOR, ETC.

DEAR SIR,—

In dedicating to you this narrative, I have been influenced by one consideration only. I have no title to your friendship. I cannot claim the most remote affinity with your career in arms. There is nothing connected with this sad fragment of history, either in fact or hope, to suggest any association with your name or achievements. But as my main object is to show that Ireland's failure was not owing to native recreancy or cowardice, I feel satisfied that of all living men, your position and character will best sustain the sole aim of my present labour and ambition.

In past history, Ireland holds a high place; but her laurels were won on foreign fields, and the jealous literary ambition which raised adequate monuments to these stormy times denied to her swords the distinction they vindicated for themselves in the hour of combat. The most brilliant, unscrupulous and daring historian of France degraded the niggard praise he accorded them by making it the medium of a false and contemptible sneer. "The Irish soldier," says Voltaire, "fights bravely everywhere but in his own country."

Without pausing here to vindicate that country from such ungrateful slander, it is enough to say that you were not placed in the same unhappy position as the illustrious exiles from the last Irish army—soldiers of fortune in the service of a foreign prince. You were a citizen of this free Republic, and a volunteer in its ranks; it was *your* country, and you and your compatriots who followed the same standard did no dishonour to those who were bravest among the brave on the best debated fields in Europe.

In the wreck of every hope, all who yet cherish the ambition of realising for Ireland an independent destiny, point to your career as an encouraging augury, if not a complete justification for not despairing of their country. It is because I am among those that I have claimed the honour of inscribing your name on the first page of this, my latest labour in her cause.

I remain, dear Sir,

Very respectfully and sincerely yours,

MICHAEL DOHENY.

New York, Sept. 20, 1849.

PREFACE

The Irish Confederation still awaits its historian. Three of its leaders have left narratives of its brief and momentous career, but, of the three, Doheny alone participated in the Insurrection that dug the political grave of Young Ireland. In "The Felon's Track," written hot on his escape from the stricken land, he tells the story vividly and passionately. It has morals deducible for all manner of Irishmen, and one for those English statesmen who comfort themselves with the illusion that Irish Nationalism, like Jacobitism, is a platonic sentiment. The man who, roused from his bed at midnight by tapping fingers on his window and a voice whispering that insurrection was afoot, rose and rode away in the darkness to join himself to its desperate fortunes was no young man ardent for adventure. Michael Doheny, when he left his home and his career to engage in the fatal enterprise, was a sober middle-aged barrister, a man of weight and fortune into which he had built himself by the hard toil of twenty years. His social anchorages were deep-cast—and no mere sentiment provokes such a man to throw aside the hard-won harvest of his life and risk the rebel's or the felon's fate.

In the leadership of the Young Ireland party Michael Doheny was, save Smith O'Brien, the oldest man and, like O'Brien, his counsels while courageous were always restrained. There was little other likeness between the men. Doheny sprang from the poorest class of the Irish farmers. At Brookfield, near Fethard in Tipperary, where he was born in May, 1805, he followed the plough on his father's little holding, earning literally his bread in the sweat of his brow, and educating himself how he could, for his people were too poor to pay for his schooling. His indomitable perseverance and his thirst for knowledge overcame the formidable obstacles of fortune, and at thirty years of age the poor peasant boy had become a barrister of reputation for ability and fearlessness. He returned to his native county to become the most popular and trusted of its "counsellors"—the advocate who did not fear to face and beard Influence and Ascendancy in its courts. The city of Cashel had had much of its property alienated and long enjoyed by local magnates whom none were willing to offend. Doheny fought and defeated them and regained the purloined estates for the people. He was made Legal Adviser to the Borough of Cashel and when later the pestilence fell upon the place, and even the men employed to carry the sick to hospital lost courage and fled, Doheny showed the same manly example of citizenship and duty which years later forced him "on the Felon's path," by carrying in his strong arms to shelter and relief the deserted victims of the plague. Davis who marked his character, and knew that on such men a free and self-respecting Ireland must be rebuilt induced him to enter the Repeal movement of 1842, and in its councils he swayed the influence of a strong, sincere, able and incorruptible man until the Association fell into the toils of the English Whigs. Then he quitted it and formally adhered to the Young Irelanders. To them he was invaluable for his eloquence— less brilliant and polished than that of Meagher, but more effective in its appeal to the heart of the peasantry whom Doheny knew better than any of his colleagues. On a platform he triumphed, but with the pen he was often ineffective. His admiration and reverence for Davis misled him into laboriously imitating Davis's style, and the result was what it must always be when one man attempts to express his ideas not in his own way but as he thinks a greater man would express them. Much that would have been impressive and lucid as Doheny becomes unimpressive and clouded as Doheny-Davis. In a few of his verses and "The Felon's Track" Doheny the writer will survive. As a man who gave up all to help his country and served her like a gallant son, his memory must be honoured while Ireland has virtue.

The Irish Confederation, on whose council Doheny sat, was noble in conception, true in policy and able and honest in its membership. Never in the leadership of the modern Nationalist movement has there been the peer in genius and character of the men who founded and inspired that brilliant and short-lived organisation. In its career it went nearer to bridging the differences of class and creed in Ireland than any previous organisation since the Volunteers at Dungannon proclaimed themselves Irishmen and hailed their oppressed Catholic countrymen fellow-citizens. But the Confederation was not yet six months old when it was called on to face a situation in Ireland as terrible as that which confronted Irishmen when Eoghan Ruadh O'Neill lay dead and Cromwell marched at the head of his iron legions to the conquest of a distracted country. The failure of the potato-crop which menaced Ireland with serious loss at the birth of the Confederation in January, 1847, threatened the destruction of the people by the middle of 1847. The Relief measures provided by the English Whig Government set up a system under which places, large and small, were provided for some thousands of persons of political influence. Their tenure of employment depending upon the ministry, they used that influence to the end of sustaining the ministry, while the unfortunate small farmers who had hitherto kept on the right side of the line between poverty and pauperism were forced to the wrong side. Of all the measures passed under the guise of relieving "the famine-stricken Irish" the most infamous was that measure which provided that no farmer should be accorded relief if, the produce of his farm having gone to discharge his rents, rates and taxes, he hungered and yet strove to hold his farm. Before he was permitted to receive any help from the public funds he was required to surrender his land and become a pauper. Thus under pretext of relieving famine, pauperism was propagated.

Be it remembered that all this time there was no *famine* in Ireland. The potato-crop, indeed, had failed as it had failed in Great Britain, France, Germany and other countries at the same period, but the corn crop was fat and abundant. Each year of the so-called famine, food to maintain double the whole population was raised from the Irish soil. It was exported to England to feed the English people. Nobody starved in Germany. The German governments ordered the ports to be closed to the export of food until the danger had passed. The Irish Confederation demanded the same measure. "Close the Irish ports," it called to the British Government, "and no man can die of hunger in Ireland." The British Government, instead, flung the ports wide open. The great principle of Free Trade required that the Irish should export their food freely. Relief ships from foreign countries laden with the food subscribed by charitable people to succour the starving Irish met occasionally ships sailing out of the Irish ports laden with food reaped by the starving Irish. On the quays of Galway the unhappy people wailed as they saw their harvests borne away from them, and were admonished by the butt-ends of British muskets, the British Government meantime passing Relief measures which provided employment for hordes of English officials and Irish understrappers, and pauper-relief for those who surrendered their manhood and their property—the cost of this relief, like the cost of the passage of the Act of Union, being debited to Ireland—a generous loan in fact.

No doubt a union of the whole Irish people would have rendered all this impossible. The Irish Confederation worked hard to bring about this essential union. Directly and indirectly it achieved for a moment a semblance of national unity. The Irish Council, composed largely of the resident landlords—who mostly endeavoured to alleviate the distress—came into being, reasoned with the Government and, when the Government ignored reason, fell to pieces. George Henry Moore, a young sporting landlord and a Tory (afterwards, as a result, to become a Nationalist leader), conceived the design of getting all the Irish members of the British Parliament to act together against the existing British Government or any British Government which did not deal honestly and effectively with the crisis. With the Marquis of Sligo, a nobleman who did his duty to his tenantry during the Famine, Moore travelled around Ireland and secured between sixty and seventy Irish members of Parliament and forty-five Irish peers to subscribe to his independence programme. They met in Dublin, resolved boldly, departed for London cheered by the nation, and crumbled there at the Premier's frown. When the Tory Lord George Bentinck proposed that instead of pauperising the Irish by a vote of four or five millions for relief there should be a vote of sixteen millions for railway construction, the Premier, Lord John Russell, threatened the Irish members with his displeasure if they supported Bentinck, and the majority of them thereupon opposed the proposal of reproductive work for the people in lieu of pauper relief.

It was in these circumstances Mitchel put forward his policy in the Confederation of arming the people and bidding them hold their harvests. The Confederation rejected the policy, still hoping to effect a national union. Through such a union alone, it declared, could national independence be achieved. Doheny strongly opposed Mitchel on this ground. Mitchel's reply was simple. He had been and was ready to follow the aristocrats of Ireland if they would lead. They would not lead, and meanwhile the people perished. Therefore he would urge the people to save themselves. The policy of the Confederation in normal times would have been nationally sound. The circumstances had become abnormal, and Mitchel's policy was suited to the abnormal circumstances. His conviction that the British Government was deliberately using the potato-crop failure for the purpose of reducing the Irish population—which then was equal to more than half the population of England and a menace to that country, as one of its statesmen incautiously admitted—was a conviction not shared by the bulk of his colleagues. They shrank from it as men will shrink from a conclusion that horrifies the human nature in them. Mitchel went outside the Confederation to preach his policy, and he might have preached it without result had not the French Revolution turned men's minds to the contemplation of arms and armed opinion. The arrest, indictment and conviction of Mitchel, Doheny has described graphically. The reasons that prevailed against attempting Mitchel's rescue,

Doheny cogently states. There is no reason to doubt that an attempt to rescue Mitchel would have been a failure in its object. But there are occasions when it is wiser to attempt the impossible than to acquiesce. The unchallenged removal of Mitchel in chains from Ireland had a moral effect on the country that was worth 20,000 additional troops to the Government.

Thereafter, the Confederation vacillated in its policy and finally permitted itself, in its desire for Unity as the potent weapon, to be extinguished in favour of an Irish League which was to combine O'Connellites and Young Irelanders. The Irish League met once, and died. The Confederation had been hoodwinked. Doheny who opposed the amalgamation, retired to Cashel, severing his connection with the former Confederation. He was, therefore, free in honour to have taken no part in the insurrection, since it was begun by men from whom he had withdrawn. But when the voice in the night whispered through his window that his former colleagues had crossed the Rubicon, Doheny, like the man he was, rose and rode forth to make the fatal passage and stand or fall with them.

From this point, Doheny's narrative may be supplemented and corrected by information that was not at the time he wrote available to him. Meagher, Leyne, M'Gee, O'Mahony and MacManus, have left in newspaper articles and in MS. accounts of what happened in the light of which Doheny's narrative must be read.

On Thursday, July 20th, 1848, the British Government issued a proclamation ordering the people of Ireland to surrender their arms. Thomas Francis Meagher, who was at the time in Waterford, issued a counter-proclamation to the people of that city bidding them to hold them fast. He then hurried to Dublin to consult with his colleagues and he arrived in the metropolis the next day. There had been a strong division of opinion in the Confederate clubs as to how the Government proclamation should be treated, the general feeling of the rank-and-file inclining to open resistance. The leaders counselled a waiting policy until the harvest had been gathered, the arms to be concealed meanwhile. This counsel prevailed against the remonstrance of one of the Dublin leaders that if heaven rained down loaded rifles they would wait for angels to pull the triggers. If the insurrection could have been postponed until the harvest the counsel would have been sound. The Young Ireland leaders forgot, however, that the Government had one powerful weapon in reserve with which it might force their hands—the Suspension of the Habeas Corpus Act. On July 21st Meagher and his comrades and the Dublin leaders discussed and arranged the outline of a contingent insurrectionary plan for the autumn. O'Brien left for Wexford and O'Gorman for Limerick to organise those counties. The next morning the news reached those who remained in Dublin that the Habeas Corpus Act had been suspended, and that a warrant was on its way to Ireland for the arrest of Smith O'Brien. The choice left was to fight, to become fugitives, or to surrender. Dillon, M'Gee, Reilly, P.J. Smyth and Meagher decided hurriedly on the first course. They rejected the proposal to begin the fight in Dublin, as they believed it would be hopeless with the resources at their disposal to contend against a disciplined garrison of 11,000 men in a city a large proportion of whose population was hostile. Kilkenny was regarded as a stronghold of the Confederation, and Dillon suggested it should be the objective. Dillon and Meagher quitted Dublin to seek O'Brien; Reilly and Smyth started for Tipperary, and M'Gee for Scotland where it was hoped the Glasgow Irish could be induced to rise, seize some of the Clyde steamers and effect a landing in Sligo or Mayo which might rouse Connacht and western Ulster to the assistance of the South.

Dillon and Meagher left Dublin on the night of the 22nd of July by the mailcoach for Enniscorthy. Neither had the slightest hope of a successful insurrection, but they felt that honour and its future survival demanded that a nation must reply to the command of a foreign power to gag its mouth and throw down its arms by drawing the sword. They found Smith O'Brien at Enniscorthy and he joined in their views. Father Parle and the people of Enniscorthy undertook to defend O'Brien by force of arms if any attempt were made to arrest him there, and agreed that if he went into Kilkenny and Tipperary and succeeded in arousing those counties Wexford would take up arms. O'Brien and his colleagues moved towards Kilkenny through Graiguenamanagh where the people received them with enthusiasm, and they arrived in what they hoped to make again the provisional capital of Ireland in the evening of the 23rd of July.

Terence Bellew MacManus

The considerations in favour of beginning the insurrection in Kilkenny were sound. It was the one Irish city of importance inaccessible to British naval power, it offered a convenient rallying-centre for the counties of Tipperary, Waterford, and Wexford upon which the Young Ireland leaders relied, the country around it was well-adapted for defensive fighting against superior forces, and it had an historic appeal to the Irish imagination. The arrival of the insurgent leaders was hailed with joy by the people, and there was no doubt of the readiness of the populace to fight. But an examination of the military resources of the place showed that the British forces consisted of 1,000 troops in a strongly-defended position, while amongst the Irish there were but 200 armed men and the gunsmiths' shops in the city could not arm a hundred more. The decision not to strike the first blow at Kilkenny in the circumstances was inevitable. It was agreed to make for Carrick-on-Suir, another Young Ireland town, seize the place and march at the head of the elated Tipperarymen on Kilkenny. On Monday, July 24th, O'Brien, Meagher and Dillon left for Carrick-on-Suir, and on the way they were received with enthusiasm at Callan, where the 8th Hussars—mainly composed of Irishmen—manifested sympathy with the insurrectionary propaganda. Near Carrick they were joined by John O'Mahony, a landed proprietor of the neighbourhood, afterwards to become famous as the founder of Fenianism. By descent, education and character a leader of men, O'Mahony had thousands of followers among the people ready to rally to any venture for Ireland at his call. "His square, broad frame," wrote Meagher, "his frank, gay, fearless look; the warm forcible headlong earnestness of his manner; the quickness and elasticity of his movements; the rapid glances of his clear full eye; the proud bearing of his head; everything about him struck us with a brilliant and exciting effect, as he threw himself from his saddle and, tossing the bridle on his arm, hastened to meet and welcome us. At a glance we recognised in him a true leader for the generous, passionate, intrepid peasantry of the South." O'Mahony strongly advised them to begin the insurrection that night in Carrick, and he left to collect the peasantry. O'Brien and his comrades proceeded to the town where the people received them with frenzied enthusiasm, calling out to be led immediately to the fray. "A torrent of human beings rushing through lanes and narrow streets"—such is Meagher's description of the scene— "surging and boiling against the white basements . . . wild, half-stifled, passionate, frantic prayers of hope . . . curses on the red flag: scornful delirious defiances of death . . . It was the Revolution if we had accepted it." But it was not accepted. The local leaders were unworthy of the people. They persuaded O'Brien to go elsewhere. It was a cardinal and egregious mistake which he regretted within twenty-four hours. Had he brushed the quavering local leaders aside and given the word to the imploring people of Carrick the insurrection of 1848 would have become respectable. O'Mahony's followers to the number of 12,000 were on the march to Carrick when the news reached them of O'Brien's departure. Disheartened they broke up and returned to their homes.

Doheny's account of what happened after the fatal retreat from Carrick needs to be amplified in connection with the final error of O'Brien's leadership. At the Council of War on the 28th of July O'Brien rejected the proposal to seize for the use of his followers all things needful, paying for them with drafts on the future Irish Government, and he declined the other practical proposal to offer farms rent-free to all who fought for Ireland. Neither would he assent to the suggestion that he and the other leaders should go into hiding until the harvest was reaped. Willing to fight and ready to die, he would not consent to conduct a revolution on revolutionary lines. The departure of Doheny and others—save Devin Reilly, who urged the abandonment of the insurrection as hopeless—was in pursuance of their plan to await the gathering of the harvest.

O'Brien's attitude at the Council of War destroyed the last hope of the insurrection. He expected to get men to fight under his standard while he essayed no adequate provision for their support in the field, and interdicted them from interference with private property to supply them with the necessaries of the campaign. No nobler and braver man has appeared in modern Irish history than William Smith O'Brien, but at the head of an insurrectionary movement he was incompetent. There was none of his lieutenants who, in his position, could not have made the insurrection to some extent formidable.

That it could have been successful, few will believe. Mitchel and Meagher agreed that 1848 would not have been the year of Liberation. But the former held very justly that the insurrection if it grew to respectable dimensions might have forced terms from England. The attitude of France at the time was a factor in the situation. The pro-Irish minister, Ledru-Rollin, had been checked by the pro-English minister, Lamartine, but General Cavaignac and Louis Napoleon were, for divergent reasons, inclined to help Ireland against England, and assurances had been given that if an Irish insurrection gained considerable initial successes the French Government would exert influence on England. A successful blow at Carrick and a subsequent seizure of Kilkenny and proclamation of Irish independence from that city was possible, and if realised would have probably led to the counties of Waterford and Tipperary rising en masse. How far the insurrection would have spread outside those counties is problematical, but in the year 1848 they were counties which presented difficulties to regular troops and advantages to insurgent forces. According to M'Gee, Sligo was willing to rise if the South made a good beginning and the Bishop of Derry, Dr. Maginn, sent a message to Gavan Duty that he was willing to join in the insurrection at the head of his priests once the harvest was reaped. Doheny's criticism of the action of some of the Tipperary priests is justified. But of others it is to be remembered that they were not in sympathy with Young Ireland, that they were not bound to support an insurrection undertaken irrespective of them, and that they could not be expected to take the initiative. There were at least two priests in Tipperary prepared to lead their parishioners to the insurgent standard if O'Brien struck at any point a successful blow. O'Brien's indecision was the real cause why the insurrection died in its birth.

If courage and devotion could have saved Ireland in 1848, O'Brien and his comrades would have saved the land. No braver gentlemen could any nation produce. They asked their countrymen to take no risks they did not take themselves in the forefront. But courage and devotion alone can never make an insurrection into a revolution. 1848 was a failure—in one sense—because there was no second Mitchel in Ireland when the first Mitchel was hurried off on a British gunboat.

But 1848 was not a failure in the true sense of failure. For years the Irish people had submitted to any and every imposition of foreign tyranny, taught to believe that forcible resistance to outrage on their national liberties was in itself immoral. The sneer of the satirist that the Irish were:—

"A nation of abortive men
Who shoot the tongue and wield the pen,"

seemed to have grown a reality. Young Ireland evoked the fighting tradition of the nation once again. Without 1848 the spirit that freed the Irish Catholic from being tributary to another Church and regained the land for the farmers would have slept for a century—perhaps for ever.

Driven from his country, Doheny with the companion of his fugitive wanderings, James Stephens, and the chivalrous O'Mahony, founded the Fenian brotherhood in the United States. Once more before his sudden death in April, 1862, he saw Ireland—on the occasion of the MacManus Funeral.

Let me, said a wise man, always be surrounded by men of sanguine temperament. Defeat and exile could not dim the faith of Doheny in his country. The fugitive who had wrecked his fortunes in Ireland's cause and witnessed a failure which English statesmen believed ended for ever the dream of Irish independent nationhood, set his foot in exile only to begin anew to plan Ireland Independent. So long as the sanguine heart that carried Michael Doheny undaunted along the Felon's Track beats in the breast of his country the Irish Nation will be indestructible.

ARTHUR GRIFFITH.

CONTENTS

ILLUSTRATIONS

AUTHOR'S INTRODUCTION

There are few facts detailed in the following pages that need explanation here. If my motive in writing them were personal gratification, or simply a desire to preserve a memorial of scenes in which I took an anxious part, I might labour to make the narration more interesting to my readers, without any care for future consequences.

But through every disaster I preserved unbroken faith in the purpose and courage of my country. I believed, and still believe that her true heart is faithful to liberty and hopeful for the future; and this conviction involved me in a struggle with the apparently opposite tendency of the facts I was bound to narrate. Had I to write for a new generation, upon whom these facts could have made no false impressions, my task would be easy. I am persuaded that a simple statement of all that occurred would satisfy any candid mind that no disgrace attached to Ireland in her recent discomfiture. But I must needs confess that it is a task of extreme difficulty to reconcile her fall with the pre-conceived notions or present prejudices of those who read her story through the false medium of the press; nor do I hope for more than partial success from the details I have been able to give of the circumstances of which she was the victim and the dupe.

It is impossible fully to appreciate the pernicious effect of Mr. O'Connell's teaching, without reviewing in minute detail the leading circumstances of his wonderful career and the matchless and countless resources with which he upheld his fatal system. In dealing with this part of my subject my difficulties have been multiplied and enhanced by a strong desire to do him no injustice, and to leave untouched by doubt or suspicion a character so intertwined with my country's love. But it became necessary to refer to those acts which chiefly tended to increase the obstacles which beset our endeavours. In doing this, whether here or elsewhere in my narrative, if I use phrases which would seem to imply harshness to his memory, I wish them to be understood as applied in reference to the attempt to effect the deliverance of Ireland by force of arms, and establishing her entire and perfect independence. I have avoided this question, assuming that I wrote only for those who agreed with me in the belief that such is her true destiny, and the end for which her children ought to strive.

In this view of her recent struggle, there can be no doubt of the tendency of Mr. O'Connell's policy to demoralise, disgrace, enfeeble and corrupt the Irish people, and it is in that sense, and that only, I have always spoken of him.

Another subject, of perhaps greater delicacy and difficulty, was the part taken by the Catholic clergy. On my arrival in America, I found a fierce contest agitating, dividing and enfeebling the Irish-American population. It was asserted on one side that the entire failure was attributable to the Catholic priests, and that in opposing the liberation of Ireland they acted in accordance with some recognised radical principle of the Church.

I could not assent to either of these propositions. I knew several priests who were fully prepared to take their share in an armed conflict; in fact, the vast majority of those I met at the time. And again, with respect to such as did interfere, and opposed the efforts of the people's chiefs, I do not believe that one man was influenced by considerations connected with, or emanating from the Church, in its corporate capacity. Of Mr. O'Connell's policy, already referred to, none were blinder victims than some of the priests. It had made such an impression on them that they scarcely could believe anything was real, or any sentiment was true; and when they admitted its truth it was only to prove its madness. Of other and more questionable motives I shall say nothing here.

But while I feel the injustice of the sweeping charge made against the whole body of the priesthood, I would be unfaithful to my purpose and my convictions if I concealed the acts and language of those among them, who interposed and unhappily exercised baneful influence on the abortive attempt of their unfortunate country. I shall only say further that what relates to them is the only part of my narrative which gave me shame to tell.

I have only a word to add in reference to certain proceedings in the Committee of the Association now made public for the first time. It may be said, and, I doubt not, will be said, that these were matters which we were morally pledged to keep secret. I readily admit that, although there was no obligation whatever, either expressed or implied, as to any subject discussed in committee any more than in the public hall, still, I should not disclose any part of its proceedings if I were not compelled by an imperative necessity. Upon one subject, and that the most important to the character of my illustrious friend, no other proof was available. And the tacit understanding, in virtue of which I would be disposed to admit any obligation of secrecy, does not and could not extend beyond such matters as would, if divulged, endanger the safety or impair the efficiency of the Association. What I tell of the proceedings of the Committee, even if it yet existed, would scarcely have any such effect. But every one knows it not only does not exist, but that is has left no memory which it would be possible to degrade. Its physical existence long survived the last spark of moral vitality, and its efficiency now consists in this, if it warn all men against the species of terrorism which finally prevailed in its councils and effected its overthrow.

In certain circumstances which I relate, I may possibly make some mistakes in the dates, owing to the difficulty of finding those dates in odd numbers and broken volumes of the Journals to which alone I have had access.

It would have given me the sincerest pleasure to add to the collection of heads, which I have been able to procure, those of others who took an honourable part in the Irish struggle. Foremost among them are John Martin and Kevin Izod O'Doherty, who followed in the footsteps and shared the fate of John Mitchel. But I am not aware that there are any likenesses of them in existence; at all events they are not to be obtained in this country.[1]

There are others, too, mentioned in my narrative, whose likenesses I would feel delighted to present to my readers, and some, who although cursorily or not at all mentioned, acted a noble and devoted part. Of the first, are the companions of my wanderings, James Stephens and John O'Mahony; and of the second, Doctor Antisel, Richard Dalton Williams, James Cantwell, Richard Hartnet, Patrick O'Dea, and indeed many others, of whose efforts and sacrifices it would be a source of pride to me to make honourable mention.[2]

I may be permitted to take this opportunity to assure them and others of whom I have not spoken that no name has been omitted by me from any feelings of dislike or any desire to depreciate the services and sacrifices of a single man among the hundreds, whose exile or ruin attests the sincerity of their convictions and the purity of their patriotism. Even with men who do not take the same view of last year's history as I do, their names and characters will go far to redeem its darkest traces from shame and obloquy. They are now scattered over the wide earth, and there is not one among them from the highest to the humblest, whom I do not hold in the utmost honour and esteem.

New York, September 21, 1849.

FOOTNOTES:

1   I am glad it has been found easy to supply these in this edition of the work.— Ed.

2   Some of these will also be found in the present gallery—Ed.

William Smith O'Brien

CHAPTER I

RETROSPECT—COMMENCEMENT OF THE REPEAL STRUGGLE.—ARLY DAYS OF THE ASSOCIATION.

The appearance of this narrative will surprise no one. For apology, if any be needed, the writer may trust to his own share in the transactions with which it deals; and still more so perhaps to the misrepresentation to which, during their progress, he had been personally subjected. But personal vindication imparts neither interest nor importance to history, while it necessarily detracts from its dignity and good faith. Besides, time with the disastrous events marking its more recent course, have silenced the voice of calumny; and the writer undertakes his task with no personal feeling to gratify or even to consult. The character of others, now unable to be heard, is far dearer to him than his own: and while he aspires to justify, before the world, their singular career, distinguished throughout by generous and lofty passions, surpassing intellect and measureless love of their country and countrymen—a career so brilliant and instructive even in the last hours of gloom—he will endeavour to infuse into the history of their struggles and their fate, that generous tenderness toward others, that spirit of self-sacrifice and supreme love of truth, which were among their noblest characteristics.

The undertaking suggests but one painful consideration—the impossibility of treating the subject fully and fairly without investigating facts far anterior to the late struggle, but coincident in their effect with its progress and development, and stamping their pernicious and fatal influence upon the spirit and conduct that led to a final overthrow. This will necessarily involve an inquiry into the late conduct and teaching of Mr. O'Connell, which the writer would most willingly avoid. Mr. O'Connell's name and character fill a mighty space in history. They are the most cherished recollections in his country's memory; and she clings to them with loving pride in this her hour of utter desolation. The hand that traces these recollections would be the last to aim a blow at the object of her sacred affections; and if in obedience to a more binding obligation, Mr. O'Connell's policy be questioned and condemned, his influencing motive shall be unchallenged and unarraigned. What his final purpose was, and how he had determined to effect it, had his life been spared, and his course left unimpeded, now rest with him in his grave. It is for others to write his history and vindicate his career. By me even his mistakes shall be treated with forbearance.

A brief reference to the struggle for Catholic Emancipation becomes here imperative. That struggle has had no equal in history—nor for its moral grandeur, nor for its triumph—but for the singular difficulties which the position of the Irish Catholic imposed on those who engaged in it. It is an error to call it emancipation. It was neither the first nor the last, nor even the most important in the train of concessions, which are entitled to the name of emancipation. The pains and penalties of the *"penal laws"* had been long abolished, and that barbarous code had been compressed into cold and stolid exclusiveness. But the vices which a long and unrelenting slavery had burned into the character of the country, remained. The lie of law, which assumed the non-existence of the Catholic had infused itself into his nature, and while it was erased from the statute book, it was legible on his heart. That terrible necessity of denying his feelings, his property, his religion and his very being, had stamped its degrading influence on his nature. In a moral sense the law had become a truth—there was no people. The Catholic gentry, giddy by their recent elevation, had only changed for that semblance of liberty their old stern spirit of resistance and revenge. Their new concessions hung gracefully around them, but they were like grafts on an ash stock—their growth was downward, and they wanted the stature and dignity of the native tree. Such were the means at Mr. O'Connell's disposal. His enemies on the other hand were false, powerful, dexterous and unscrupulous. His efforts necessarily partook of the character both of the weapons he was obliged to wield and the foes he struck down. As he advanced to eminence and strength, means, the most crafty and cruel, were taken to overthrow him, every one of which he foiled by a sagacity infinitely above that of his oppressors. So successful had he been in deceiving the champions of intolerance, that of all the great qualities displayed in that wonderful struggle, that which was most prized was the cunning of evasion. It left behind it an enduring and destructive influence. Dissimulation in political action began to be regarded as a public virtue, and long afterwards, when men sought to assert the dignity of truth, their candour was charged against them as a heinous crime. It will be seen hereafter how fatally this fact operated against their efforts.

The very character of Emancipation has assumed an exaggerated and false guise. The joy of the nation was boundless—its gratitude immeasurable. In the shout that hailed the deliverer, earlier deliverers were forgotten. No one remembered the men whose stupendous exertions wrung from the reluctant spirit of a far darker time the right of living, of worship, of enjoying property, and exercising the franchise. All these, and more, which were once, and not very remotely, denied to the Catholics had been before this accorded to them. Yet the interest and importance of winning access to Parliament, to the higher ranks of the army, and, perhaps a stray seat at the Privy Council, acquired the name of Emancipation, and Mr. O'Connell monopolised its entire renown. He was styled the "Liberator," and his achievement designated as "striking the fetters from the limbs of the slave, and liberating the altar." In truth, the import of Emancipation was so exaggerated, and its history so warped, that even now at a distance of more than twenty years, both the act and the actors are so misunderstood that it requires no little daring to approach a question involving the sensibilities, prejudices and passions of an entire generation.

A truer appreciation might have given Mr. O'Connell a different and higher destiny. Not alone the boundless exultation of the Catholic but the mortified pride of the baffled Protestant also stamped its influence on his fortunes, prospects and career. In proportion as he was to the former an object of adulation and pride did the latter hoard up in his heart for him enduring envy and insatiable hate. Another circumstance, too, which Mr. O'Connell did not create and could not in the beginning control, contributed to mar his future glory. This was the pecuniary compensation which the emancipated Catholics kneeled to present him. It is far from being intended here to disparage the offering or decry its acceptance. On the contrary, if this were the proper place, both would be vindicated with zealous pride. But the effect of the continued collection, on Mr. O'Connell's conduct and efficiency was baneful in the extreme. And it was among the most prominent circumstances in shaping his career.

Mr. O'Connell entered the House of Commons under auspices more flattering and encouraging than ever smiled on the advent to that assembly of any other man. In whatever light he was regarded, he was far the foremost personage of his time. How his subsequent career might justify the hushed awe with which a proud senate received him if he had devoted himself to the broad and comprehensive questions of imperial jurisprudence, for which he seemed so eminently fitted, it would be idle now to conjecture. Certain it is that no act of his after life, varied and wonderful as it was, realised the promise of that glad and glorious morning.

Lord Anglesea, who had been removed from the viceroyalty for suspected treachery to the cause of intolerance, was restored to his office, by more distinguished converts, and was received by the people with tumultuous acclaim. His popularity was short-lived. The present Chief Justice, Doherty, was then Attorney-General. He incurred the wrath of Mr. O'Connell in consequence of treachery which he had exhibited in conducting a trial at Clonmel. This led to a fierce encounter in the House of Commons—the first great trial of Mr. O'Connell's powers—in which Doherty's friends claimed for their champion a decisive victory. However unjust may be that judgment, Mr. O'Connell's admirers were compelled to admit that he failed in his impeachment and principally in consequence of a letter written by Mr. Shiel, then second to no other Irishman. Mr. Shiel had been associated with the Attorney-General in the prosecution at Clonmel, and his letter boldly justified the conduct which the great popular tribune vehemently and indignantly impugned. This was quite unexpected, and greatly affected Mr. O'Connell's cause. But whether Mr. Doherty failed or succeeded, he was rewarded, and almost avowedly, by the Chief Justiceship of the Common Pleas. The appointment was a direct insult to Mr. O'Connell, and scarcely a less direct insult to the Irish bar, and the Irish nation. Mr. Doherty was regarded as a man of great forensic ability, but no legal attainments. He had scarcely acquired any practice, and no distinction whatever: so that his elevation to a post he was so inadequate to fill gave universal dissatisfaction, and was read as evidence that the Government of Ireland was subservient to an unscrupulous and audacious faction.

Soon after the date of this appointment the first Repeal Association was established by Mr. O'Connell. His motives were at once bitterly assailed. By some he was charged with being influenced by personal mortification. By some his conduct was attributed to a love of turbulence and money. By some it was said he only intended the agitation as a threat, by means of which he could enforce a wiser, more liberal, and just administration of the law and government in Ireland. Few, if any, believed him to be in earnest and sincere. But the condition of the country and the principles of Mr. O'Connell's early life would suggest higher motives; and the perseverance and intensity of feeling and purpose, with which he urged the deliverance of his country in after times, proves that he was a stranger to the sordid considerations which envy or fear coupled with his first labours in that direction. Certain it is that, whatever were his motives, it could be no tempting ambition that determined him to transfer the exercise of his abilities to the tribune of angry agitation from that more legitimate and loftier arena which, with unsurpassed energy, he had won.

The agitation succeeded rapidly. The Government became at once intolerant and impotent. They proclaimed down the agitation; but this only imparted to it activity, energy and strength. The Government gave way to a furious storm which had been long gathering elsewhere. The great Reform Ministry succeeded with Earl Grey at its head; and in the struggle for Imperial parliamentary Reform, Ireland and her independence were forgotten.

During the intellectual conflict that followed, Mr. O'Connell asserted his pre-eminence, and won a lofty name. He made far the most successful speech on the question of Reform. It not only exceeded the ablest orations of the British leaders, but was, perhaps, the most triumphant he himself had ever delivered. But his position soon changed. From being the unanswerable champion of the ministerial majority in the House of Commons, he took the lead of a small opposition which resisted the Government on the Irish Bill. Although the minister was the exponent and stern advocate of the widest liberality, in applying the reform to England, he undertook to defend, on the very opposite principle, the niggard liberty he was prepared in the same measure to extend to Ireland. In this unnatural and unexpected turn of affairs, Mr. O'Connell took a proud and bold stand, against the Government, and for his country. The ministry succeeded, but he had more than ever acquired the confidence and unbounded gratitude of his countrymen. Thenceforward, he was their acknowledged chief, and his words expressed not more his own than the public will.

His remonstrances were vehement and angry, but they were vain. The ministry disregarded the claims of justice, as well as the voice of the orator. The quarrel became personal and vindictive to so great an extent, that Mr. O'Connell's support would almost ensure the defeat of any measure at the hands of the English Whig faction.

While this was his position in the House of Commons, he was preparing the elements of an organisation which was destined to embrace the whole island. He started the first great Repeal Association, which was at once attended with marvellous success. Forty-four members of Parliament were under its control if not in its ranks. A discussion of the merits of Repeal was forced in the House of Commons by the intemperate zeal of the member for Cork.[3] The motion was resisted by the whole weight and influence of the Ministry. But in a resolution proposed as an amendment, both Houses concurred in acknowledging that Ireland's complaint was founded in justice, and in solemnly pledging themselves to the practical redress of her grievances. The resolution was carried to the foot of the throne, and there received the sanction of royalty.

But that resolution remained and remains unfulfilled. The ministry which proposed it, redeemed their promise by an Algerine measure of coercion, which Mr. O'Connell denounced as "base, bloody and brutal." His opposition, and their own recreancy of principle, tended rapidly to their overthrow. Lord Stanley, in hatred to Mr. O'Connell and his country, abandoned the Government, which he charged with truckling to the great demagogue's will. The country, on the other hand, withdrew its confidence from them on the ground that they truckled to their hereditary foes, and allowed the principles of the Tories to influence Parliament in the name and through the agency of the Whigs. Division and weakness followed; and the result was a break-up of the administration, which was remodelled, with Lord Melbourne for its chief, on the understanding that more liberal views should govern its future course. An alliance was entered into with Mr. O'Connell, whose support the Prime Minister openly claimed and as openly boasted of. Then was formed what was known as the "Litchfield House Compact." This compact, if such the understanding that existed can be called, was based upon the assurance that the most liberal measures of justice should be extended to Ireland, and that in the administrative department, the Government should apply itself diligently to the reform and purifying of all public functions and functionaries. What was the nature or extent of Mr. O'Connell's engagement, I do not pretend to know. But whether he pledged himself to abandon for ever the struggle for independence, or only to place it in abeyance for a season to facilitate the action of the Government in reference to their good intentions and favourable promises, he so far fulfilled his engagement as to dissolve the Association.

That Association was composed of various and very conflicting elements. The motives which influenced many of its leaders were equally varied. Many joined it merely because Mr. O'Connell was its founder and its guide. Many among the middle ranks of society had acquired a sort of interest in agitation they could not easily surrender. It had gained them local distinction, and gratified a morbid vanity. Profuse votes of thanks were their incentive and reward. To correspond with Mr. Ray, or perhaps the Liberator, consummated their ambition, and for aught beyond that they felt no concern. Others there were, corrupt by nature and cunning in design, whose political exertions had personal advancement for their sole aim; and others still who never believed Mr. O'Connell sincere, but joined the Association and shouted their approval, because too contemptible and feeble to acquire distinction except through the echo of his voice or under shelter of his fame. To the false and the sordid and the indifferent, the dissolution of the confederacy was a welcome event: but the people, yet uncorrupted, looked on passively with agonised hearts.

Physical contagion generally begins at the bases of society, and trails its way slowly to the upper ranks, occasionally dealing doom to some hard hearts that mocked, it may be, its first uncared-for victims. But moral corruption begins with the highest, and embraces the whole circle of society in its descent. So it was in this instance. Members of Parliament who had solemnly pledged themselves to the disenthrallment of their country, accepted the wages, and entered into the service of the Government who had one and all vowed they would prevent the fulfilment of the hustings pledge, even at the risk of a civil war. Among them was Mr. O'Connell's son, who had taken that pledge before the assembled people of Meath, his son-in-law, Mr. Fitzsimon, who had sworn it to the freeholders of the metropolitan county, Mr. Carew O'Dwyer who, in virtue of the same pledge, obtained the unanimous suffrage of Drogheda, and several others. Many relatives and friends of Mr. O'Connell obtained rewards adequate to their services. Agents who had been successful against Whig candidates now retired into Whig places. The corporate towns were made over to the Whigs, who held out the understanding that the sons, nephews and kindred of the leading and deserving citizens would be provided for in the departments suited to their different capacities, and varying from the post of tide-waiter, to that of stipendiary magistrate. Fierce was the struggle which followed, and sore the disappointment, and many a scalding tear of baffled ambition watered the way to the aspirant's ruin.

This is not said for the purpose of disparaging the legitimate ambition of those who sought advancement in the altered circumstances and sentiments of the time. But the effect of such a state of things on the morality of the nation was incalculably injurious. The most solemn resolution was openly violated, and that by the very men who were foremost in recommending the national vow. Nor would its tendency be less fatal, assuming that Mr. O'Connell was correct in supposing that the experiment would be vain, and that its failure could not fail to supply new and more urgent reasons for the nation's independence. The compact, if even entered into with that view, would shake all faith in public men; because it would only change the parties with whom a false obligation was contracted, leaving the obligation itself and its violation exactly where they were.

Mr. O'Connell's support was doomed to be as fatal to the Whigs as his opposition. He unhappily assisted them during his period to carry one measure, against which they had recorded several solemn decisions in Parliament, namely, the Tithe Bill, without an appropriation clause, which was a direct falsification of their own resolution, whereby they defeated Sir Robert Peel's short-lived administration, in 1835. And what was still more lamentable, he supported them in renewing in a modified form the very Coercion Act for the introduction of which he designated them as "*base, bloody and brutal.*"

But other elements were secretly sapping the influences for which he made these sacrifices. The storm of disaffection, a long while gathering among open foes and disappointed retainers, was about to burst on the devoted heads of the Whigs. With their accustomed fickleness and treachery of character they prepared to sacrifice, for the sake of power, the man whom they conciliated and deceived in the same hope of retaining it. If he foresaw that this would be the result of his experiment, never was augury more fully realised. Whatever may be the exact engagements of the Whigs, he was able to allege that not one was fulfilled, while he was in a position to prove that he more than kept his own: unless indeed, it could be assumed that for the few places obtained by his friends, and others, some of them honourable men, he surrendered the lofty and nearly impregnable position he occupied in 1834, and which, in one sense at least, he never afterwards attained.

From whatever cause, his influence over the Whigs visibly declined, and his counsels no longer swayed their Irish policy. Once more they relied on the false expedient of yielding to their enemies and allowing them to wield the *power*, while they were themselves content with the spoils of the country. Again the quarrel with Mr. O'Connell became bitter and personal, and again had he recourse to Repeal.

From the time of the first Repeal Association to that of the Precursor Society several other associations or societies were established, which have left behind them scarcely the memory of their very names—that of the second association alone excepted. Yet each had an ample treasury, and was composed of the same or nearly the same elements, and the same members. There is many an honest man and many a fool, whose boast it is that they contributed a pound to each of them, and had their respective cards.

At last the late Repeal Association was formed. Its birth was received with sneers. Mr. O'Connell's sincerity was questioned, and his motives canvassed with vindictive vigilance. The warmest Nationalists looked on with doubt and coldness. Not one man of rank, outside the members of the defunct society, joined its ranks. The routine of business, the receipt of money, the resolutions, the speeches, were exactly identical with those of its predecessors. The Government seemed neither to dread it nor care for it. It lingered on, unsustained by the country and despised by its enslavers. The contributions of the members did not suffice to pay half the ordinary expenses of its machinery. Debts accumulated, and the revenue did not increase. While the body was thus situated, Mr. O'Connell had recourse to an expedient at once singular and decisive. It was to build Conciliation Hall. The Association was at the time seriously in debt, and he proposed to multiply that debt four-fold by engaging in this costly undertaking.

While persons who affected to be in his confidence were amazed at this step, the Government regarded it as an evidence of purpose which it was indispensable at once to check. They saw that their opponents had formerly menaced and coerced in vain, and they determined to proscribe. Accordingly the newly appointed viceroy, Lord Ebrington, being waited on by the Dublin Corporation with some address of congratulation, delivered them a lecture on the disloyalty of the Corn Exchange, and announced his purpose never to employ in the service of the Government any one who frequented that pestilent locality. The corporation returned abashed to their council-rooms to record the viceregal threat. But from end to end of the land rose one shout of indignant defiance. Suspicion, doubt and hesitation gave way to the taunt involved in the insolent challenge. The ranks of the Association were filled, and its treasury replenished; and the viceroy soon discovered how little was to be gained by a vulgar appeal to the meanest passion when it was addressed to the Irish people.

FOOTNOTES:

3   Mr. Feargus O'Connor, afterwards leader of the English Chartists.—Ed

CHAPTER II

THOMAS DAVIS, HIS EARLY LABOURS.—THE "NATION" NEWSPAPER.—PROGRESS OF THE ASSOCIATION.—CLONTARF MEETING.—THE STATE TRIALS.—THE YOUNG IRELAND PARTY.—SMITH O'BRIEN.—FEDERALISM.—THE BEQUEST ACT.

Even before this great occasion, gifted spirits were insensibly moulding the character and destiny of the Association. The hurried but firm step of a pale student of Trinity College might be daily seen pacing the unfrequented flagways that led to the Corn Exchange. His penetrating glance, half shrouded by its own shyness, his face averted from the crowd, and his mind turned within, he would come, and sit, and hear, and suppress the emotions that swelled his proud young heart as he caught glimpses of a bright future for his country. He had the richest store of practical knowledge, an imagination fruitful as a sunny clime: faith, hope and courage boundless as immortal love. That he could realise all things which came within the scope of his own fond yearnings, he had no doubt. But most of the men with whom he took his place were stinted in acquirements, and not over-gifted in intellect, and had no conception or ambition beyond admiring or applauding the behests of one predominant and controlling will. With the passionate aspirations of the young student they felt no kindred sympathies. In their hands, political action, for whatever end, sank into a traffic or parade. Even with such materials he determined to work out his country's redemption, though already satisfied that before such a thing were possible, their habits, feelings, passions and hearts should be entirely changed. In order to do this, it was necessary he should stoop to the level of their conceptions and capacities. Thus for many weary months, with his energies, as it were, chained down to a cold stone, toiled and strove Thomas Davis. His influence first began to be felt as chairman of a sub-committee on the registers. This position afforded him an opportunity of entering into correspondence with the leading politicians of the party, and whenever he saw in any man's replies evidence of depth, capacity or earnestness, he at once entered into friendly and unreserved communication, exhorting him in language full of passionate entreaty. In these, his early efforts, John Dillon shared his labours, his ambition and his heart.

Truly yours, Thomas Davis.

About this time Mr. Stanton, proprietor of the *Morning Register*, committed to the two young graduates the writing of his journal. His preference was not so much owing to their character as politicians as it was to their pre-eminence in literary attainments. The press of Dublin had then sunk to the lowest level. Newspaper literature had even fallen, too. It was divided into three sections, each of which was the whining slave of one or other of the great predominating factions of the country. The *Register* was generally regarded as ranking among the mercenaries of the Castle. But no sooner did it fall into the hands of the college friends than all Dublin was startled by the originality, vigour and brilliancy of its articles. When the Whigs were about retiring they determined on a gross and scandalous abuse of power for the purpose of rewarding an unscrupulous partisan, even though it involved an affront to one of their oldest and ablest friends, the then Irish Chancellor. That man was Lord Plunket, who had served the Whigs so faithfully, honourably and fearlessly. He was commanded to retire in order to make room for Sir John Campbell, who was thereby to be qualified for the English peerage.

The stipendiaried journals of the Castle exhausted their adulation, and had received their last reward for upholding the appointment. The Tory press, hungry for the spoil which it maddened the others to lose, paid back the compliments by intense vituperation. The slang of party warfare was bandied in the usual fashion, without thought or a care beyond the interest of party. The *Register*, to everybody's astonishment, took up the one cause not represented, namely, that of the country. Davis denounced the appointment as an insult to that country, and with a bold hand vindicated the superiority of its Bar, without any reference to party, above the adventurers whom each faction placed over it in turn.

Soon after he and his friend ceased to write for that paper; but not until satisfied by the experiment that a journal devoted to Ireland, guided by truth, and sustained with earnest ability, would supersede the whole jaundiced literature of the metropolis, and create a new era in the progress of the country's civilisation and ambition. They immediately busied themselves to establish such an organ. Charles Gavan Duffy, late editor of the *Belfast Vindicator*, entered into the spirit of the enterprise, and after an evening's ramble in the Park, during which the terms and the principles of the paper and the spirit in which it should be conducted were canvassed, the publication of the *Nation* was determined on. Mr. Duffy was convicted for having written a libel in the *Vindicator*, and his friends earnestly advised him to compromise the matter with a view of bringing more powerful energies to the same task in a wider field.

The first number of the new journal appeared on the 12th of October, 1842. It had been announced under auspices calculated to ensure its success, but its unexpected ability, the ground it broke in the national policy, and the vast intellectual resources it developed eclipsed the prestige under which it was deemed necessary to usher it into existence. It was at once a proof of greater powers than the country had yet witnessed, and a prophecy of a different fate from what she hoped for. The aims, the logic, the very language of factious diplomacy were eschewed. It seemed as if a light had streamed down from heaven, fresh from God, to give the people hope, comfort and assurance. The genius of Davis seized the opportunity as though he were His deputed messenger in the great work of regeneration. For the first time men awoke to the consciousness of what they were or might be. Harnessed to the triumphant car of one gigantic intellect, they had forgotten the dignity of their own nature, and were astonished to find how transcendant its resources and sufficient its strength. The publication of the *Nation* was really an epoch which marked a wonderful change, and from that day forth self-reliance and self-respect began to take the place of grateful but stultified obedience and blind trust.

The change became more marked as the publication proceeded. In speech, article, song and essay, the spell of Davis's extraordinary genius and embracing love was felt. Historic memories, forgotten stories, fragments of tradition, the cromlech on the mountain and the fossil in the bog supplied him substance and spirit wherewith to mould and animate nationality. Native art, valour, virtue and glory seemed to grow under his pen. All that had a tendency to elevate and ennoble, he rescued from the past to infuse into the future. His songs, so soft and tender, and yet so redolent of manliness and hope, inspired the ambition to compose a minstrelsy as wild and vigorous as themselves. They were read and learned and sung with an avidity and pride heretofore unknown.

The monster meetings were long a design of Thomas Davis, John Dillon and the present writer. One great object with them was to train the country people to military movements and a martial tread. This object it would be unsafe to announce, and it was to be effected through other agencies than drill. The people should necessarily come to such rendezvous in baronial, parochial or town processions, and under the guidance of local leaders. Order is a law of nature; and, without much trouble on the part of those leaders, it would establish itself. The present writer left Dublin early in the spring of 1843 to carry this design into effect. Sir Robert Peel, then Prime Minister of England, alluding to the fact in the House of Commons, said that the first Monster Meeting was purposely held on the anniversary of the very day, the 22nd of May, destined for the rising of '98. Sir Robert was wrong in his inference, though it was a natural and nearly justifiable one; for at that Cashel meeting were offered unmistakable evidences of the tendency of the agitation. Upwards of £1,100 were handed to Mr. O'Connell. Each parish came in procession, headed by a band and commanded by some local leader; and those who took part in the public procession marched in excellent order for upwards of eight miles. A military and magisterial meeting had been previously held in the barracks of Cashel to consider whether the people should not be routed at the point of the bayonet. But though the committee were fully aware of this consultation, they decided unanimously that the meeting should go on. The meeting itself passed the strongest resolutions, and adopted a petition to the Legislature, consisting of a single line, something to this effect: "You have robbed us of our Parliament by fraud and blood; pray restore it, or—." And finally, Mr. O'Connell said at the dinner that evening, alluding to an armed strife; "Give me Tipperary for half a day." This simple wish, enunciated in accents familiar to that great ruler of men, elicited a cheer, a shout, a wild burst of enthusiasm, so long and loud as almost to suggest the idea that it would be seconded by naked steel and a deadly blow. One would think it had a significant meaning, and yet there was no wrathful ban. Not one pronounced that terrible anathema against shedding a single drop of blood, which afterwards became the canon of peaceful men. Nay, if memory be not very treacherous, amidst that roar was loudly distinguishable the voice of him who on an after day, yet to be spoken of, cursed from God's altar those who wished to realise his simulated aspirations and in the endeavour had forfeited their lives. A doggerel ballad had been written for the occasion by Thomas Davis, to the air of the "Gallant Tipperary," over which himself and his friends afterwards indulged in many a hearty laugh. One verse runs as follows:—

The music's ready, the morning's bright,
Step together left, right, left, right,
           We carry no gun,
           Yet devil a one
But knows how to march in Tipperary O!
By twelves and sixteens on we go,
Rank'd four deep in close order O!
           For order's the way
           To carry the day,
March steadily, men of Tipperary O!

It is here introduced as a proof and a justification of what has been stated in reference to one great object of the projectors of the monster meetings. Possibly it will be said that this is an admission of the truth of a charge frequently urged by Mr. O'Connell against the *Nation* and its writers, namely, that they having intentions of which he knew nothing, had committed him to breaches of the law, of which he was not only not guilty but not cognisant, but which by a perversion of judgment were given in proof against him at the celebrated State Trials. It is quite true that they did entertain the intentions which he afterwards so vehemently repudiated. But they never once concealed them. In the Association, and where Mr. O'Connell was committed with them, they abstained from giving them utterance; but they did so because they felt bound to act in accordance with the resolution of that body. And with respect to the proceedings of the Cashel meeting and the more wonderful and significant meetings that followed, they always submitted to him and had his entire sanction for every act done at and every line written for these meetings. In fact, if he were in any way mistaken as to them, they were still more grievously deceived as to him. All their acts and speeches were in the direction of their intentions; all his acts and speeches were in the same direction, and went further. In truth, they believed that he fully concurred in the sentiments which they cared not to conceal, but which he had the cunning or caution not to avow. One justification of this belief has been already given; another and a more pregnant one was the Mallow defiance which the greatest poet and the greatest sculptor of our time and nation have immortalised. In reference to proofs not published, however conclusive, this history shall be silent.

Succeeding events shall be briefly glanced at only. Some of them have already attained a place in history; and the scope of my narrative only embraces the facts, incidents and tendencies which led to an armed crisis and governed its explosion. Meeting followed meeting in rapid succession, and each was marked by some signal manifestation of a healthier, holier and more resolute national purpose. Numbers, calmness, order, obedience, bespoke an advanced discipline, and prefigured future victory. The crowds that attended the Halls of the Association no longer consisted of idle brawlers; they were listening, thoughtful mechanics, conscious of the toil and danger that lay before them, and braced for the encounter. Dignitaries of the church and the ablest men among the second order of the clergy appeared on the platform, and added sanctity and dignity to the proceedings. Members of Corporations through the country, and private gentlemen of rank brought to the imposing confederacy the weight of their office, rank and name. The existing Government in a splenetic attempt to crush it, had dismissed certain magistrates for having their names enrolled on its books. This new aggression gave a fresh impetus to its progress. Men who had previously looked on it with doubt or fear, now embraced it as the only safeguard for the remaining liberties of the island. The parliamentary committee which had been instituted by Mr. O'Brien, had exhausted every source of information within the reach of industry in developing the resources and capacities of the country. The committee of the Association counted within its members one hundred lawyers who preferred the fortunes of Ireland to professional or political advancement. Many of these and others who were not of the party brought to the popular tribune rare endowments, the most generous passions, and the noblest eloquence. Poetry, fresh, vigorous and full of heart, shed her harmonising and ennobling influence upon the whole, and imparted to patriotism the last pre-requisite of success. Amidst this grand movement stood Mr. O'Connell, erect, alone, its centre and its heart. He was not its guide, but its god, until he slept within a prison, and came forth less than man.

During this period two events occurred deserving particular notice— the only facts upon which Mr. O'Connell's supremacy was questioned, or his advice audibly condemned. These were, first, his refusal of French contributions and French sympathy, of which M. Ledru Rollin, since so celebrated, was to be the bearer; and secondly, his acceptance of contributions from America under protest, against the "infamous institution" of slavery. He rejected the first with indignant scorn, because it was the offering of "republicans," and spoke of the latter with contempt, as "smelling of blood."

These two acts alienated from his cause the only foreigners in the world who were willing to espouse it. His wisdom was questioned and condemned. It was urged upon him that he should not intermeddle with foreign institutions or with the political predilections of individuals.

Enough for Ireland, he was told, to find that Frenchmen and Americans were ready to do battle in her cause, and it ill became her to spurn their advances with indignity and a sneer. The argument failed, his hatred of slavery and republicanism out-weighed all other considerations.

I have fixed upon the State Trials as an epoch in this history, marking a distinct phase in the character of the Repeal Association. The proceedings of that extraordinary inquest are familiar to most men. It is not my intention to refer to them, except as a sort of pivot upon which public sentiment veered. When they were commenced there was untold wealth in the coffers of the Association. There was still a greater store of public purpose in the country. Threats, hot and violent, had been uttered. Pledges had been made which could only be violated in shame and death. A challenge had been given from which it would be baseness to shrink. The world looked on in wonder and awe. Each successive act was more and more gigantic; each resolution bolder. When the meeting at Clontarf was projected, the heart of the nation beat quick and hotly. Yet no man was surprised; none condemned. The associations of the spot suggested a perilous future. Still the hazards it prefigured created no alarm; the directions of a sub-committee respecting the military order of the processions towards the place of meeting was but the expression of the public hope that lay at every heart.

While the bustle of preparation was at its height; while the flushed capital was dizzy with wild excitement, a proclamation appeared on the walls—'twas nearly evening's dusk—forbidding the proposed demonstration. For that proclamation there was no law; scarcely any object. It could not render the meeting illegal. It would not entitle the chief magistrate to disperse it; for if it were proved to be constitutional, he would be answerable before the laws of his country. It was simply a warning utterly inefficient for good or ill in any trial that may follow. In this state of things, a responsibility of the greatest magnitude devolved on the Association, or its committee. They were hastily summoned or came together spontaneously. Alarm, surprise, disappointment, chagrin, swayed their hurried consultation. The decision was weak, and it was fatal. It was only carried by a small majority, but in that majority was the great spirit of the confederacy. Never after did he stand on equal terms with his adversary. He was driven before him amidst broken hopes, and broken promises—his challenge, a boast unfulfilled, his prestige withered.

What the issue might have been if the decision were different, it would be rash to conjecture. It might have been carnage; it might have been a triumph. The historian has nothing to do with conjecture. But in this case was involved a mighty question, palpable, self-created and conclusive. The wisest forethought may fail to arrive at a sound conclusion as to the result of holding the meeting. The risk existed, no doubt, that some ill-disposed or hired villains, or even rash enthusiasts may provoke the troops, and thus afford a pretext for carnage. But opposed to that were the dictates of prudence, honour and fear on the part of those in command of the army; and it seemed a more probable result that either the meeting would be allowed to proceed, or it would be illegally dispersed in the usual way by reading the Riot Act. Even if the weight of conjecture were the other way, the consequences should be risked rather than falsify the national pledge. To recede was cowardice; not the vulgar cowardice arising from personal weakness, but the moral cowardice which shrinks from an imperious obligation, because it is perilous. The meeting should be held; every possible precaution should be taken to prevent an armed conflict. If Power, drunk with its own advantage, risked an outrage, the people should be taught to yield; but only to yield with the purpose of entering a court of law, as prosecutors and avengers. Even if worse consequences ensued after every effort to prevent them had been exhausted, the issue should be left to God. Recriminations, painfully petty in their nature, followed. The Government were charged with a premeditated design to commit wide and indiscriminate slaughter, and the weakness, in which were shrouded deep national shame and guilt, was made matter of indecent boast. The Government, aware of the unexpected advantage, followed up the blow. Mr. O'Connell took shelter in the sacredness of the Hall, which, he imagined, he had guarded against the encroachments of arbitrary power, and thither they followed him. Having abandoned a position where he could act on the offensive, he was forced to contend against the aggressive attacks of Government flushed with its first success.

The trial that followed already occupies a large space in history. Its effects were immediate and disastrous. The personnel of the accused assumed the nation's place. Exhortations full of intense eloquence were addressed to the people from which the question of the country's deliverance was entirely excluded. Technicalities of law absorbed the attention which was due to Liberty. A demurrer, a motion in abatement, or in arrest of judgment, was canvassed with a deeper interest by the people of the provinces than by even the distinguished Bar, which were arrayed on either side. Mr. O'Connell's infallibility in law engaged the anxious solicitude, the pride, the passions of Ireland. Yet throughout that long trial the question which would test it was not mooted. The indictment was a subtle net-work, which excluded such argument. The objections to the indictment also were objections of form merely, and the final issue upon which the judgment was reversed was not even remotely connected with the main enquiry, whether or not the charge of conspiracy was sustainable in point of constitutional law. During the progress of the trial, a fraud, a swindle, a petty theft, was perpetrated by the officers of government, which more than one man, high in office, had a hand in suborning. This fact had supreme influence on the decision of the House of Lords. But the plain truth is, the judgment was reversed as an essential move in a great party game.

Ireland triumphed. Her triumph was a just and a great one.

But her exultation was on a fallacious basis. She believed Mr. O'Connell's infallibility was re-established. No one cared, or perhaps dared to correct the error. In itself it seemed little worthy of notice, yet it had its share of evil influence. First, it diverted men's minds from the one question; secondly, it left behind it the demoralising effect inseparable from untruth. Were it even what the public eagerness chose to shape it, its relative value, weighed against the triumph of courage and virtue, would be contemptible.

Mr. O'Connell himself did not seem to share in the nation's pride. His spirit was broken. He anticipated the glad wishes of the metropolis, and walked home from the penitentiary clouded and gloomy. It was evident something within him had died. However, he went back the next day, and left the prison the second time in the midst of public rejoicings never surpassed on any occasion in his life. His addresses on that day, and subsequently while in town, were not such as they were wont to be; and he soon retired to his wild mountain home to invigorate a mind and body, borne down by gigantic labours, fearful responsibilities, some alarms, and perhaps a chilling sense of defeat and weakness. His health was soon restored, but his political vigour never. The first time his voice was heard from that retreat, it was to recommend a compromise; and, for the first time, his advice was openly opposed. Charles Duffy answered his letter, which recommended to fall back on Federalism—a question in the mouths of many, but in the brain of none—respectfully and firmly remonstrating against such a course. In a great many circles, Mr. Duffy could not be looked at with more wonder if he had recommended to cut off Mr. O'Connell's head.

Hitherto, this condensed retrospect has been almost exclusively confined to the name and fortunes of O'Connell. It is time now to revert to other actors in the scene. Even before the trial, elements of antagonism had begun to manifest themselves. With the party since called "Young Ireland," every consideration was subordinate to the great question of national deliverance. They laboured incessantly to elevate the morals, the literature, the taste, passions, genius, intellect and heart of the country to the sublime eminence of a free destiny. Far the foremost man in urging and encouraging this glorious endeavour was Thomas Davis. From sources the most extraordinary, and the least known, there welled forth abundant and seductive inspiration. He struck living fire from inert wayside stones. To him the meanest rill, the rugged mountain, the barren waste, the rudest fragment of barbaric history, spoke the language of elevation, harmony and hope. The circle, of which he was the beloved centre, was composed of men equally sincere, resolute and hopeful; there was not one of them undistinguished. Some of them had now the first literary distinction. The character of each was remarkable for some distinctive and bold feature of originality. I, of course, exclude myself from this description. I know not to what circumstance I owe the happiness of their trust and friendship. My habits, my education, my former political connections, disqualified me for such association. Since first I took my place among them, seven or eight years have now rolled by. They have been years of severest trial, years of suffering and sorrow, years of passion and prejudice and calumny, years of rude and bitter conflict, years of suspicion and acrimony, and finally of defeat and shame; still, in that eventful course of time, to me at least, there has occurred no moment wherein I would exchange the faintest memory of our mutual trust, unreserved enjoyment and glad hope for the hoarse approval of an unthinking world. There was no subject we did not discuss together; revolution, literature, religion, history, the arts, the sciences—every topic, and never yet was there spoken among us one reproachful word, never felt one distrustful sentiment. Our confidence in one another was precisely that of each in himself; our love of one another deeper than brotherly. When we met, which was at least weekly, and felt alone, shut in from the rude intrusion of the world, how we used to people the future with beauty and happiness and love. Little did we dream that those for whom we toiled, and thought, and wove such visions of glory, would shun and scorn, and curse us. But had that bitter cup, which afterwards we were forced to empty to the dregs, been then presented to us, there was not one of us who would not have drunk it to the last drop; drunk it willingly and cheerfully, without further hope or purpose than our own deep conviction that we owed the sacrifice to truth.

Those who took immediate part in the proceedings of our circle before the State Trials, were Thomas Davis, John Dillon, Thomas MacNevin, Michael Joseph Barry, Charles Duffy, David Cangley, John O'Hagan, Denis F. MacCarthy, Denny Lane, Richard Dalton Williams, with one or two others whose names I cannot mention. To this list was afterwards added Thomas Francis Meagher, Richard O'Gorman, John Mitchel, Thomas Devin Reilly, and Thomas Darcy M'Gee. I do not include several distinguished men who lived in the provinces with whom we communicated, and from whom we received sympathy and sustainment; and I omit others who took a leading part, in deference to the position they are now placed in.

John Blake Dillon

With the first section above named, originated the idea of publishing the *Library of Ireland*. It was proposed, discussed, and determined on one evening, at the house of Thomas MacNevin, while some one sat at the piano, playing the lovely Irish airs, of which the soft strains of Davis suggested the conception to William Elliot Hudson. The music was as true to the Celtic genius as the lays of Davis to its character and hopes; and amidst the entrancing seductiveness of their association, was born the generous resolution of rescuing the country's literature from the darkness in which it had long lain. The *Library of Ireland* was proposed as a beginning, and so diffident did its promoters feel, that they deemed it indispensable to engage the recognised genius of William Carleton, whose name and abilities they pledged to the public, as an assurance for the undertaking. Mr. Carleton promptly undertook his share of the task, and James Duffy, the enterprising bookseller, assumed all the risk and responsibility of the enterprise.

John Mitchel, then known to few, and appreciated only by Thomas Davis, was by him associated with those who were willing to engage in the new and difficult labour. He pledged himself for him, and selected his subject. Most nobly was that pledge redeemed; but its fulfilment dawned on the fresh grave of him who made it. Other men, and first in order, as well as eminent in ability, was Thomas MacNevin, who has also sunk into a too early grave, more than realised the most sanguine hopes of an exulting country. Death first interrupted this new current of life, even in its day of most sparkling promise. Disunion haunted the petty jealousies of little and narrow minds; famine, pestilence and defeat have done the rest. The labourers are dead, exiled, immured in dungeons, or scattered over the face of the earth as fugitives; and how far they had capacity to fulfil their inspiring promise, can never be tested more. A few, however, remained, and amid greater gloom, and nearer to utter death, they stand out redeeming beacons to the future.

I have not mentioned the name of Mr. O'Brien, as associated with us at this early stage. He joined the Association in a time of great excitement.

The *Nation* hailed the accession with the fondest joy. The consistency of his politics, the purity of his intentions, and the unvarying rectitude of his life gave abundant assurance, not alone that he was deeply sincere, but that his purpose could only be changed by death. But to those who looked beyond the expediency of the hour, those who had cherished fervently the passionate aspirations for true liberty his name and character became an augury of success: nor would they intrude for any consideration on the attitude of lofty dignity he assumed.

It has already been stated that elements of antagonism between Mr. O'Connell and the Young Ireland Party had at this time (the period of the State Trials) manifested themselves. It will be remembered that this period embraced a space of nine months, from the date of Mr. O'Connell's being held to bail in September, 1843, to that of his sentence the 30th of May, 1844. As the events of this or the previous year do not, properly speaking, range within the historical scope of my narrative, I have excluded chronological and historical order. My object has been to group together the great features of the confederacy without other reference than that of pointing out their moral influence, operating through a long space of time. Thus I have referred to the Parliamentary Committee instituted by Mr. O'Brien among incidents which belong to an anterior period, because the vigour of these incidents, which left moral seeds in their track, continued to co-exist and blend with the powerful agencies of that Committee. As I now approach the period when the differences with Mr. O'Connell, which hitherto developed themselves in the distinctive characteristics of the respective opinions of both parties rather than in any direct collision, became tangible, it is necessary to observe strict historical and chronological accuracy.

Before proceeding to details of succeeding events, a brief recapitulation of important facts, with the dates of their occurrences, become necessary. A few others, not heretofore alluded to, must needs be added.

The date of the imprisonment is the 30th of May, 1844: that of the release the 6th of September in the same year.

In the intermediate period the amount received in the Repeal treasury during four weeks was, £12,379 14s. 9d.

About the close of August was passed the Charitable Bequest Act, against the indignant remonstrances of the priesthood and Catholic population of Ireland. This Bill was obnoxious in all it's provisions, but the enactment which was received with most scorn was the clause that annulled a Catholic charitable bequest, unless it had been duly made six months at least before the decease of the testator. The prohibition was attributed to an insulting assumption that the Catholic clergymen abused their influence over dying penitents, for sacerdotal or religious, if not for personal aggrandisement, and the impeachment was repelled with bitter execrations. Others objected to the Bill on grounds involving more alarming considerations. They regarded it as the first infringement on the liberty of the Catholic Church—the first criminal attempt to fetter her free action and sow dissent among her prelates and priests. The Repeal Association offered, from the beginning, its undivided, unqualified and indeed vehement opposition. But amidst the storm and rage of the nation, it became the law, and three Roman Catholic prelates of the highest reputation undertook the duty of its administration.

One party there was who regretted the Bill still more deeply, but in a different point of view. At the head of these was Thomas Davis. He regarded it as an instrument of dissension and weakness, cunningly adapted to that end by Sir Robert Peel, and he deplored the diversion of the public mind and energy from the grand national object. Mr. O'Brien, to a certain extent, shared this feeling, but never obtruded the opinion or ventured to check the Association, while Mr. Davis confined his efforts to passionate warnings addressed through the columns of the *Nation*.

This question is introduced here because it was important and fatal in its consequences. A still more important one taken in the same light must interrupt its discussion for a moment: Mr. O'Connell's Federal letter, already referred to. The leading sentiments of that letter are subjoined. It is dated the 2nd of October, 1844.

After stating what Simple Repeal and what Federalism respectively meant, he proceeded to contrast their value.

"The Simple Repealers are of the opinion that the reconstructed Irish Parliament should have precisely the same power and authority which the former Irish Parliament had.

"The Federalists, on the contrary, appear to me to require more for the people of Ireland than the Simple Repealers do; for besides the local parliament in Ireland having full and perfect authority, the Federalists require that there should be, for questions of imperial concern, colonial, naval and military, and of foreign alliance and policy, a Congressional or Federal Parliament, in which Ireland should have her fair share and proportion of representatives and power.

"It is but just and right to confess that in this respect the Federalists would give Ireland more weight and importance in imperial concerns than she could acquire by means of the plan of Simple Repealers.

* * * * *

"For my own part, I will own that since I have come to contemplate the specific differences such as they are, between Simple Repeal and Federalism, I do at present feel a preference for the Federative plan, as tending more to the utility of Ireland and the maintenance of the connection with England than the plan of Simple Repeal.

* * * * *

"The Federalists cannot but perceive that there has been upon my part a pause in the agitation for Repeal since the period of our release from unjust imprisonment."

I have only extracted from Mr. O'Connell's most elaborate letter, his distinctly expressed preference for Federalism, and the single reason upon which the preference is founded. The remainder consists for the most part of a sort of logical equation, balancing the component elements of both plans, from which is deduced the above conclusion.

Charles Duffy's answer, dated October the 18th, was triumphant and conclusive, at least in Mr. O'Connell's own mind, for he did not afterwards repeat the same sentiments. But a blow had been given the Association from which it never recovered. The newspaper press, taken under three distinct heads, first the blind and heedless echoers of Mr. O'Connell's doctrines, secondly the Whig organs in Ireland, and thirdly the papers in the English interest, gave way to unrestrained exultation. The wisdom, the prudence, the holiness of the "great Liberator," were extolled as unmatched in the annals of statesmanship. A few whose self-interest constrained their subserviency, shrugged wisely and said nothing, while several provincial journals stoutly maintained the undoubted and enduring supremacy of the great national aim over every weak expedient.

Whatever hopes may be entertained by Mr. O'Connell, his suggestions met with no sustainment and no response, save the empty echoes of an adulating press. Among the great party to whom he appealed, not one voice was heard to suggest a practical step in the direction intimated. The project fell, if indeed it were ever seriously entertained, leaving no memory and no regret. The first place Mr. O'Connell afterwards appeared in a public capacity, was at the Limerick banquet, given on' the 20th of November. His speech on that occasion contained scarcely a reference to Federalism, and both his sentiments and those of the other speakers, including John, Archbishop of Tuam, as well as the Toasts and Mottoes, were distinguished for loftiness of tone, unflinching purpose and highest enthusiasm. But other elements were at work furtively sapping that purpose and dimming that enthusiasm.

Prominent among these was the spirit of religious dissension already under discussion, to which it is now time to recur.

At and after the period when the Roman Catholic prelates accepted the functions of administering a law insulting and obnoxious to the Catholics generally, much angry controversy prevailed. A report was rife that the Government not alone succeeded in deluding the Irish Bishops, but had accredited a minister plenipotentiary, whose mission was to conciliate the Court of Rome to a "Concordat" with England. A rescript said to be received by the Most Reverend Doctor Crolly, the Primate, was adduced to prove not alone the existence of the intrigue, but its partial success. The rescript contained an admonition to restrain the intemperate violence of political priests, and an advice to confine themselves more generally to the sacred functions of their holy office. The English press magnified the advice into a command, and exulted over the failure of the Repeal movement whose extinction they augured from the withdrawal of the Catholic priesthood.

Mr. O'Connell, alarmed at the import of a command so fatal, pronounced the rescript "uncanonical." This led to greater dissensions and bitterer recriminations. The prelates who condemned the Bequest Act, denounced those who accepted the task of administering it. One of the body thus writes:—

"The resolution [referring to one passed at a meeting of the prelates, which was pronounced by the ministerial press a vote of unanimous approval of the bishops' acceptance of the office of Commissioners] did not meet the approval of all the Bishops, neither could it convey to any one of the Episcopal Commissioners the most distant notion that in accepting the office he did not oppose the views and wishes of many of his Episcopal brethren. When the resolution was moved, there were six of the protesting Bishops absent, and a moment was not allowed to pass after it was seconded, when it was denounced in the strongest manner by two of the Bishops present. They solemnly declared before the assembled prelates that, in the event of any prelate accepting the odious office, they would never willingly hold any communication with him in his capacity as Commissioner."[4]

But, while disunion reigned at the council board of the Catholic Hierarchy, the Government plied their task of seducing, dividing and misrepresenting bishops, priests, people and nation. Out of all the elements of disunion, distraction and disaster over which they in turn gloated, the British newspapers, with wonderful accord, predicted and boasted of the complete overthrow of the Repeal Party. It was amidst these circumstances of gloom and evil augury the year 1844, a year within which range the most startling, extraordinary and trying events of Ireland's recent history, came to a close.

Before I conclude this chapter, I must revert to a fact which, although unimportant in relation to the view of the question under consideration, deserves to be remembered in connection with future events. The date I cannot fix, as it was confined to the private circle of the Association Committee, and no record of it remains. Immediately after the close of the State trials, as well as I can remember, Mr. O'Connell proposed the dissolution of the Association, with a view of establishing a new body, from which should be excluded all the "illegal" attributes and accidents of the old. The suggestion was resisted by Mr. O'Brien, and all those understood to belong to what was called the Young Ireland Party. They protested against such a course as false, craven and fatal, and Mr. O'Connell at once yielded to their vehement remonstrances.

FOOTNOTES:

4   Doctor Cantwell to Mr. O'Connell. Given in the *Nation*, Vol. III., No. 119.

CHAPTER III

FURTHER EMBARRASSMENT CAUSED BY THE RESCRIPT—
DIFFERENCES BETWEEN MR. O'CONNELL AND THE
PRIMATE.—FINANCIAL REFORMS IN THE COMMITTEE OF
THE ASSOCIATION, AND CONSEQUENT DISSENSION.—
'82 CLUB.—THE COLLEGES BILL.—DIFFERENCES AND
CALUMNIES CONSEQUENT UPON IT. QUARREL WITH MR.
DAVIS.—THE GREAT LEVEE AT THE ROTUNDA.—DECLINE
OF THE AGITATION.—CLOSING LABOURS AND DEATH OF
THOMAS DAVIS.

Thus wrote Thomas Davis at the opening of the new year:—

"Hitherto our dangers have been few and transient. The product
of mistake or enthusiasm, they were remedied by explanation and
kindliness. There are dangers threatened now, and against them we
shall try the same prompt and frank policy which never failed us yet.
Already the English press are quarrelling for the spoils of the routed
Repealers. They are almost unanimous in describing the people as
disgusted, the leaders as exhausted, and the policy of the ministers as
rapidly levelling the defences of the once great party.

"We do not quail. We remember that whenever the rent[5] has
fallen, the same press cried out the people are sick of the agitation.
Whenever righteous discussion took place in our councils, they
exulted over our 'fatal divisions,' and at the beginning of each new
blunder of the cabinet, they sang victory.

"If the Irish be a hot or capricious race, who plunge into a new policy because it is new, and abandon their dearest interests and most solemn vows because their success needs time, then indeed Repeal was hopeless and was always so. If the leaders have not sagacity enough to embrace the business of an empire and pierce through time, unwearied industry, pure hands and resolute spirits, then to repeal is hopeless until a new race of chiefs appears."

Almost contemporaneously with this article, the Catholic Primate contradicted Mr. O'Connell's assertion respecting the rescript, and laid rescript and contradiction before the public. "I was surprised and sorry," he writes, "to find that you had ventured to assert that a letter sent to me some time past from the Propaganda was not a canonical document." He adds that he laid the document before the assembled prelates, and appends the resolution in which they acknowledged its authenticity and approval of its counsel.[6]

Mr. O'Connell at once expressed his entire acquiescence and deep contrition. He bowed reverentially to the resolution of the prelates, retracted the hasty opinion, and apologised for his error, which, he said, resulted from his great anxiety of mind, caused by the avowal of the *Morning Chronicle* that the Whigs had a secret agent in Rome.

But the prelates were far from unanimous in their construction of the rescript which they promised unanimously to obey. With the resolution among his papers, the Archbishop of Tuam proceeded directly from the Episcopal meeting to the Repeal banquet at Limerick, where he delivered a speech stronger in language and more violent in character than any he had ever uttered. Some passages in that speech, wherein he eulogised the heroism of the women of Limerick who cut their long hair to supply the defenders of the city with strings for their bows, excited the wildest enthusiasm and most rapturous applause. Doctor Cantwell, in the letter already referred to, gives his construction, which he says was that of the majority.

"The Cardinal only evidently censures violent and intemperate language, in either priest or bishop, whether they address their flocks in their temples, or mix with their fellow-countrymen in banquets or public meetings. We inferred, and I think we were justified in the inference, that conduct and language at all times unbecoming our sacred character, and not our presence on such legitimate occasions, were the object of this salutary caution."

His construction was sustained more clearly and forcibly by Thomas Davis. "It [the rescript] announces the undoubted truth that the main duty of a Christian priest is to care for the souls of his flock, and both by precept and example to teach mildness, piety and peace. It does not denounce a Catholic clergyman for aiding the Repeal movement in all ways becoming a minister of peace. Nowhere in the rescript is the agitation as a system, or repeal as a demand, censured; but some reported violence of speech is disapproved."

The coincidence seems a strange one, that in the same paper, which thus disposes of the rescript, the same paper wherein appear the letters of Doctor Crolly, Doctor Cantwell, and Mr. O'Connell, the same paper in which is published the official denial of a Concordat with the Pope, under the viceregal seal, are also published the proceedings of the Repeal Association, which consisted, to a great extent, of a violent attack on the exploded Concordat. At the meeting held on the 13th of January, it was denounced especially by two of Mr. O'Connell's friends, Mr. O'Neill Daunt and Mr. John Reilly, in terms the most vehement and indignant. Mr. Daunt used these words. "On that day fortnight he had proclaimed from the chair of the Association, that if a rescript should emanate from Rome denouncing the national movement, the Catholics of Ireland would treat it as so much waste paper." This statement was made on the 13th, Doctor Crolly's letter is dated on the 11th, Mr. O'Connell's on the 14th, and Lord Heytesbury's denial of the Concordat on the 15th of January. Contemporaneously with all these was also published an address of his clergy to the Archbishop of Dublin, deprecating in the strongest language certain calumnies against him, which they attribute to priests and people, Protestant and Catholic.

From these proceedings one inference is inevitable, namely, that they who have so strongly inculcated obedience to the Holy See, and denounced as an infidel any Catholic who refused blind obedience to its decisions, in reference to secular education, were not then troubled with the same sensitiveness or scrupulousness of conscience in regard to the authority of the Roman Pontiff. But of that one word hereafter. I here reproduce the historical facts connected with these letters, for another object. Although the excitement about the threatened Concordat was allayed, and the invectives against the Archbishop of Dublin abated in intemperance, the bitterness of feeling which swept over the country like an avenging scourge, left behind it germs of discord and weakness.

Publicly or privately the Seceders did not interfere. At the meeting of the Association already alluded to, Mr. O'Brien made a most noble speech, inculcating education, self-reliance, organisation and progress, without stooping to refer to the perplexed question, which filled his audience with angry passions, and supplied the other speakers with intemperate enthusiasm.

The whole endeavours of the Seceders were at this time devoted to the organisation of clubs or reading rooms on an educational basis. Connected with this object was the augmentation of the Repeal revenue, which was anticipated from the extended action of these political and social schools. The funds were greatly diminished, and the weekly collections had fallen to an average of about £150. It became necessary, as much as possible, to curtail the expenses, and a reduction of a very serious amount was effected during Mr. O'Connell's absence at Derrynane. The effort was continued after his arrival in town, which led to differences of opinion with him, in committee. Sinecure situations, created by him, were abolished, and inquiries were instituted which gave him great annoyance. He particularly resented and resisted the removal from one of those offices of Doctor Nagle. Doctor Nagle was appointed to be "curator of manuscripts", the ostensible duty of which was to superintend the reports (then daily issuing from the press, and written for the most part by the Seceders) for the purpose of preventing the publication of anything illegal or dangerous. In effect, he was nominally, literary, legal and moral censor. But the unanimous and loud indignation of the essayists rendered his task a light one. He was content to accept the salary and leave those gentlemen the guardians of their own safety, their character and literary fame. Doctor Nagle continued to act as librarian and, weekly, delivered to the secretary certain lists of contributions that had been previously furnished him by that gentleman. His salary and certain fees given to other "patriots," came under the cognisance of a sub-committee consisting, as well as I remember, of the present member for Dublin, a Mr. O'Meara and someone whose name I now forget. Their report adjudged the office useless, and recommended its immediate abolition. A motion was accordingly made in committee for Doctor Nagle's dismissal. Mr. O'Connell was in the chair. All his sons were present, one of whom, I think, moved an amendment to the effect that he be continued at his then salary. A division took place, when the majority against the amendment was considerably over two to one. Mr.

O'Connell expressed himself deeply mortified at this result. Another amendment to the same effect was then proposed and negatived by a majority numerically somewhat less, when Sir Colman O'Loghlen moved, and John Loyd Fitzgerald seconded, an amendment to the effect that he be continued as clerk of the library at half his salary, that is £50 a year. The result would have been the same as before but that many of the majority had withdrawn under the impression that the question was disposed of; the number for the amendment was twenty-two, and the number against only twenty-three. Mr. O'Connell assumed the right to give two votes, one as member, which made the numbers equal, and a casting vote as chairman. It was then proposed and carried that every chairman should in future have two votes, and Sir Colman's amendment was allowed to pass in the affirmative. Doctor Nagle continued to fill his office until his appointment to a more lucrative one under the Whig Government.

The Eighty-Two Club which was projected in prison was finally organised in January, 1845. The differences which manifested themselves in Conciliation Hall imperceptibly extended to this body. The original members constituted the committee and were self-appointed. The others had to submit to a ballot. Some few were rejected, at which Mr. O'Connell's friends took umbrage, and the rejected aspirants were sure to attribute their decision to their devotion to the "Liberator." Thus it happened that most objectionable candidates could not be resisted without incurring the imputation of opposing and thwarting the "saviour of his country."

Charles Lavan Duffy (1846)

Mr. O'Connell himself, although he warmly approved of the club in the commencement, soon ceased to feel an interest in its proceedings. For the first year, its action was confined to some routine dinners, which attracted a very fashionable attendance, and furnished an occasion for some brilliant speaking. Yet the fame and respectability of such a body were seductions which few of the leading men in the confederacy could resist. The Eighty-Two Club became a standard toast at public dinners, and its members were received as distinguished guests or visitors wherever they appeared. Without having yet performed any distinct service, or realised the promise involved in its establishment, the club became a very important and imposing body.

Mr. O'Connell was its president, and Mr. O'Brien, Mr. Grattan, Sir Colman O'Loghlen and others, vice-presidents. The first committee was composed of the Members of Parliament, Mayors of cities, and men eminent in the different professions and literary pursuits. Complaints of inattention were made against some of its members, and at the election for officers after the expiration of the first year, others were substituted for the inattentive and inefficient. The change for the most part was made by unanimous consent; but when a ballot was called for, other names were substituted for those on the house list, recommended by the former committee, and the contest resulted in the rejection of Richard Barrett and one or two others. This was taken as an affront to Mr. O'Connell, though personally he neither took part in, nor was present at, the meeting. Whether it was owing to Mr. O'Connell's aversion to the green-and-gold uniform, to which he sometimes expressed his dislike, or his objection to the rejection of his soi-disant friends, or to his consciousness that the club was not subservient to his control, he took very little interest in its progress, and frequently spoke of it in terms of derision.

But that which produced the first sensible and vital difference between Mr. O'Connell and the Seceders was the Colleges Bill. Education had long been a subject of anxious solicitude with Mr. Davis, and he was in continual communication with Mr. Wyse, its great parliamentary champion. He had repeatedly urged upon him the indispensable necessity of the principle of mixed education, as the basis of any collegiate system for Ireland. That basis was recognised in the system of national education which was accepted and approved of by the whole Catholic Hierarchy, with one exception, and most warmly sanctioned by the Catholic priesthood and laity. Extreme bigots of the Protestant school opposed and denounced it as unscriptural and Godless, and one extreme bigot of the Catholic school echoed the objurgation. It was not to be supposed that a principle thus sanctioned, tried, and efficient as applicable to the children of the poor, would be objected to when applied to those who were higher in station and older in years. When, therefore, the Bill was introduced and its principal provisions announced, it was received with the utmost delight and, even, triumph. Mr. O'Connell proclaimed in a meeting of the committee his emphatic approval of the principle of the Bill.

As soon as its details were published, it was submitted to the parliamentary committee, and, during its discussion there, he expressed for the first time some doubts as to the practicability of a mixed system of education. Mr. O'Brien, Mr. Davis and others expostulated, and deprecated in unmistakable terms the fatality of engaging the Association to a principle so sectarian, narrow and illiberal. He said he would take time to consider, and would meantime consult with Doctor MacHale. He was reminded that Doctor MacHale could not approve of the system without gross inconsistency, and requested to take the opinion of all the other Bishops as well. How far he was governed by this advice is unimportant and impossible to tell. But the bishops met in solemn synod and published the result of their deliberations in the following memorial:—

> "That memorialists are disposed to co-operate on fair and reasonable terms with her majesty's government and the legislature, in establishing a system for the further extension of academical education in Ireland.

"That a fair proportion of the professors and other office-bearers in the new colleges should be members of the Roman Catholic Church, whose moral conduct shall have been properly certified by testimonials of character, signed by their respective prelates. And that all the office-bearers in those colleges should be appointed by a board of trustees, of which the Roman Catholic prelates of the provinces in which any of those colleges shall be erected shall be members.

"That the Roman Catholic pupils could not attend the lectures on history, logic, metaphysics, moral philosophy, geology, or anatomy, without exposing their faith or morals to imminent danger, unless a Roman Catholic professor will be appointed for each of those chairs.

"That if any president, vice-president, professor, or office-bearer, in any of the new colleges shall be convicted before the board of trustees of attempting to undermine the faith or injure the morals of any student in those institutions, he shall be immediately removed from his office by the same board."

It will be observed that the principle of mixed education is not here directly approved or condemned. But approval is an inference, as clear and emphatic as words could express. The memorial prays for distinct and specific alterations in the details of the Bill. It demands that certain branches of secular education should be taught to the Catholic students by Catholic professors approved of by the prelates, and it insists upon other guarantees to secure the Catholic youth from the danger of all and every species of interference with the tenets of their faith.

How far the demands of the bishops were just or extravagant, is not a fit subject of inquiry here. But the fact of making the demands stamps the principle of the bill with their incontrovertible approval. The argument which denies it involves an accusation against those Most Reverend and Right Reverend divines, of evasion, treachery and untruth.

Any defence which implies that they avoided the direct condemnation of the principle because they knew their memorial would be disregarded, which would enable them to interdict the whole Bill, principle and details, on the ground of the immorality of the latter, involves an implication that moral and Christian turpitude is synonymous with Catholic zeal. Such an implication, inevitable from the premises assumed by the opponents of the mixed system, would be foulest calumny. The Catholic prelates were eminently sincere; and had they been warmly seconded they might have obtained such ameliorations in the details of the system as would be satisfactory to every rational, liberal and honest man. But the old jealousy, division and calumny which had grown out of the Bequests Act, obtruded themselves on every attempt at calm consideration, and scattered the elements indispensable to successful moral combination. The principle and details of the academic project became confused and confounded, and while some clamorously opposed, others unthinkingly supported, the entire. Thus the minister was enabled to balance the voice of public opinion as he found it arrayed for and against his measure, and under pretence of indifference to despise both parties. For a long while, the action of the Association was paralysed. There were deeper questions at issue there than even those which appeared on the face of the bill. The educational party insisted that any measure which did not embrace the University was scanty and illiberal. They claimed its honours, advantages and emoluments for all the youth of Ireland alike; and they sought to make the academic subordinate to and parcel of the collegiate system. The Dublin University and Trinity College are separate and distinct foundations and establishments. They proposed that Maynooth and Trinity College should be both sufficiently endowed for all purposes of ecclesiastical education, without any interference, direct or indirect, from each other or the Government, while the University should be open alike to all who had obtained distinction in the provincial colleges. Any measure of narrower scope would, they contended, leave dullness and bigotry where it found them.

74

Mr. O'Connell, on the other hand, insisted on the inviolability of Dublin College as a Protestant institution, inaccessible to Catholics, except through the slough of perverted and perjured faith. He would then have new colleges purely Catholic and entirely under the control of the Catholic bishops, but endowed by the State, and chartered to confer literary degrees. He would extend the same right to the members of other religious persuasions. It was answered that these positions and his arguments addressed to the academic question were irreconcilable and incompatible. Catholics were already admissible to Dublin College, and entitled to certain degrees and a vote. He either intended that they should be thenceforth excluded or he did not. If not, then the argument against mixed education would hold for nothing: if he did, then he attempted what was impracticable, or, if not impracticable, preposterous and absurd. It is not conceivable that Catholic young men, of laudable ambition, would be deterred from entering the lists with their Protestant contemporaries where most honour was won by superior eminence, or that they would be swayed by a warning that a college course would be attended with risk to their faith and morals, when they remembered that for the past century, while the risk was infinitely more imminent, no such warning had been ever heard from council, synod or conference. It is a strange fact in the history of these troubled times that no voice of denunciation against Dublin College could be heard in the polemical din, although it was well known that its literary honours stamped preliminary degradation on the Catholic aspirant, and were used at once to mock his political condition and pervert his faith—no voice was heard although one at least of the prelates had obtained degrees in the University, while the bishop and priests of an entire diocese, in conclave assembled, solemnly resolved that they would refuse sacraments to any Catholic parent who sent his son to one of the Godless colleges. But supposing it were practicable to exclude Roman Catholics from the University, and that the system of exclusive education among the middle and upper classes were applied in all its rigour, when were Protestant and Catholic to meet? If it were dangerous to faith and morals that they should discuss together the properties of an angle or the altitude of a star, it could hardly be safe to have them decide together a principle of law or determine the value or limits of a political franchise. All this was urged on Mr. O'Connell, and sometimes apparently with success, for he more than once consented to forego the discussion of the question in the Hall; and he would have strictly adhered to that engagement had he not been goaded by the intemperate counsels of others.

In the desultory history of this question, two facts have been stated requiring distinct proof. They are:—First, that Mr. O'Connell was favourable to the principle of mixed education in the commencement.

And, secondly, that the Seceders—those who were afterwards so glibly denounced as infidels for their support of the Godless bill—were as much opposed to that bill as he was.

How Mr. O'Connell expressed himself when the bill was first announced has been already stated. It is at once conceded that the writer's memory of a conversation, in its nature almost private, were he even above all suspicion, would not be a safe authority. In this instance there is no need to rely on it—the statement is more than sustained by Mr. O'Connell's recorded words. From a number of occasions, equally available, I select one, because of its solemnity and importance.

In a prolonged and most earnest debate in the House of Commons, on motion for going into Committee on the Bill, June 2nd, Mr. O'Connell, after eulogising the Maynooth grant, says:—

> "Take one step more, and consider whether this bill may not be made to accord with the feelings of the Catholic ecclesiastics of Ireland. I ought not to detain you: I am not speaking here in any spirit of hostility. I should be most happy to give any assistance in my humble power to make this bill work well. I have the most anxious wish to have this bill work well, because I am desirous of seeing education promoted in Ireland; but even education may be misapplied power. I admit that at one time I thought the plan of

a mixed education proper, and I still think that a system of mixed education in literature and science would be proper, but not with regard to religious education."

And further on: "Again I repeat I am most anxious for the success of this bill, but I fairly tell you it cannot succeed without the Catholic bishops . . .

"There may have been harsh expressions in the public papers, but depend upon it great anxiety exists in Ireland to have such a measure."

The second proposition would be abundantly sustained by a single sentence in Thomas Davis's commentary on the speech from which I extract the above.

"On our part we had feared O'Connell conceded almost too far."

But the testimony of Mr. O'Connell himself will be considered more conclusive.

Speaking in the Association on the 6th of July, he said:—

"I may remark for the present that on this subject a question of difference has arisen among ourselves. Some of the members of the Association are for what is called mixed education, and others of us are against it, but that difference of opinion ought not to create any division among us, for neither the one nor the other of us is gratified by the bill as it stands."

Again, in the course of the same speech, he said:

"We (Mr. O'Brien and himself) did our best to avert such a calamity. We called upon the Government not to persist in working out this bill in all its details of blackness and horror."

He concluded by lauding Lord John Russell for his valuable assistance in the attempt to amend the bill, and finally said that, having failed in this attempt, he "flung the bill to the ministry, to deal with it as they pleased."

Mr. O'Brien continued in London, and proposed amendments to the bill in every stage of its progress. It was during that time he was assailed by Mr. Roebuck with all the little malevolence of his envenomed nature. He failed in every attempt to remedy the defects of the bill, which passed its last stage in the Commons on the 10th day of July. On the 17th of the same month, Mr. O'Connell, speaking in the Association, said:

> "In the resolution I am about submitting to the Association, we have not inserted one word about mixed education. This is a question upon which there exists some differences of opinion. I have my opinions upon the subject, I am the decided enemy of mixed education . . .
>
> "I fully respect the contrary convictions entertained by others, and I am the more ready to proclaim that respect because at present all possibility of discussion on the matter is out of the question."

It will be observed that Mr. O'Connell's opinions underwent a serious and important change during the time over which these speeches range. That change was produced gradually, and not without infinite trouble on the part of his son whose inveterate zeal knew no bounds. In his father's presence, and more particularly so in his absence, he denounced the bill, and held up any Catholic who dared to support it to public indignation. He called on the people of Waterford to demand Mr. Wyse's resignation, not because he was an unfaithful representative, but because he was unchristian. If he had not determined to divide the Association on this question, he did all a man could do who had so determined.

I shall only trouble the reader with two quotations more. They refer to the question immediately under discussion, namely, that the Seceders were as much opposed to the obnoxious clauses of the bill as those with whom they differed. But while they are unequivocal and conclusive on that branch of the subject, they go still further and attest the sincere forbearance with which they treated language and conduct which appeared to them in the utmost degree narrow and intolerant. Discussion among the bishops naturally produced discussion among the chiefs of the Association, and it was agreed that the Association should confine its objections to those provisions of the bill upon which there could be no disagreement. The first petition of the Association was confided to me. I endeavoured to embody in the petition what appeared to me the true basis of a comprehensive system of education. Some persons on the Committee objected to certain phrases as susceptible of an inference favourable to the principle of mixed education. Mr. O'Connell joined in the objection and succeeded in reducing the petition to a single paragraph, deprecatory of the Tenth Clause of the Bill. I refused to have any more to do with the petition, and it was dropped. After the lapse of a fortnight, Mr. Maurice O'Connell proposed another, simply praying that the tenth clause, which vested the appointment of the professors of the college in the Government, should be rejected.

Upon the occasion of this petition being submitted to the Association (9th June, 1845), Mr. J. O'Connell delivered one of his usual invectives against the bill and its abettors. Mr. O'Brien deprecated the ill-feeling and discord such language was calculated to provoke. In the course of his observations he said:—

> "In seconding the motion of my hon. friend, the member for Kilkenny, for the adoption of this petition, it is not my intention to follow into any of the polemical questions which, in the course of his protracted speech, he has raised in this Association. I am obliged, however, to say in candour that in some of the

views he has put forward I cannot agree ... We have given a general concurrence in this Hall to the recommendation that has emanated from the Catholic Hierarchy ... I am not disposed to assist the Government in making those seminaries, which ought to be seats of learning, filthy sties of corruption. It is because I believe that such would become their character if this tenth clause were to remain a legislative enactment that I shall oppose it to the utmost."

The Reverend John Kenyon, then little known, rose to protest against the course pursued by Mr. J. O'Connell, which he characterised as not only uncatholic but unchristian. Mr. J. O'Connell, in the blandest tones, deprecated any discussion tending to division, which induced Mr. Kenyon to sit down. Having spread with dexterous industry the most baleful elements of discord, he begged they should not be disturbed.

I will be pardoned for transcribing here a few observations of my own on that occasion.

"I am exceedingly anxious, having the misfortune to differ most widely from my honourable friend the member for Kilkenny, on the subject of academical education, to express my cordial concurrence with him in reference to the subject of this petition. I shall not say one word about our difference of opinion. I shall enter into no disturbing or dividing discussion, and the more so because any difference we may express could not fail to impair the efficiency of our action where we are thoroughly agreed. I condemn this clause as strongly as the hon. member can. Nay, I will go a step further, and say that if there be no provision made by the bill for religious instruction and moral culture, Protestant and Catholic ought to unite in struggling for its rejection. No matter how splendid may be the accommodations provided by these academies—no matter how richly they may be endowed—

if there be no provision made for the religious education of the pupils, I trust they will remain silent, unattended Halls."

Numerous other proofs to the same facts are accessible, but these are abundantly conclusive. The history of the struggle itself, the slow and evidently reluctant change in Mr. O'Connell's opinions, and the intolerant spirit with which the enemies of the bill pursued the name and character of those who, although they approved of the mixed system, were as inveterately inimical to the dangerous provisions of the bill as they were themselves, sufficiently attest that faction swayed the troubled movement of clerical and popular passion alike. The vulgar and virulent anathemas of some tongues and pens not only swept unsparingly over the unhappy crowd, but aimed at the lofty sphere of Episcopal authority, even where most identical with purity and piety. A malignant charity extended to the errors of the Primate that palliation which perverted reason otherwise refused to admit. Too lofty to be accused of treachery, he was not too sacred to be pronounced mad.

The Committee of the Association alone nearly escaped the influence of the fierce spirit of the times. There the voice of reason for a while held sway. The forbearance and respect for conflicting opinions which preserved its dignity were, with the one exception, extended to the proceedings in the Hall, where even the most unscrupulous were checked by a petition which recognised and welcomed the principle of united education, but strongly deprecated the objectionable provisions of the "Godless Bill." To this petition was affixed the signature of almost every educated lay Catholic in Dublin. The number of Catholic barristers alone whose names are found among those signatures amounts to seventy-two. At the same time, a remonstrance addressed personally to Mr. O'Connell was signed by the leading Catholics of the Association. Its object was to preclude all discussion on the subject of the disputed principle in Conciliation Hall. It was signed for the most part by men who theretofore had taken but little part in the dispute. But against all these precautions passion by degrees prevailed, and when Mr. O'Connell was reminded by Mr. Barry, of Cork, that in reply to the remonstrance he had pledged himself to abstinence from the irritating discussion, his apology was, that he thought the document in question and all proceedings connected with it were strictly private; as if the privacy of a solemn pledge dispensed with its obligation.

An episode in this strife deserves specific notice. At a meeting of the Association, held on the 26th of May, the question was incidentally introduced. Mr. Michael George Conway, a man of considerable literary and oratorical powers, but not distinguished for any very rigid piety, introduced the subject, evidently with the view of exciting Mr. O'Connell's impulsive character against the species of restraint under which his sinister friends were continually hinting he was held. The speech breathed the most fervent spirit of Catholic piety, seasoned with bitter invectives against what Mr. Conway described as a baffled faction in the Association. Mr. O'Connell took off his cap, waved it repeatedly over his head, and cheered vociferously. Few, if any, of the Catholic gentlemen who were opposed to Mr. O'Connell, were present. Mr. Davis rose, and commenced by saying: "My Catholic friend, my *very* Catholic friend." The allusion was intelligible to almost every man in the assembly, but the practised and dexterous advocate saw and seized the advantage it presented for exciting the active prejudices of the audience. He started up and exclaimed, "I hope it is no *crime* to be a Catholic." The whole meeting burst into a tumultuous shout which bespoke a triumph rather than admiration. Mr. O'Connell did triumph, but not in the sense understood by his applauders. He apprehended the effect of the honest, frank and manly exposure which, if he were not rudely interrupted, would be made by Mr. Davis, and he was too keen to allow an opportunity, so tempting to his object, to pass, though he should violate all the observances of good feeling and decorum. Mr. Davis, on the other hand, felt the blow to be a stunning one. He was shocked at the same time by Mr. O'Connell's disregard, not alone of friendship, but of common courtesy, and by the intemperate exultation of the audience. To his loving nature, both seemed, especially in such a place, utterly unintelligible and grossly unkind. He was the last living man to offer insult to the belief or even the prejudice of a Catholic, and he felt that this was thoroughly known to Mr. O'Connell, and that it ought to be known to his audience. The disappointment and the rudeness were too much for his susceptible heart, and he so far yielded to wounded feelings as to shed tears. Mr. O'Connell, whether gratified by success or influenced by his better impulse, caught him by the hand and exclaimed: "Davis, I love you." Although the first struggle closed amidst cheers, there were carried away from that meeting in the breasts of many, seeds of bitterness and hate which ripened in after times and under gloomier auspices. I dwell on it as important, although a casual incident, frequent and almost inevitable in political excitement. There were two parties from whose memory the scene never passed. These were the blind followers of Mr. O'Connell, to whom it seemed blackest guilt to question his supremacy or infallibility, on the one hand, and on the other, all who sympathised with genuine and lofty emotions, and regarded the attack on Mr. Davis as wanton, brutal and contemptible. The miserable little faction that existed on the spoils of the Association magnified the difference and fanned the discontent. That Young Ireland had received its death-blow passed into a watch-word among them.

An event of mighty augury and most trifling results, which distinguished the year 1845, must not be passed unmentioned. This was the celebrated levee, held in the Round Room of the Rotunda, on the 30th of May, the anniversary of the imprisonment. It was referred to a sub-committee, on which Mr. Davis and Sir Colman O'Loghlen were principals, to devise the most appropriate celebration for that important day. They determined on a public levee, to which were summoned whatever there was of respectability, authority, genius and worth in the island, which recognised the wisdom, justice and holiness of the struggle for Nationhood. All the corporations, every delegation which derived public authority from the popular voice, besides citizens of the unincorporated towns, answered the summons with alacrity. That day witnessed a scene the most extraordinary, imposing and formidable of the kind in modern annals. The Round Room was thronged to excess, but preconcerted arrangements had provided for the convenience of its favoured visitors, while the public streets, abandoned to chance, presented an immovable mass of human beings, swaying to and fro, but governed by a single and omnipotent impulse, which steeled them to the pressure and broil as if they felt themselves in presence of a speedy deliverance and free destiny.

Richard O'Gorman, Jun. (1848) & Patrick O'Donohoe (1848)

The preparations engaged the vigilant activity of a large committee for two entire days and nights. Yet these preparations bore an infinite disproportion to the display of wealth of mind, of energy of thought, and national pomp, which ushered in the glorious morning. Those who scoffed at the project when it was first announced came to mock the scene but went away admiring. The spirit of the hour infused itself into the public heart, which appeared to throb but to one impulse and one aim: at all events no one was, no one could be, found obdurate enough to question the significance or importance of the proceeding.

Mr. O'Connell's fellow-prisoners shared his state and the homage which was paid to him. But in the outward crowd no one dissociated him personally from the minutest detail of the day's proceedings, or admitted for a moment that any other human being partook of its glory, or directed its end. High above the multitude they saw him receive the nation's homage, which seemed but the expression of the liberty he had already achieved. How he felt the influence of the scene there is no record to tell. His demeanour while exercising the prerogatives of his position was such as became a man conscious that he occupied a throne loftier than ever yet was decked by a kingly crown. But when his official functions were discharged, he addressed the impassioned throng in language too tame for the most ordinary occasion.

The great act of the day was the adoption of the following pledge. It had been prepared and approved by the Committee of the Association, and every word was canvassed with the most scrupulous regard to the trying circumstances which the committee found themselves in presence of. The virulent hostility of the Tory Government had been baffled, and its utmost strength discomfited. It was understood at the time that a Whig Government was in the advent of power, and the great object of the pledge was to record the solemn conviction of the Nation that they were faithless and treacherous as the others were unscrupulous and vindictive, and that to the corrupting influence of the one and the unmasked hostility of the other the same resistance should be shown. The pledge was preceded by this resolution:—

"Resolved, That in commemorating this first anniversary of the 30th of May, we deem it our duty to record a solemn pledge that corruption shall not seduce, nor deceit cajole, nor intimidation deter us from seeking to obtain for Ireland the blessings of self-government through a national legislature, and we recommend that the following pledge be taken:—

"We, the undersigned, being convinced that good government and wise legislation can be permanently secured to the Irish people only through the instrumentality of an Irish Legislature, do hereby pledge ourselves to our country that we will never desist from seeking the Repeal of the Union with England by all peaceable, moral and constitutional means, until a parliament be restored to Ireland.

"Dated this 30th day of May, 1845."

This pledge was adopted formally in the Pillar Room of the Rotunda, in presence of most of the Irish mayors, the leading delegates of the country, the members of the Eighty-Two Club, and a vast concourse of gentlemen both from the metropolis and the provinces. It was proposed by William Smith O'Brien, seconded by Henry Grattan, and put to the meeting from the chair by the eldest son of Daniel O'Connell. The cheer that hailed its adoption was a shout not of approval, but defiance. But alas! many voices mingled in the chorus which have since been attuned to the meanest whine of mendicancy. That they vilely belied their solemn promise were of little moment. Nay, more, it is bootless to consider whether they were more false-tongued and false-hearted in that great pageant, or on the recent occasion of their kneeling in their own shame to pledge a faith they do not feel, in expectation of some royal notice or royal favour. What is mournful in both instances is this, that a show of wealth, a practice of successful chicanery called good sense, or public trust won by intrigue and falsehood, should so blind the world to the *man's* rotten and vulgar heart as to raise them to a position where their acts should be regarded as indicative of the feeling or important to the destiny of a nation.

With the 30th of May, passed off the excitement of which it was the cause and scene. Those who arranged the grand pageant of that day, and invested it with attributes, suggestive, imposing and useful as ever decked a public spectacle, would have wrought it out into a sterner purpose: but the heart upon which they counted had, even then, died. Mr. O'Connell's speech too painfully bespoke his utter inability to guide the nation in any higher effort. The energy that should have seized the occasion to confirm the people in their strong purpose, and elevate their hopes to the level of the great stake at issue, exhausted itself in balancing the routine details of cold and empty statistics. The curtain fell, and nothing remained but grotesque figures, withered garlands, broken panels and desolate dust, which mingled confusedly behind the scene, over the dark, deserted stage. The journals, of course, preserved, for a few days, very glittering reminiscences of the scene. With one accord, they pronounced it surpassing in interest and importance. Great results were anticipated in the newspaper world; and many imagined they had fulfilled the last obligations they owed their country. But with the men, who had fondly hoped to date therefrom a new era and begin a nobler task, the 30th of May, was of dark, despairing augury. They clearly saw that from that hour forth there remained but the alternative of abandoning their cherished hopes, or attempting to realise them without the aid, perhaps in opposition to the wishes, of Mr. O'Connell. It was a gloomy and sad conviction, but it was no longer to be blinked.

Meantime, Mr. O'Connell returned to the Hall, and repeated to a jaded audience, week after week, the same stale list of grievances. From any other man the repetition would be intolerable. But the public ear had become attuned to his accents, to which, whatever the sense of his language, men listened as to a messenger of heavenly tidings. Mr. Duffy strongly urged upon his fellow labourers the improbability of success, and advised a distinct change of policy. In this he was overborne by their united opinion, and the *Nation* continued to promulgate the same bold, unwavering course. By degrees the feeling of bitterness entertained by the anti-education section of the priests found utterance, and the paper was, almost openly, denounced as an infidel publication. At first indeed, the charge was shrouded in mysterious insinuations; but it soon gained strength and audacity, and received the unblushing sanction of at least one prelate. The answer of the *Nation* was confined to one indignant line. Proof was demanded and was not offered; but its very absence only deepened the malignity of the slanderers. Even in the midst of this storm the muse of Thomas Davis sang no discordant strain, nor did his pen trace one angry word. On the contrary, he summoned his whole energies to the task of harmonising the jarring elements around him. His inspiration rose to that unearthly height, whereon guidance becomes prophecy. Great, strong and unselfish convictions, entertained holily and uttered sincerely, are assurances of new creations, pledges of the destiny to which they tend. In this spirit, spoke and sang Thomas Davis during a time of bitterness and dissension. And his counsels had been successful, but alas! in that last effort his fond, faithful, trusting heart was broken.

There was a perceptible lull in the agitation. The country gradually relapsed into a state of inactive and vague hope, which centred in the mental resources of Mr. O'Connell. The difficulties which the people should have appreciated and learned to overcome, they transferred, with easy and trusting indifference, to the energies of the "Liberator," which they not only deemed boundless but immortal. From all educated and thoughtful men, however, hope in those energies had passed away. Davis seduously endeavoured during the summer months of 1845, to gather these, and others of the same class from the Conservative ranks, round some common object or endeavour, outside Mr. O'Connell's path, and not calculated to wake their prejudice or jealousies. The Art Union, the Archaeological Society, the Royal Irish Academy, the Library of Ireland, the Cork School of Design, the Mechanics' Institute and every effort and institution, having for their aim the encouragement of the nation in arts, literature and greatness, engaged his vigilant and embracing care. Of each of these institutions he became the great attraction, the real centre and head. While he successfully wrought to give a national and steady direction to Irish intellect and enterprise—Hogan, in Italy, Maclise, in

London, and others like them, who were bravely struggling and nobly emulating the highest efforts of the genius of other lands, were vindicated, encouraged and applauded by his pen. Among the sterner natures, who urged their way through the stormy elements of agitation, his accents, though low and diffident, commanded the deepest attention and most lasting memory. While thus engaged, compassing by his "circling soul," every sunward effort and immortal tendency of the country, death came, sudden and inexorable, and struck him down in his day of utmost might. His last work on earth was the brief dedication of the memoir of Curran, and edition of his select speeches, which he had prepared, to his friend, William Elliot Hudson. This he wrote during a pause of delirium, and soon afterwards passed to a brighter world. He died on the 16th of September, 1845, when yet but thirty-one years old. How sincere and deep was the public grief, no pen can ever tell. In the mourning procession that followed his hearse there was no parade of woe, but every eye was wet and every tongue silent. If ever sorrow was too deep for utterance, it was that which settled above the early grave of Thomas Davis.

During the summer, no effort of the Association rose above the hacknied level of the usual weekly meetings and the repetition of the same stale grievances, except a gathering of Tipperary at Thurles, which took place on the 23rd of September. This was the largest of the monster meetings: but, although the crowd was enormous and the shouting loud, it seemed without purpose or heart. During the preparations for that meeting I had to encounter difficulties of the most extraordinary kind. First, the meeting was opposed by certain influential clergymen; and when they found themselves too feeble to resist, they transferred all their opposition to me. There is no petty cavil they had not recourse to, to thwart and discourage, and even when all had succeeded I was treated with personal discourtesy and annoyance at the public dinner. The seeds of strife, afterwards destined to bear such deadly fruit, had already begun to manifest themselves, and petty calumnies were insinuated in the name of religion and morality. From that great meeting the crowd retired quickly, and, almost as instantaneously, its effect faded from the public heat. All that remained was soreness and distrust.

No event worth a memory marked the close of 1845, or the first months of 1846. The Colleges Bill had passed, without a single important amendment, and a Roman Catholic priest accepted the nomination of Government, as president of one of the institutions. Some of the prelates, too, were said to be favourable to the colleges, even as they were then constituted, and the divisions supposed to exist among them were imparting their acridity to the deepening distractions of the time, when an event occurred—the advent of the Whigs to office—which broke up the great confederacy on which the hopes of the nation were staked.

FOOTNOTES:

5 The Repeal "Rent." The weekly contributions to the funds of Conciliation Hall.—Ed.

6 Moved by the Right Reverend Dr. Brown of Elphin; seconded by the Right Reverend Dr. McNally of Clogher. Resolved: That the Most Reverend Dr. Crolly be requested to reply to the letter received from the Holy Father, stating that the instructions therein contained have been received by the assembled prelates of Ireland with that degree of profound respect, obedience and veneration that should ever be paid to any document emanating from the Apostolic See, and that they all pledge themselves to carry the spirit thereof into effect."

   Dr. Crolly had previously explained what he considered true obedience to the rescript. He writes in reference to a former one in 1839: "In obedience to the injunction of the Holy See, I endeavoured to reclaim those misguided clergymen;" adding that the present was "in order that I should *more efficaciously* admonish such priests or prelates as I might find taking a prominent or imprudent part in political proceedings."

7 John Reynolds.

* * * * *

CHAPTER IV

IMPRISONMENT OF O'BRIEN FOR CONTEMPT OF THE
BRITISH COMMONS.—CONDUCT OF THE ASSOCIATION.—
DEPUTATION FROM THE '82 CLUB.—MR. O'CONNELL RETURNS
TO IRELAND.—DISCUSSIONS IN THE COMMITTEE.

Before proceeding to detail the circumstances which led to the
celebrated secession, it is essential to dispose of an episode in the struggle,
which, more than any other, stamped its impress on the acts and feelings
of that unfortunate period; I allude to the imprisonment, by the House
of Commons, of William Smith O'Brien. There is no act of his life upon
which there has been so much acrimonious criticism; none on account of
which he has been subjected to so much intemperate misrepresentation.
And yet, perhaps, his great career, fruitful in good actions, never
furnished a purer or more unselfish example of sound judgment as
well as intrepidity and devotion. The history of his incarceration ranges
over a great portion of the time which has been already passed, and
enters largely into the leading events, hereafter to be related. A clear
understanding of the whole—of Mr. O'Brien's influencing motives and
his tenacity of principle—would be impossible without a distinct recital
of the circumstances out of which his purpose first grew, and which, to
the end, controlled his resolution.

In the spring of 1845, the committee of the Association passed a vote
to the effect that the Parliamentary representatives, who were members of
that body, should withdraw from the British Parliament. It was proposed
by Mr. Davis and received Mr. O'Connell's entire approval. Though at first

sneered at, it had a stunning effect. The supercilious British Commons, who would have answered the just remonstrance of the Irish Repealers with a jeer, shrank from the consequences of legislating for the country in the absence of the men, whose efforts, if present, they would not hesitate to scoff at. The disturbing influence of the resolution became at once perceptible, and the earliest means were taken to bring the question to an issue. Mr. Hume, a parsimonious economist, of niggard principle and grovelling sentiment, undertook the office of coercing the Irish. He gave notice of a motion for a call of the House. This man, a mean utilitarian, had been rejected by the country of his birth and the country of his adoption, and found refuge in an Irish constituency, that returned him without solicitation and without expense. He repaid them and the country by a vulgar jest, and now assumed the responsibility of their public prosecutor.

The Association heard his threat with calm indignation and resolved at once to defy him. The great importance of the position in which it was placed suggested the necessity of a deliberate consideration; first, of the constitutional question at stake and, secondly, of the steps proper to vindicate its own dignity and resolution. As on all such occasions, a sub-committee was appointed to whom the question was referred. Mr. O'Connell had to some extent formed an opinion favourable to the object of the Association. He stated that he had considered the question in a two-fold point of view.

First, "Whether the controlling power of the English House of Commons over its members, which admittedly it possessed before the Act of Union, was extended to the Irish portion of the members by that Act, there being no express provision creating it?"

And secondly, "Whether even if the House possessed the power, it was competent to enforce it, or, in other words, whether the Speaker's warrant would receive Ireland?"

To report on these two questions, thus framed, the following gentlemen were elected as a sub-committee: James O'Hea, Sir Colman O'Loghlen,

Robert Mullen, James O'Dowd and myself. Of that committee, each approached his task with that instinctive bias, inseparable from ardent minds, excited by a darling hope. They read the precedents, the cases, the arguments and judgments applicable to their enquiry with the aid of such a hope, and still they came to the reluctant decision that the ground taken against the authority of the British Parliament was not maintainable. With regard to the first branch they were unanimous. With regard to the second, Sir Colman O'Loghlen alone entertained some doubts. As chairman of the committee, I drew up a brief report, embodying our opinion. One reason alone we thought conclusive, namely, that the formidable jurisdiction claimed by the House of Commons was indispensable to the unimpeded fulfilment of its functions, as a coordinate branch of the supreme power and controlling authority of the State. In its very danger and extravagance consisted its supremacy; for it showed that it was only admitted from its overruling and overmastering necessity. And as the Parliament was recognised in Ireland in all things else we thought it would be absurd to deny it functions indispensable to its vitality.

On handing in the report, I mentioned the doubts entertained by Sir Colman O'Loghlen. Mr. O'Connell suggested that the report should be deferred until he could consult Sir Colman. The suggestion was agreed to, and time given for reconsideration. Mr. O'Connell himself examined the question, he said, with great attention. He was assisted by Mr. Clements in his researches, and at the end of the fortnight he came down to the committee with a report of his own, distinctly and emphatically contradicting ours, upon both branches of the case. He delivered it to the chairman (Mr. S. O'Brien), with exultation, as a great constitutional discovery of unspeakable importance to the liberties of Ireland. The committee received it in the same spirit. I ventured to question the soundness of his opinion, and maintain my own, it was considered a daring thing to do in those times; but the question seemed to me so clear that I could not abandon my views without treachery to my conviction. The discussion was very short, and ended in personality, wherein he insinuated something about unworthy motives. No scene of my life made the same impression on me. I felt keenly his reproaches, but still more keenly the impolicy and imprudence of the step into which the country was precipitated. I requested that the question should be again postponed, and the opinion of some eminent men outside the Association taken. I was overruled, and even laughed at—it was "doubting Mr. O'Connell." Mr. O'Connell said, "I'll test this question *'meo periculo.'*" The resolution passed amid cheers, and was recorded next day amid the louder and more vehement cheers of the Association. The country re-echoed the boast, and the House of Commons was, by a formal and solemn vote of the entire nation, set at defiance. The conflict was pre-arranged, even to its minute details. Mr. O'Brien was to proceed to London, where disobedience would be more marked and decisive; and Mr. John O'Connell was to remain in Ireland, where he could take advantage of an additional obstacle to the exercise of its authority to the House. So the matter stood when Mr. Hume, through what motive it is not easy to see, neglected or abandoned his notice. The country regarded this as a confession of weakness by the House, and gloried in a new triumph achieved by the genius of Mr. O'Connell. He himself thought he had found a great and solid basis for future action, and hinted at the prospect of being able to raise upon it a parliamentary structure, having imprescriptible and indefeasible authority, and only requiring the sanction of the crown.

A short time after the withdrawal of Mr. Hume's motion, the question was again raised in another form. The chairman of the Committee of Selection for Railways addressed a circular, among others, to Messrs. S. O'Brien and John O'Connell, requiring their attendance at the selection of special Railway Committees. The correspondent of the *Freeman's Journal*, thus writes in forwarding their replies:—

94

London, Monday, June 30.

"The authority of the British Senate over Irish representatives is now fairly placed at issue. By my letter of yesterday evening, you were apprised of the determination of Smith O'Brien and John O'Connell, to refuse to comply with the summons of the parliamentary selection committee.

"The course I suggested as that which it was probable would be adopted, has been since finally resolved upon, and in part carried into execution. John O'Connell, for the purpose of taking the chances of a judgment in the Irish court, will not forward his answer till he shall have reached Ireland. Smith O'Brien delivered his reply to the clerk of the House of Commons this day, at one o'clock."

Here follows Mr. O'Brien's letter:—

OXFORD AND CAMBRIDGE CLUB, PALL-MALL.

"June 30, 1845.

"Sir.—I had the honour of receiving on Saturday afternoon a letter dated 28th June, and signed 'Henry Creed,' to the following effect: 'I am directed by the committee of selection to inform you that your name is on the list for which members will be selected to serve on the railway committees, which will commence their sittings in the week beginning Monday, the 14th July, during which week it will be necessary for you to be in attendance, for the purpose of serving, if requested, on a railway committee.'

"I trust that the committee of selection will not think that I am prompted by any feeling of disrespect towards them, or towards the House of Commons, when I inform them that it is my intention not to serve on any committees except such as may be appointed with reference to the affairs of Ireland.

"I accepted a seat in the House of Commons, in the hope of being thereby enabled to assist in improving the condition of the land of my birth. So long as I continued to believe that I could serve Ireland effectually in the House of Commons, I shrank from none of the labours which are connected with the varied functions of that assembly. During twelve years I attended Parliament with an assiduity of which I might feel disposed to boast, if the time so consumed by the House and by myself had been productive of results useful to my native country.

"Experience and observation at length forced upon my mind the conviction that the British Parliament is incompetent through want of knowledge, if not, through want of inclination, to legislate wisely for Ireland, and that our national interests can be protected and fostered only through the instrumentality of an Irish legislature.

"Since this conviction has established itself in my mind I have felt persuaded that the labours of the Irish members, though of little avail in the British Parliament, might, if applied in Ireland with prudence and energy, be effectual in obtaining for the Irish people their national rights.

"I have reason to believe that in this opinion a very large majority of my constituents concur. To them alone I hold myself responsible for the performance of my parliamentary duty. If they had disapproved of my continued absence from the House of Commons, I should have felt it my duty to have withdrawn from the representation of the county of Limerick; but I have the satisfaction of thinking that I not only consult the interests, but also comply with the wishes of my constituents in declining to engage in the struggles of English party, or to involve myself in the details of English legislation.

"While such have been the general impressions under which I have absented myself during nearly two years from the House of Commons, I yet do not feel myself at liberty to forego whatever power of resistance to the progress of pernicious legislation my office of representative may confer upon me. Upon the present occasion, I have come to London for the purpose of endeavouring to induce the House of Commons, or rather the Government, who appear to command the opinions of a large majority of the House, to modify some of the Irish measures now before Parliament in such a manner as to render them beneficial, instead of injurious, to Ireland.

"Desiring that none but the representatives of the Irish nation should legislate for Ireland, we have no wish to intermeddle with the affairs of England, or Scotland, except in so far as they may be connected with the interest of Ireland or with the general policy of the empire.

"In obedience to this principle I have abstained from voting on English and Scotch questions of a local nature, and the same motive now induces me to decline attendance on committees on any private bills, except such as relate to Ireland.

"I am prepared to abide with cheerfulness the personal consequences which may result from the course of conduct which I feel it my duty to adopt.

"I speak with great diffidence upon any question of a legal kind, but I am supported by very high professional authority when I suggest to the committee that no power was delegated to the House of Commons by the Act of Union, or by subsequent statutes, to compel to attendance Irish members on the deliberations of the British Parliament. Neither do I find that any authority has been given by statutory enactment to the House (except in the case of election petitions) to enforce the attendance of members upon committees.

"I refrain, however, from arguing legal questions which may be raised before another tribunal, in case it should become necessary and advisable to appeal from the decision of the House of Commons to the courts of judicature, and conclude by assuring the committee that I take the course which I propose to adopt, not from any desire to defy the just authority of the House of Commons, but in obedience to my sense of the duty which I owe to my constituents and my country.

"I have the honour to be, your obedient servant,

"WILLIAM S. O'BRIEN.

"To the Chairman of the Committee of Selection."

Thomas Devin Reilly

Mr. O'Connell's letter bears date on the next day, as announced in the correspondent's notice, because it was intended it should not be delivered until the honourable gentleman was beyond the pale of English jurisdiction.

"BRITISH HOTEL, JERMYN STREET,

8 a.m., *July 1st.*

"Sir.—I have to acknowledge the receipt of a notification by order of your committee, to the effect that my attendance in Parliament will be required during the week beginning Monday, 14th July, for the purpose of serving, if chosen, on a parliamentary committee.

"With every respect to you, Sir, and the gentlemen of your committee, I absolutely decline attending.

"I, like some others, came to London the first time this session about a fortnight ago to remonstrate against and endeavour to resist the plan of infidel education which the Government are forcing upon Ireland. We had not, nor for some years have had, the slightest hope of obtaining any measure of good from a foreign parliament; but we came against our better judgment, that it might not be said we had not gone all lengths to endeavour to deter the Government from a scheme so redolent of political corruption, social profligacy and religious infidelity.

"We came armed with multitudinous petitions of the people, and the strong, unanimous and most decided protest from our revered prelacy and clergy.

"We were of course mocked at, derided and refused; but, what is of infinitely more consequence, the voice of our prelates and of the faithful people of Ireland have been treated with utter contempt—even Irish Catholics (yielding to the unwholesome influences around them) joining in the contemptuous refusal.

"Under these circumstances, Sir, I certainly will not suffer that portion of the people of Ireland who have entrusted their representation to my charge to be further mocked at and insulted in my person. I go to where I can best discharge my duty to them and to Ireland—*in Ireland.* There struggling, with doubtless as little ability, but with more energy and, if possible, more whole-hearted devotion than ever, to put an end to the present degradation of my country and obtain for her that which can alone ensure protection to her interests, relief to her many wants, and peace, freedom and happiness to her long oppressed and long enduring people,

"I have the honour to be, Sir,
"Your obedient servant,

"JOHN O'CONNELL.

"To the Chairman of the Committee of Selection."

These documents were entered on the minutes of the Association, and remained on its records with the original resolution. But no more was done in the matter until the beginning of April, 1846.

Mr. O'Connell and his son were in London, and Mr. O'Brien remained in Ireland. They had been all summoned to attend on committees. When Mr. O'Brien reached London, he found that the Messrs. O'Connell, without any previous communication with him or with the Association, and without reference to the solemn resolution, to the contrary, of that body, were acting on committees. This deeply disappointed and mortified him, and he at once resolved to remain faithful, at all risks, and though he stood alone, to the obligation which he had contracted with the sanction and approval of his country. Whatever may be the temper and resolution of the House of Commons, had it been resisted by the unbroken strength of the Association, it felt confident of its power to crush Mr. O'Brien alone, separate from, nay, abandoned by, the great leader of the Irish people. It must be acknowledged that the course pursued by the Commons was considerate and moderate. A principle involving their liberty of action was in issue; to vindicate it was indispensable; but finding themselves only opposed by a single man, of all those who had provoked the encounter, they proceeded with caution and forbearance. They forewarned, counselled and remonstrated during the time that intervened; and several members of the House, including Mr. O'Connell, urged Mr. O'Brien to give way. He refused, determinedly, and it may be supposed not the less sternly, when he found, among those who advised him to falsify his solemn promise, the man upon whose authority and through whose influence he had made it. The result was, his arrest and imprisonment, for disobedience to the House. Circumstances more trying never beset the fortitude of a great man. Personal liberty was his slightest loss. The sneers of his enemies, the pity of his personal, and the desertion of his political, friends poisoned the very air of the miserable cell to which he was consigned, and what completed his agony was a notion that he had been abandoned by his country.

During the early part of his imprisonment, a motion was made questioning the authority of the House. In the course of the discussion, Sir Thomas Wilde, then Attorney-General, dared any constitutional lawyer to impugn the jurisdiction assumed by the House. Every member felt that the challenge was offered to Mr. O'Connell, who replied as follows:—

> "I am sure that the House will give credit to my assurance that I should not rise to advocate the cause of my honourable friend, if I thought he had had the slightest intention of being disrespectful towards the House. It has not been his intention to be guilty of any contempt towards it: he thought he was entitled to make the exception to which he adheres. He has acted from a strong sense of duty, and I am sorry to see it is a sense of duty he is not likely to give up."

I add to this an extract from his speech delivered at the Corn Exchange, when, in spite of the most earnest remonstrance, the Association offered its defiance in solemn form to the British Parliament.

"Mr. O'Connell rose amid loud cheers, and said:—Our usual course of proceeding in this hall is to commence with handing in money, and then to go on with business of inferior importance, the business of making speeches (hear! hear! and laughter); but among the passing events of the day, there is one of such signal importance, that I am sure you will readily admit that I am right when I claim for it, on the present occasion, a right of precedence over any donation or subscription, no matter from what quarter they may come. The matter I allude to is a menace held out for the intimidation (as it is supposed) of the Irish members who are given to understand that there is about to be a call of the House, and that it is intended that the Speaker's warrant shall issue to compel them to go over to London. Now, sir, I think it right to apprise the Association and the country that, having considered this question attentively, I have made up my mind that the Speaker has no constitutional authority whatever to issue any such warrant."

But what pained Mr. O'Brien the deepest was the apparent coldness, apathy or cowardice of the Irish people. Among them, and them only, he calculated an enthusiastic sustainment. But those who felt the deepest in his regard were constrained by the responsibility of coming to an open rupture with Mr. O'Connell, at a time when union in the ranks of the Association was indispensable to even partial success. A vote was proposed to the committee, approving of Mr. O'Brien's act, and pledging the Association to an identification with the principle by which his conduct was governed. That vote was resisted by the whole of Mr. O'Connell's family, and personal friends and by all the pensioners and employes of the body. It was carried, nevertheless. But a motion to consult Mr. O'Connell as to its legality was passed, and the resolution was transmitted to him accordingly. His reply was an urgent remonstrance against the resolution on the ground of illegality. Meantime, representations were made that a certain party in the Association, intolerant of Mr. O'Connell's sway, were using that occasion to undermine his authority and overthrow his power. The great responsibility of causing disunion determined the supporters of the resolution to compromise with its opponents, and it was finally shaped thus:—

"Resolved, That having learned with deep regret, that by a resolution of the House of Commons the country has been deprived of the eminent services of Mr. William Smith O'Brien, and that illustrious member of this Association himself committed to prison, we cannot allow this opportunity to pass without conveying to him the assurance of our undiminished confidence in his integrity, patriotism and personal courage, and our admiration for the high sense of duty and purity of purpose which prompted him to risk his personal liberty in assertion of a principle which he believed to be inherent in the constitution of his country."

It was again, in its modified form, transmitted to Mr. O'Connell, and returned with his disapprobation. Captain Broderick read a letter from him, to that effect, at a meeting of the committee, suddenly summoned on Monday, the 4th of May, a few hours only previous to the public meeting of the Association, deprecating the passing of the resolution in any form. The present writer was the proposer of the resolution, and, feeling that he had already made too great a compromise, he refused to accede to this last request of Mr. O'Connell. The resolution was proposed and adopted with acclamation, and a letter was read from Mr. O'Connell, by Mr. Ray, in which he stated that the resolution did not go far enough.

In the provinces, the timid policy of the Association was decried with bitterness, and the men who struggled, against great odds, to identify the whole island with Mr. O'Brien, and pledge it to sustain him to the last, were subjected to the most virulent denunciations. Because the compromised resolution was moved, seconded, and spoken to by them, the whole country regarded them as the betrayers of their own avowed chief, and the violence with which they were attacked was unmeasured and unscrupulous.

They made no reply. No unjust aspersions from a people in ignorance of the resistance offered to them, and the motives that influenced them, could induce them to explain the position they had taken. But when they saw while they were subjected to the storm that Mr. O'Connell's friends, on the authority of his published letter, took credit for neutrality, they resolved once more to test the question in a body, whose proceedings were of a more private character, and where the most marked difference of opinion could lead to no fatal result—the Eighty-Two Club. Mr. O'Connell was the president of this club, and Mr. O'Brien one of its vice-presidents. A meeting was called. The attendance was unusually large. Men who had never before, and have never since, appeared at its meetings, were present. The question proposed was that an address be presented to Mr. O'Brien, in which his principles and his conduct would be fully recognised, approved of and adopted. This led to a discussion that lasted two days, but the motion was carried in the end by a majority of two to one. One man, and one only, unconnected with Mr. O'Connell, either by personal friendship or personal obligations, voted against the resolution. That man is Sir Colman O'Loghlen. His name is mentioned, because he was the only member of the minority whose motives could be regarded as unquestionable. For the rest, the minority was composed of Mr. O'Connell's sons and relatives, with Mr. Ray and Mr. Crean, officers of the Association, and one or two members whom he had caused to be returned to Parliament, amounting to twelve. A committee was appointed to prepare the address and resolutions, which were written by John Mitchel, and adopted by the committee without the change of a word. They also determined that the address should be adopted in its integrity by the club, or not at all. When it was proposed, objection was again taken to its principle, on the ground that it would commit the club, and involve it in a hopeless conflict with the House of Commons which of itself, it was averred, would be a misdemeanour at common law. The proposition was eminently absurd in common sense, as well as law, but it was sustained by the practised ingenuity and great skill of Mr. O'Hea, who, to do him justice, seemed deeply to feel the hopelessness and shamefulness of the task that was assigned him. But no other argument could prevail, and this appeal to the fears or selfishness of its wealthiest members was had recourse to in consequence of the utter poverty of reason and argument, which could otherwise be presented against the principle of the address. But such an obligation led to a novel difficulty and bitterer conflict. A discussion involving principles of the greatest moment narrowed into a technical disquisition of abstract law. Mr. O'Hea was driven from his position by the unanimous and unqualified opinion of every barrister present, and even by his own silence, when dared to allow the address to pass in the negative, and assume the responsibility of its rejection on the avowed ground of his legal opinion, as expressed to the meeting. The address was adopted by a greater majority than that which had confirmed the principle on the previous day, and a deputation was appointed to present it to Mr. O'Brien in his prison.

The members of that deputation, who proceeded to fulfil their mission, were William Bryan, of Raheny Lodge; John Mitchel, Richard O'Gorman, Thomas Francis Meagher and the present writer. They were accompanied by Terence Bellew MacManus and John Pigot, who joined them in London. They waited on Mr. O'Connell, as the president of the club, produced the address and requested he would proceed with them to present it. He admitted, without question, that as it was adopted by so very large and influential a majority, he was bound to do so. But he added that Mr. O'Brien refused to receive a visit from him, owing to the part he had taken, and further said, if Mr. O'Brien expressed a wish to see him, that he would accompany us. The deputation on their way to the House of Commons consulted for a moment, and, as well as I remember, Doctor Gray and some others were present: the result was a determination to present the address without Mr. O'Connell, feeling that an explanation between him and Mr. O'Brien, could not fail to lead to unpleasant recriminations, if not to more serious differences. The address and answer were as follows:—

"TO WILLIAM SMITH O'BRIEN, ESQ.
"RESPECTED VICE-PRESIDENT AND BROTHER.

"Heartily approving of the course you have taken in refusing to devote to the concerns of another people any of the time which your own constituents and countrymen feel to be of so much value to them, we, your brethren of the '82 Club, take this occasion of recording our increased confidence in, and esteem for you, personally and politically, and our determination to sustain and stand by you in asserting the right of Ireland to the undistracted labours of our own representatives in Parliament.

"We, sir, like yourself, have long since 'abandoned for ever all hope of obtaining wise and beneficial legislation for Ireland from the Imperial Parliament'; nor would such legislation, even if attainable, satisfy our aspirations. We are confederated together in the '82 Club upon the plain ground that no body of men ought to have power to make laws binding this kingdom, save the Monarch, Lords, and Commons of Ireland. From that principle we shall never depart, and with God's help it shall soon find recognition by a parliament of our own.

"Upon the mode in which the House of Commons has thought fit to exercise the privilege it asserts in the present instance—upon the personal discourtesy which has marked all the late proceedings in your regard, we shall make but one comment, that every insult to you is felt as an insult to us and to the people of Ireland.

"It would be idle and out of place to offer condolence to you, confined in an English prison for such an offence. We congratulate you that you have made yourself the champion of your country's rights, and submitted to ignominy for a cause which you and we know shall one day triumph.

"(Signed)
"COLMAN M. O'LOGHLEN,
Vice-President, Chairman.

"May 9th, 1846."

"BROTHERS OF THE '82 CLUB.—I receive this address with pride and satisfaction.

"I recognise in the '82 Club a brotherhood of patriots, who have volunteered to take the foremost place in contending for the liberties of Ireland, and who may vie, in regard of ability, integrity and sincerity of purpose, with any political association, consisting of equal numbers, which has ever been united in voluntary confederation.

"The unqualified approval accorded to my conduct by such a body justifies me in entertaining a sentiment of honourable pride, which I am not ashamed to avow.

"Nor shall I attempt to disguise the satisfaction with which I receive this address.

"If you had approached me with language of condolence, I could scarcely have dissembled my grief and disappointment; but you have justly felt that such language would be unsuited to the occasion, and unworthy both of yourselves and of me.

"On the contrary, you *congratulate* me upon being subjected to reproach and indignity for having aspired to vindicate the rights of my native land; you deem, as I deem, that to suffer for Ireland is a privilege rather than a penalty.

"In acknowledging your address, I shall not dwell upon the many important considerations which are involved in my present contest with the House of Commons. I cannot but think, indeed, that the constitutional questions at issue are of the highest moment, not alone to the Irish people, but also to each member of the legislature, and to every parliamentary elector in the United Kingdom. Upon the present occasion, however, I am contented to waive all reference to collateral issues, and to justify my conduct upon the simple ground upon which it has received your approval—namely, that until a domestic legislature shall be obtained for Ireland, my own country demands my undivided exertions.

"Be assured that those exertions will not be withheld so long as life and liberty remain to me, until Ireland shall again *fiat* the Declaration of 1782: 'That no body of men is entitled to make laws to bind the Irish nation save only the Monarch, the Lords, and the Commons of Ireland.'"

On my way home I was invited to address a public meeting of Repealers in Liverpool. I accepted the invitation, and in the course of my observations, emphatically repudiated all compromise on the subject of my country's deliverance. I disclaimed the idea that any concessions, any equalization with England in political franchises, any amelioration of our political or social condition, could ever be accepted by Ireland in compromise of her inalienable independence. When I arrived in Dublin, I attended the Association, and, happening to read a letter from the Rev. Mr. Walshe, of Clonmel, couched in the warmest terms of admiration of Mr. O'Brien's purity and heroism, the cowardice or jealousy of a certain party in the Hall found expression through its proper organs, and I was called to order in the name of the law. A violation of law to *praise* William Smith O'Brien! The chairman decided it was. To such decision I scorned to submit, and I read the letter to the end, amidst the most enthusiastic cheers of the audience. I was proceeding to read another letter from another clergyman of the same town, written in a very different spirit, when I was besought to withhold it, and entreated not to read it. I complied. It is but fair to add here that on the Saturday previous, an article was published in the *Nation*, some expressions of which Mr. O'Connell considered personally insulting.

Whether Mr. O'Connell was influenced by one or all of these occurrences, cannot be affirmed here. But he proceeded to Ireland in the course of the week, and suddenly called a meeting of the Committee of the Association, before which he arraigned us of discourtesy to him in London, found fault with the meeting at Liverpool, accused the *Nation* of attacking him, and, finally, expressed his unequivocal disapprobation of my resistance to the order of the chairman in the Hall. The deputation explained their conduct in London, and the motives that governed them, with which he appeared to be satisfied. All connection with the proceeding in Liverpool with which he took offence, was disclaimed, and, finally, Mr. Duffy satisfied him that no offence was meant him in the *Nation*, and that the passage of which he complained had no reference to him.

The discussion was a long and, to some extent, an angry one. It ended, however, as we thought, amicably. Mr. O'Connell had proposed at the outset two objects, namely, to express a solemn condemnation of the proceedings in Liverpool, and to expel the *Nation* from the Association. The rule of the Association was to send to every locality, at the expense of the body, whatever papers the subscribers of a certain sum desired. There were then three other weekly papers in Dublin, The *Register*, the *Freeman*, and the *Old Irelander*. The *Nation* had a circulation nearly equal to that of all the others. Its expulsion from the Association would at once deprive it of all the circulation it had through its agency, thus involving a very serious pecuniary loss to Mr. Duffy.

The two positions were abandoned, and the Committee separated on amicable terms. Another subject of importance was under discussion. This was, what suitable mark of national respect should be offered to Mr. O'Brien; and it was proposed that the committee should re-assemble on the following day (Sunday), at two o'clock. At the second meeting the disagreeable topics of the former evening were revived and discussed in a more acrimonious spirit and tone. The Committee was differently composed, most of the treasurers connected with the Committee being present, and most of the professional men, who attended on Saturday, being absent, Mr. O'Connell saw his advantage, or those under whose guidance he unfortunately was, saw it, and urged him on. He clearly had a majority. But having satisfied himself he could succeed, with a resolution refusing to circulate the *Nation*, he generously conceded the whole matter; and once more the Committee separated on good terms.

It was hoped that, as the concession was entirely voluntary, Mr. O'Connell would be content. This was a vain hope. On the next day, he referred to the subject in terms of unmitigated animosity; and on Tuesday the resolution of exclusion, in effect, though not formally, passed in the absence of most of those who were well known to be opposed to it.

One word of concession would have saved the *Nation* at this juncture; but that one word would not be written, had the consequence of refusal been the loss of every subscriber it had in the world. It maintained its high position in face of the two despotisms which had combined to crush it. The resolution of the Association was not formally recorded, but it remained in readiness to be re-asserted as soon as the trial in the Queen's Bench would be over.

That trial was for the celebrated railroad article, written by John Mitchel. When the article first appeared, Mr. O'Connell came to the *Nation* office. He seated himself familiarly, and, seeing all its contributors around him, he said: "I came to complain of this article." He then read through until where certain principles, previously promulgated, were recommended to Repeal wardens as the catechism they should teach. "I do not object," said he, "to your principles; but I object to your coupling them with the duties of Repeal wardens who are the officers of the Association." Mr. Duffy promised, at once, to explain the matter, to Mr. O'Connell's satisfaction, in the next number. He did so accordingly, and no more was said of it until after the prosecution was commenced.

On the 17th of June, Mr. Duffy was placed at the bar, on an information or indictment setting forth the entire of the obnoxious article. The Government was vehement and imperative, and the Bench constitutionally jealous of the law. The prosecution was conducted with malevolent ability, and the court charged, with pious zeal, for the crown. Robert Holmes was counsel for the accused and, in an impassioned speech, on every word of which was stamped the impress of originality, vigour and beauty, vindicated not the "liberty of the press," but the truth of the startling propositions Mr. Mitchel had propounded.

In the Hall, the speech was regarded as triumphant for the country, but conclusive against Mr. Duffy. It was said that for sake of his client he should confuse, confound and deny. The fact, however, justified the advocate. When Mr. Mitchel first promulgated his principles, they grated strongly on the public ear. Men openly pronounced the doctrines pernicious and bloody. But the veteran of the bar, speaking in the spirit of the more glorious times he remembered, denounced as a slave and a toward any one who thought them too strong for the occasion on which they were used, and the provocation to which they applied. For a brief moment he awoke in other hearts the spirit that lived in his own. The jury refused to convict, and were discharged. But the prosecution in which the Attorney-General failed, was transferred before a more loyal tribunal, and Mr. Duffy was condemned by the judgment of *Conciliation* Hall; a judgment of which something remains to be said hereafter.

It has been stated that the subject of testifying the respect of the *Nation* for its chivalrous advocate, after his release from the prison of the House of Commons—he was discharged without compromise or submission on the 26th of May—was under discussion.

A public and triumphal entry was determined on. But Mr. Smith O'Brien, desirous that the State prisoners of 1844 should be participators in any tribute of respect offered to him, requested that the 6th of September, the day of their release from prison, should be fixed on for a public triumph, in which all alike could share.

John Mitchell

Mr. O'Brien passed through the metropolis quietly on his way home; but in Limerick and Newcastle was received by hundreds of thousands with boundless joy. When he returned to town, it was to be expelled from that body to which he, of all living men, gave most firmness, and for which he alone acquired most respect. In the events which followed, the public dinner was forgotten.

It is now time to recur to those events, some of which at least range behind those already detailed—to which the following preliminary may be necessary. Early in June, a meeting was held at Lord John Russell's, when the minister-expectant explained the grounds on which he claimed the support of the entire Liberal Party. The English Liberals, generally and enthusiastically, acquiesced. The correspondent of the *Evening Mail*, writing from London, stated that Mr. O'Connell added to his adhesion, a voluntary promise to sink the cause of Repeal provided measures of a truly liberal character were carried into effect. He, moreover, said that he never meant more by Repeal than a thorough identification of the two countries. The *Nation* indignantly repelled the insinuations of the correspondence, and pronounced it a lie. Mr. O'Connell and his friends passed the *Mail* by unnoticed, but bestowed on the *Nation* their measureless wrath. It was never afterwards forgiven.

CHAPTER V

DEFEAT OF PEEL.—ACCESSION or THE WHIGS.—MR. O'CONNELL'S COURSE.—DEBATES IN CONCILIATION HALL.—MR. O'CONNELL DENOUNCES THE YOUNG IRELAND PARTY.—CONTINUED DEBATES.—QUESTIONS AT ISSUE.—PHYSICAL FORCE.—THE SECESSION.—WHIG ALLIANCE.—DUBLIN REMONSTRANCE.—FORMATION OF THE CONFEDERATION, ITS CAREER.—MR. O'CONNELL'S DEATH.—CLOSE OF THE YEAR 1847.

On the 25th of June, Sir Robert Peel was defeated in the House of Commons on a motion that the Irish Coercion Bill be read a second time.

The majority against him was seventy-three, and was composed of the Whig party, the extreme Conservatives, the ultra-Radicals and Irish Repealers. In ten days after, Lord John Russell assumed the seals of office. During the preliminary arrangements that led to Peel's defeat, there was much coquetting between the Whig and Irish leaders. Alarmed by this startling aspect of affairs, and somewhat, perhaps, by the uncontradicted correspondence of the *Mail*, heretofore alluded to, Mr. Meagher, in the midst of vociferous cheering, announced from the tribune of Conciliation Hall, "that Irish Repealers would teach an honest lesson to the Whigs." This took place on the 15th of June. A short discussion followed, in which Messrs. Mitchel, O'Gorman and Barry took part, denouncing in the strongest language all idea of compromise with the Whigs. On the next day of meeting (June 22nd) a letter was read from Mr. O'Connell, expressing "the bitterest regret at the efforts being made by some of their juvenile members to create dissension in the Association." "To silence all unworthy cavilling," he desired that the solemn pledge of the Rotunda be read after his letter, and copies thereof posted in the Hall. This letter was the signal for an attack on the Seceders by James Fitzpatrick, who is now enjoying his reward in shape of a lucrative office on the coast of Africa. Another discussion followed, in which Messrs. Mitchel, Barry, O'Gorman and myself repelled the charge urged against us by Lord John Russell, to the effect that we were separatists.

The discussion which followed was an angry one. Fierce denunciations against the Whigs proceeded from the Seceders, which were answered by the Old Irelanders, as they called themselves, with clap-trap allusions to the name and fame of the "Liberator." The audience were indisposed to be duped, and so strong and general was the aversion to a Whig compromise, that Mr. D. O'Connell, jun. was denied a hearing, and even the Secretary found it difficult to command a moment's attention.

The next letter from Mr. O'Connell, was written after the accession of the Whigs. It, too, evidently bore the impress of that controlling fact. The writer enumerated twelve measures (excluding Repeal) "without which no British minister should dream of bidding for the people of Ireland." On the whole, the letter, which was long and elaborate, was an unmistakable though very guarded advice to give another trial to the Whigs. Mr. O'Brien, in moving that it be inserted on the minutes, pressed his conviction that the "millions would never abandon Repeal." He concluded by reading a resolution, pro posed in 1842 and seconded by Mr. O'Connell himself, to the effect that the Whigs were as inimical to Repeal as the Tories; and that no honest Repealer could vote for a Whig representative. Mr. O'Brien, on this occasion, took a wrong course. Instead of moving that the letter be inserted on the minutes, he should have moved its rejection, as containing doctrines subversive of principle and inconsistent with the solemn pledges of the nation. He was, no doubt, influenced by a desire to preserve unanimity; but the unanimity which is based on the disruption of most binding obligations is weaker and more fatal than any division. One paramount advantage would result from at once joining issue with Mr. O'Connell—the question would be placed on its true ground, and the preposterous folly of the physical and moral force abstractions would never have been heard of.

Mr. O'Connell appeared in Conciliation Hall on Monday, the 6th of July. He stated that his object was to ascertain the state of the registries, so as to resist the return of the anti-Repealers in any of the towns where a vacancy was likely to occur. But he added, "I will give no vexatious opposition." Here a voice cried "Dungarvan," with significant emphasis, a question Mr. O'Connell evaded with his usual dexterity. Four seats were then actually vacant; Dungarvan, Drogheda, Dundalk and Roscommon county. In the three former, there were clear majorities in favour of Repeal. That question admitted of no earthly doubt. It had been long before enquired into, and assurances the most unequivocal were transmitted to the Association. On motion of Mr. O'Connell, the question was referred to the committee.

Daniel O'Connell, jun., was a candidate for Dundalk, where a public dinner was given him on the 7th. His father attended, and said, "*I tell you there is another experiment to be made, in which every honest and rational man, of every party, will join.*" Similar doctrines were to be found in his former letter and speech, above referred to; and the other members of the Association awoke to a sense of the danger that threatened the body. Meantime, the Dungarvan committee proceeded with its labours. A deputation from that town waited on them—the parish priest and two others. They paid their first visit, however, to the Secretary, at the Castle. They found it as easy to satisfy the committee, or its majority, as the Secretary found it to satisfy themselves. They advised there should be no opposition given to Mr. Shiel on these two grounds: First, because success was then impossible, owing to the shortness of the time for preparation. And secondly, because a failure then would endanger the cause at the general election which was to take place in a few months. The sincerity of these reasons was tested by the facts, that, at the general election, the same parish priest stood at the hustings to propose and sustain the same official of the Whigs, insolently proclaiming his steadfastness in O'Connell's *glorious principles*, while he was huckstering away the honour and independence of his country; and that at that general election, when the people of Dungarvan were more openly betrayed and trafficked on by John O'Connell, and when they had to contend against the treachery of the priest, the treachery of the Association and the whole strength of the Whigs, they were only defeated in their opposition to Mr. Shiel by three votes. But, sincere or not, absurd or not, they were conclusive with the committee, or its chairman, who reported that it was not advisable to oppose Mr. Shiel, and this report was published just two days after Mr. Shiel had been returned unopposed.

No wonder that the actual return of Mr. Shiel, which the committee was charged to resist, had escaped its vigilance; for the celebrated Peace Resolutions were, at the same time, under discussion, and produced simultaneously with the Dungarvan report. Mr. Mitchel, Mr. O'Gorman and Mr. Meagher, who attended the committee, vainly remonstrated against the betrayal of Dungarvan, as well as the Peace Resolutions. They saw that the real object of the resolutions was to blind the country to the other important question, whether the Irish constituencies were to be transferred once more to Whig placemen; and they confined their opposition principally to the Dungarvan case. It must be admitted, too, that the falsehood involved in the Peace Resolutions, escaped their attention in the first instance; and they were under the impression that the pledge they contained extended no farther than the action of the Association itself was concerned. On consideration, they found it was of far wider scope, and would engage them to a false principle, embracing all men, all countries and all tunes; and having stated this at the public meeting of the Association, they allowed the resolutions to pass without further opposition.

The original resolution on which the Association was framed is this:—

"The total disclaimer of, and absence from, all physical force, violence or breach of the law."

The resolution, reported on the 13th of July, 1846, is as follows:—

"That, to promote political amelioration, peaceable means alone should be used, to the exclusion of all others, save those that are peaceful, legal and constitutional."

Sometimes, it has been averred lately that these two resolutions are, in principle and effect, the same. Mr. O'Connell himself declared the latter was introduced by him, *"to draw a line of demarcation between Old and Young Ireland."* Indeed, if there were no distinction, the introduction would be eminently absurd as well as pernicious. And if they be different, as essentially they are, there must be some strong justification for the adoption of the latter.

But before proceeding to this enquiry, it may not be amiss to point out the exact distinction between the original and the new resolution. The former embraced a rule of action whereby the members of the Association engaged their faith and honour to each other and the country that they would not use its agency to cause or promote physical force or violence of any kind, or commit one another to any act of illegality. But it went no farther—it enunciated no moral dogma—a rule of conscience rather than a pledge of conduct such as the other—and it claimed no sacrifice of one's own convictions. As a mutual guarantee, it was not only just but essential to the perfect safety of the Association.

On the other hand, the new resolution excluded the question of practical action altogether. Neither in itself nor in its preamble was there an averment, or even an assumption of its necessity, as a rule of guidance. It was a mere abstract opinion, utterly irrespective of the object or conduct of the Association, and only applicable as a test of certain speculative theories. But not alone was it inapplicable and preposterous; it was utterly untrue: at least, there are many men who could not subscribe to it without, according to their own convictions, being guilty of a lie. Supposing, however, that the seceders had attempted to violate the old constitution of the confederacy, it may be argued that Mr. O'Connell would be justified in preparing the most stringent tests for the purpose of restraining them. But no such attempt was ever made; no one proposed in the Association, no one hinted outside it, that it ought to violate one of its rules. No one complained of these rules, or said they ought to be changed, modified or, to the least extent, relaxed. Neither directly nor indirectly, openly nor covertly, was there a word spoken, nor an act done, nor a suggestion offered to that effect. The resolution was, therefore, uncalled for and unnecessary, as it was unsound and untrue.

Of this there is the clearest proof. First, the negative proof is conclusive. Mr. O'Connell did not name an act, or refer to a word of one single seceder, which would justify the imputation that they sought or desired to involve the Association in any expedient inconsistent with its fundamental rules. His only proof was this, and he did not then rely on it: Lord John Russell stated in the House, "I am told that one party among the Repealers are anxious for a separation from England." This is his solitary proof, nor does it appear that he was not himself the informant of the minister. But the positive proofs at the other side are numerous and incontestable. I select a few. On the 13th of July Mr. O'Gorman, in presence of Mr. O'Connell, said: "In order that there shall be no misconception on the subject, as far as I am concerned, I say, at once, I am no advocate for physical force. As a member of the Association I am bound by its laws. One of these is, that its object is not to be attained by the use of physical force, but by moral means only." Mr. Mitchel, on that occasion, said: "This is a legally organised and constitutional society seeking to attain its object, as all the world knows, by peaceable means and none other. Constitutional agitation is the very basis of it; and nobody who contemplates any other mode of bringing about the independence of the country has a right to come here, or consider himself a fit member of our Association." On the 28th of July, Mr. Meagher said: "I do advocate the peaceful policy of the Association. It is the only policy we can and should adopt. If it be pursued with truth, with courage and with firmness of purpose, I do firmly believe it will succeed."

Mr. M.J. Barry, on the 7th of June, said, "It is perfectly plain to all that the purpose of the Association is to work out its object by means of moral force, and that only." In my letter to Mr. Ray, written long after the secession, I used these words: "The first (original rule of the Association) implies a pledge and an obligation to which every member of the Association bound himself. Any member, who violates it, or would induce the Association to infringe it, must be false to his own vow and treacherous to the Association, whence he should be expelled with every mark of infamy."

These proofs are taken at random: they range over the time before, after and contemporaneous with the secession. They could be multiplied one hundredfold, and taken from the speeches and writings of every one of the seceders. Yet that fact availed nothing—they were told, because "they differed from the rules laid down by the Liberator, they ceased to be members of the Association."

This is, in some sort, a digression. I return to the events which directly precipitated the division. It will be remembered that the objections of the seceders to the Peace Resolutions were confined to an emphatic expression of dissent. They were not, then, informed that they ceased to be members. They attended the next meeting; and, having repeated the same dissent, they expressed their fervent wish for a perfect understanding, and pledged themselves to continue their co-operation, as if the resolution had not been passed. Mr. John Reilly repudiated these advances, and charged them with treachery to Ireland, as the natural complement of disobedience to O'Connell. He gave notice that he would put certain interrogatories to Mr. O'Brien, in reference to a speech delivered by him at Clare On the next day of meeting, Mr. O'Brien attended (July 26), and a letter from Mr. O'Connell, containing the bitterest complaints, against the "advocates of physical force," as he pleased to call them, "*who*," he said, "*continued members of our body, in spite of our resolutions*," was read.

A discussion, acrimonious and prolonged, followed. The debate was adjourned to the next day, when it was again renewed. Mr. John O'Connell spoke for nearly three hours, directing most of his arguments against some admissions of the *Nation* as to the purpose entertained by the writers in 1843. A casual expression—"*we had promises of aid from Ledru Rollin, and many a surer source.*"—supplied him with abundant material for loyal indignation. He was heard without interruption. Mr. Meagher rose to reply. He delivered that most impassioned oration, in which occurs the apostrophe to the sword. The meeting yielded to the frankness, sincerity, enthusiasm and supreme eloquence of the young orator, and rewarded him by its uncontrollable and unanimous applause. Mr. J. O'Connell rose, and, in the midst of a scene of universal rapture, coldly said, "either Mr. Meagher or myself must leave the Association." Too generous to avail himself of the enthusiasm he excited, Mr. Meagher withdrew. So did Mr. O'Brien, Mr. Mitchel and the others, with more than three-fourths of the meeting.

Thus occurred the secession. Mr. J. O'Connell simulated some stage grief, expressing his ardent hope that the "Liberator," on his arrival, would heal the wounds he had himself inflicted. How sincere was that hope is proved by the fact that, when Mr. O'Connell did arrive, which was on the Saturday following, he was prevented from proceeding farther than Kingstown, where he was detained until the hour of meeting on Monday; thus rendering it impossible to have an interview with Mr. O'Brien, or any one who could facilitate an arrangement. On Monday, instead of using soothing language and kind advice, he probed the wounds to the bottom, and infused into them subtlest poison. It is needless, as it would be painful, to recount the details of bitterness and hate with which on that day he dashed the hopes of the country. The result was deep and irreconcilable estrangement. Those who left the hall, rather than drive therefrom the son of Daniel O'Connell, finding themselves repaid by calumny, yielded to the conviction which every successive act of Mr. O'Connell conduced to establish, namely, that the country, and her great hope of destiny, were handed over to the Whigs.

The proofs of this belief were, first: The statement in the *Mail*, which remained undenied, and must, therefore, be taken to be undeniable.

Secondly: The expression used by Mr. O'Connell, in his speech at Conciliation Hall, that he would give no "vexatious opposition" to the Whig nominee.

Thirdly: His statement, at Dundalk, that "one experiment more was to be made, in which every honest man would join."

Fourthly: The following passage, which occurred in Mr. O'Connell's letter, dated London, 27th of June, 1846: "There is an opportunity to consider the Irish question as if on neutral grounds; there is a glorious opportunity (the return of the Whigs to power) of deciding if the Repealers be right in believing that no substantial relief can be given to Ireland in a British Parliament; or that they are wrong, to the demonstration that would result from PRACTICAL JUSTICE being afforded by that Parliament."

Fifthly: The assertion of Mr. Lawless, in a letter to Mr. O'Connell, dated 18th July, which the latter published, without contradiction or comment, namely: "And yet it was with difficulty you (Mr. O'Connell) prevented his (Mr. Shiel) being opposed in his election for Dungarvan,"

Sixthly: Mr. Shiel's election, without opposition, when his defeat, if opposed, was perfectly certain.

Seventhly: Mr. O'Connell's eulogy on The O'Conor Don for "accepting an office, which would enable him to serve his country."— (*Speech in Conciliation Hall, July 13th.*)

Eighthly: Mr. O'Connell's assertion, in his speech at Conciliation Hall: "I did not begin this quarrel; in my absence in London, an attack was made on the Whig ministry."

And, finally: The boasted acceptance by Mr. O'Connell of the distribution of Whig patronage, and the appointment of his personal friends to lucrative employment.

All that followed was one unvaried scene of distraction, division and enmity. Week after week, the seceders were held up to public odium, derision and scorn. One day, they were "blasphemous," one day, "revolutionary," one day, they "sang small," and one day "their nobles were come to ninepence." Now, they were challenged to establish a society of their own principles; now, they were recommended to the mercy of the Attorney-General, and again commended to the hatred of the people. Meantime a blight had fallen on the earth, and a whole people's food, in one night, perished. To the new Government, the famine that ensued was an assurance of subsistence and success. Hunger would waste the bodies of the people, as the dearth of truth had wasted their souls. The ministry affected great sympathy, great diligence, and great impotence. Among other wants of theirs, the want of practical engineers was felt the deepest. They knew and lamented that many died of starvation; but the thing was inevitable as long as they were unprovided with practical engineers. Mr. O'Connell, from the platform of the hall, announced the good intentions of the Government, and proclaimed, at the same time, his own commission to supply them with engineers. How many applied and were refused, I am not in a position to say; but there is no disputing the records of the church-yard, where many an uncoffined corpse attested the care of the "*paternal government.*" The people were guaranteed against death, and yet death came, and took them at his will; but what was left of life was taught to exhaust itself in curses against those who would save it at every risk. Wherever the seceders appeared they were hooted. Prostitutes of both sexes regarded them as fit subjects for their insolent raillery. The avowed foes of nationality looked on them as fools; its pretended friends as knaves; and the common herd of indifferent villains as a butt. The low retainers of the English garrison, who had sold their souls to the enemy but were kept in awe by bodily fear, became outrageously patriotic; and with insulted gratitude they scouted the traducers of the "saviour of their country." Alas! in Ireland, nothing was saved but death's agencies.

Doom had come upon all—her produce, her people, her hopes and her morality.

The same report, which contained the Peace Resolutions, set out with a statement dissevering the Association from the *Nation* newspaper. If the statement were embodied in a resolution of expulsion, it would clash directly with the failure of the prosecution against it, and brand the jurors who refused to find a verdict with perjury. But the admission of the *Nation* that, in 1843, it inculcated principles having a remote tendency to effect the redemption of the country, by arms if need were, supplied the Association with a pretext for expelling it altogether. Two rules had been adopted for the circulation of newspapers. The first was, when £10 were forwarded to the Secretary, the subscribers had the privilege of naming two weekly or one evening paper, which the Secretary was to forward and pay for. By the second rule, adopted after the State trials, the subscribers retained the drawback, and selected and paid for their own paper. For several weeks, the *Nation* was the only theme of Mr. O'Connell's abhorrence. He exhausted all his eloquence in warning the people against it, but in vain. The people continued to insist on it in return for their subscriptions. Accordingly, on the 10th of August, a resolution was proposed to the effect that no money subscribed for Repeal Purposes should be allocated to the payment of a subscription for the *Nation*, on the sole ground that, in 1843, it inculcated doctrines which were in their tendency treasonable. Mr. O'Connell said, after the resolution was passed, that he did not wish to injure the paper in a pecuniary point of view; and on the next day of meeting, he brought down to the Association some twenty law authorities, which he read, to prove that treason had actually been committed; and thus stamped the conduct of the Attorney-General as not alone justifiable, but lenient to excess.

The seceders determined to abide the issue. They had the fullest confidence that the insensate cry raised against them would eventually subside, and that truth would again prevail. They contented themselves, therefore, with appealing to their countrymen, through the columns of the *Nation*, then interdicted and banned through every parish in the island. But, in those appeals, there was no word of allusion to the storm of calumny and denunciation then raging against them. They sought to fix public attention on subjects of vast national importance, and to awake the energies of the people to some becoming effort where the stake was their lives. Meantime, week after week, the Government was praised, the Board of Works were praised, and the people—"*the faithful and moral people, who died, peacefully, of hunger*"—were praised, in the Repeal Association.

Robert Holmes (1848)

Late in the autumn of 1846, some men, few in number and humble in condition, undertook the desperate task of remonstrating with the

Repeal Association. Among them, Mr. Keeley and Mr. Holywood, Mr. Crean and Mr. Halpin, were prominent. Their undertaking was gigantic, considering the formidable obstacles they proposed to encounter. They proceeded silently and sedulously; and, in a few weeks, a remonstrance against the course pursued by the Association was signed by fifteen hundred citizens of Dublin. It was presented to the Chairman of the Association on the 24th of October, and ordered by Mr. J. O'Connell to be flung into the gutter. The remonstrants and the public resented this indignity alike. It was determined to hold a meeting in the Rotunda, where they proposed to defend themselves against every species of assault. The meeting was held on the 3rd of November, and was allowed to pass off without disturbance. Mr. M'Gee attended. He had never appeared in the struggle in the hall, nor was he a member at the time. His speech at the Rotunda was calm, forcible and conclusive on the points in issue; and the excitement it created was, in no small degree, enhanced by the fact that the speaker was a young man theretofore unknown. The success of the meeting suggested the practicability and safety of an experiment upon a large scale preparatory to the formation of the Confederation. The meeting was fixed for the 2nd of December. The remonstrant committee offered to defend it against any assailants. The main object was to reply to the calumnies which, for nearly six months, had been urged against the leading seceders. The meeting was one of the most important ever held in the metropolis. It was intelligent, numerous and fashionable. The entire ability of the seceders was put forth; and such was the sensation created by the proceedings that two publishers, one in Dublin and one in Belfast, brought out reports, in pamphlet form, which were read all over the country with the greatest avidity. It was that night stated, only casually, that the seceders would meet in January to announce to the nation the course of political action they would recommend. On the 13th of January, the promise was redeemed. The seceders met as before, and their deliberations were guarded by the same men, who thus a third time risked their lives—the hazard was nothing less—to secure to the

126

seceders freedom of speech and of action. On the 13th of January, the Confederation was fully established. The bases, if the phrase be applicable, were freedom, tolerance and truth. There was no avowal of war, and no pledge of peace. The great object was the independence of the Irish nation; and no means to attain that end were abjured, save such as were inconsistent with honour, morality and reason.

During the intervening time, between the first and second meetings, overtures of peace were made by Mr. O'Connell. A sudden and singular change was observable in his tone and language. He said with chagrin, and acknowledged with reluctance, that the position and strength of the party defied alike his power and his address. Every art and every effort to crush them had been exhausted in vain. The question between them, he now loudly proclaimed, was one purely of law; and he referred to several barristers, by whose judgment he was ready to abide. The question he was prepared to submit suggests the most mournful considerations. If it were not painful, it would be amusing to see to what painful absurdities he was compelled to have recourse. He would leave it to anyone at the bar, whether the "physical force principle" would not make the Association illegal; and then he would indulge in a hollow triumph over the certainty and security of his position. But that was not the question in issue. None of the seceders ever recommended the principle of physical force, in practice or theory, to the Association. On the contrary, they disavowed it, in reference to that body, and their own connection with it. The real question was this—whether it was necessary to the legality of any political society, to disavow, formally and forever, under all circumstances, and at all times, the right of men to strike down the cruellest tyranny with the strong hand. It would be absurd to submit such a proposition to a lawyer, which could only be answered by a laugh. It had been sufficiently settled by the fact that, without it, the Catholic Association, the Corn-law League, and the Repeal Association itself, up to the 13th of July, 1846, were perfectly safe and perfectly legal. But no man knew better than Mr. O'Connell that this was a feigned issue, the real one being the mendancy of the Association, and the treachery with which it abandoned the national constituencies to Whig officials. The overtures on this occasion eventuated in some negotiations, of which the Rev. Mr. Miley was the medium. His mission was singularly unfortunate, for it led to greater misunderstanding; and the negotiations terminated in mutual charges of misconception or misrepresentation.

The history of the Confederation, such as its importance deserves, is beyond the scope of my present purpose. Others may undertake to vindicate for its proceedings that enduring place in the annals of the country to which they are eminently entitled. Here, but a few words can be said.

As soon as the eclat of the first meetings had subsided, and the business began to assume a more routine character, the moral-force disciples, hitherto kept in awe by the mustered strength of the seceders and their followers, determined to give a practical illustration of the sincerity of their pledge by breaking the skulls of their opponents. On the first occasion, their onslaught was vigorous and successful. Blood was shed, and heads opened. This was deemed no infraction of the holy vow recorded in the books of the Association; for the body held its meetings without exercising its undoubted prerogative of "blotting out" the scene of outrage "from the map of Ireland." On the second occasion, the wreckers of Conciliation Hall were met as they deserved, and after a short skirmish fled through the city.

The success of the new Confederacy was certain, but slow. But, in the same proportion as their principles obtained predominance, the hatred of the Old Irelanders became unscrupulous and implacable. Often in the house of prayer, they heard themselves denounced; often in the streets, they heard their names used as by-words of scorn. Mr. O'Connell disappeared from the scene of his glory, which relapsed to the guidance of his intolerant and intemperate son. Some attempts were made to force him to a reconciliation, which in public he appeared to yield to, but which in private he exercised his utmost cunning to baffle. In the midst of this scene of distraction, Mr. O'Connell died. The news was a stunning blow to the nation. A great reaction, for a short time, ensued. Added to the other crimes of the seceders, was that of being O'Connell's murderers. They, on the other hand, resolved to treat O'Connell's memory with the greatest respect. They resolved to attend his funeral procession, in deep mourning; and they gave orders for expensive sashes, of Irish manufacture, which the members of the council were to wear. Mr. O'Brien communicated this purpose to Mr. J. O'Connell. The answer was too plainly a prohibition; and the Confederation reluctantly abandoned their design. Mr. O'Connell died at Genoa, on the 15th of May, 1847, and was buried in Glasnevin, on the 5th of August. His corpse, which was delayed some days in Liverpool, was conveyed through the streets of Dublin, during the election scene which resulted in the return of Mr. John Reynolds; being thus made subservient to the success of the man, to whom, of all his followers, he was most opposed during his life. It was a strange end, surely. Mr. O'Connell was buried with great pomp. The trustees of the Glasnevin Cemetery were generous in appropriating the fund at their disposal to the purposes of the funeral; but when the sincerity of the mourners' grief came to be tested, by the claim for a contribution to erect a suitable monument to the great champion of the age, it was found how hollow was their woe, and how lying their adulation. Daniel O'Connell is yet without a monument, save that which his own genius has raised in the liberalised institutions of his country.

The reaction in the public mind, consequent on his death, was short-lived; and the Confederation progressed rapidly, during the closing months of the year 1847. Although not formally acknowledged, every one saw that it was the only public body in the country deserving or enjoying anything like public confidence.

CHAPTER VI

THE SPLIT WITH MR. MITCHEL.—HIS TRIAL, CONVICTION, SENTENCE AND SPEECH.—THE "FELON" AND "TRIBUNE" ESTABLISHED.—ARREST OF MESSRS. MARTIN, O'DOHERTY, WILLIAMS AND DUFFY.—CONVICTION OF MR. MARTIN.—HIS SPEECH.—CONVICTION, SENTENCE AND SPEECH OF MR. O'DOHERTY.—DISSOLUTION OF THE CONFEDERATION.— THE LEAGUE

At the opening of the new year, which was destined to be its last, the Confederation, though yet regarded with coldness by the Catholic Hierarchy, was in full career. Its members had won the respect of every educated man in the land, however widely most of them may have differed from it in political faith. Among the middle classes of the Catholics, all that were left uncorrupted fell into its ranks, and embraced its belief. Men began to regard as possible everything which enthusiasm advanced with such unhesitating courage and devoted self-sacrifice. Mr. Mitchel delivered some lectures on land tenure and the poor-law system, which startled thoughtful and unthinking men alike. He had previously made an able and sincere effort in the Irish Council to compel the landlord class to some redeeming act of good sense and good will, which their own true interests required as well as the agonies of the starving tenantry. He was met by ignorance, stolidity and scorn. A timid and narrow measure of improvement in the relation between landlord and tenant had been proposed, and ably supported by Messrs. Ferguson, Ireland and O'Loghlen; and such was the obstinate aversion to all amelioration, on the part of the landlords, that they abstained from resisting Mr. Mitchel's amendment, lest they would be thereby committed to the milder reform proposed by Mr. Ferguson. His motion was lost only by a majority of two several of the five-pound Repeal representatives, who brawled at tenant-right meetings, and one member of the Confederation, Mr. M'Gee, being included in the majority.

The result of the division produced a marked change in Mr. Mitchel's career. His lectures on land-tenure in Europe, displayed the bold outlines and distinctive characteristics of his principles. His hopes from the Irish landlords, of whatever shade of politics, had ever afterwards vanished. He believed them incapable of being influenced by commonsense or good feeling; and he turned to the people, with full confidence in their fidelity and strength. All further attempts to conciliate the upper classes, he regarded as foolish, feeble and cowardly. He continued to reassert the substance of his lectures in another form, in the pages of the *Nation*, of which he was at the time editor-in-chief—that is, of which he wrote the greatest portion, especially of its leading articles. Some of these articles gave rise to a difference of opinion between him and Mr. Duffy, who, as responsible owner and editor, had the sole control of the *Nation*. There were not wanting men to take advantage of the difference and fan the flame. Charles Duffy had messages conveyed to him, to the effect that a rumour was abroad charging him with treachery; and to John Mitchel, perhaps by the same agents of dissension, it was stated that he, too, was suspected. It is unfortunately characteristic of Irishmen to be suspicious; and it was the object of one of Mr. O'Connell's eternal lessons to perpetuate and extend this degrading national vice. Whether the representations made to either of these friends were the result of national prejudice, or proceeded from a baser motive, it is scarce worth while to inquire. A separation ensued. Mr. Reilly adopted the resolution of his friend Mr. Mitchel. Mr. M'Gee adhered to Mr. Duffy; and a new career and distinct fortunes opened to the enterprise of the four men, whose united efforts elevated the popularity of the *Nation* to a height never before enjoyed by an Irish journal.

The early differences between the two great journalists suggested to Mr. Duffy, and to others, the necessity of drawing up a programme for the guidance of the Confederation. A committee was appointed, consisting of several members, including all the leading advocates of both the policy of Mr. Duffy and that of Mr. Mitchel. The report was principally the production of Mr. Duffy. It was in part modified by others; but Mr. Mitchel, who objected to its principle, refused to take any part in its modification. It was afterwards submitted to the council of the Confederation; and there gave rise to a long, earnest and, to some extent, an angry discussion. It was under consideration for several successive nights, the debate lasting sometimes until three o'clock in the morning. The principle of the report embraced the belief that moral means and agencies to effect Ireland's liberties were not yet exhausted, and should be further tried; and the agencies through which the experiment was to be tested were indicated in detail. The principle of the amendment proposed by Mr. Mitchel involved a preparation for and an appeal to arms as the only resource available to the country. After a long and anxious debate, the question of adopting the report passed in the affirmative by a considerable majority. The details then came under discussion, and, paragraph by paragraph, alterations were proposed and adopted. The discussion on these matters was still more prolonged and vehement. The principle of the entire was questioned indirectly by various amendments of form; but it was always affirmed by a majority. The report had, however, undergone such modifications and alterations that its original promoters lost all interest in its passing; and at the final stage, it was rejected, as well as I remember, without a division. At all events, it was rejected, and, I believe, with the concurrence of Mr. Duffy, who afterwards published the original draft in the *Nation*.

It was on that occasion the celebrated resolutions, afterwards the subject of the three nights' discussion at the Rotunda, were drafted and proposed by Mr. O'Brien. They were at once adopted, Mr. Mitchel alone dissenting. This may be the fittest opportunity distinctly and definitely to settle the question, which has recently arisen, in reference to these resolutions. On the several occasions of Mr. Duffy's trial, they have been given in evidence as proof of his loyalty, on the assumption that they emanated from him, and that it was through his influence the body was led to adopt them. Again, it seems to have been inferred—indeed, it has been so stated repeatedly, by persons who boast of his confidence—that it was owing to his arrest and absence from the council of the Confederation, that measure of fatal rashness was adopted, of which he became the first victim; although it was his discretion and ability that kept the "Jacquerie," who then obtained the ascendant, in check from the beginning.

This is partly a statement of fact, and partly an inference. The fact is not true, and the inference is fallacious. The resolutions were not Mr. Duffy's. On the contrary, one main object with those who adopted them, without discussion, was to avoid the expression of an opinion on several abstract principles forming the groundwork of his report. Secondly, he exercised little or no influence in the debate which led to their adoption by the Confederation. Thirdly, they were warmly sustained by the influence, personal and otherwise, as well as by the exertion and ability of the very men who, according to a recent contemptible sneer, "improvised a revolution." Every one of them, Mr. O'Brien, Mr. Meagher, Mr. Dillon, Mr. O'Gorman, and myself, spoke in favour of them, and against Mr. Mitchel's amendment. And, finally, even if this were not so and that the rashness of the outbreak really involved deep culpability, Mr. Duffy cannot claim exemption from his share of the blame.

I subjoin the Resolutions and Amendment. The division took place at ten o'clock, on Saturday morning, February the 5th, 1848, when the former were adopted, by a majority of 318 to 188:—

"Resolved: That inasmuch as letters, published by two members of this Council, have brought into question the principles of the

Irish Confederation, and have given rise to an imputation that we are desirous to produce a general disorganisation of society in this country, and to overthrow social order, we deem it right again to place before the public the following fundamental rule, as that which constitutes the basis of action proposed to our fellow-countrymen, by the Irish Confederation:—

RULE

"That a society be now formed, under the title of 'The Irish Confederation,' for the purpose of protecting our national interests, and obtaining the legislative independence of Ireland, by the force of opinion, by the combination of all classes of Irishmen, and the exercise of all the political, social and moral influences within our reach.

"II. That (under present circumstances) the only hope of the liberation of this country lies in a movement in which all classes and creeds of Irishmen shall be fairly represented, and by which the interests of none shall be endangered.

"III. That inasmuch as English legislation threatens all Irishmen with a common ruin, we entertain a confident hope their common necessities will speedily unite Irishmen in an effort to get rid of it.

"IV. That we earnestly deprecate the expression of any sentiments in the Confederation, calculated to repel or alarm any section of our fellow-countrymen.

"V. That we disclaim, as we have disclaimed, any intention of involving our country in civil war, or of invading the just rights of any portion of its people.

"VI. That the Confederation has not recommended, nor does it recommend, resistance to the payment of rates and rents, but, on the contrary, unequivocally condemns such recommendations.

"VII. That, in protesting against the disarmament of the Irish people, under the Coercion Bill lately enacted, and in maintaining that the right to bear arms, and to use them for legitimate purposes, is one of the primary attributes of liberty, we have had no intention or desire to encourage any portion of the population of this country in the perpetration of crimes, such as those which have recently brought disgrace upon the Irish people; and which have tended, in no trifling degree, to retard the success of our efforts in the cause of national freedom.

"VIII. That to hold out to the Irish people the hope that, in this present broken and divided condition, they can liberate their country by an appeal to arms, and consequently to divert them from constitutional action, would be, in our opinion, a fatal misdirection of the public mind.

"IX. That this Confederation was established to obtain an Irish Parliament by the combination of classes, and by the force of opinion, exercised in constitutional operations; and that no means of a contrary character can be recommended or promoted through its organisation, while its present fundamental rules remain unaltered.

"X. That while we deem it right thus emphatically to disavow the principles propounded in the publications referred to in the resolutions, we at the same time equally distinctly repudiate all right to control *the private opinions* of any member of our body, provided they do not affect the legal or moral responsibility of the Irish Confederation."

AMENDMENT

"That this Confederation does not feel called upon to promote either a condemnation or approval of any doctrines promulgated by any of its members, in letters, speeches, or otherwise; because the seventh fundamental rule of the Confederation expressly provides, 'That inasmuch as the essential bond of union amongst us is the assertion of Ireland's right to an independent legislature, no member of the Irish Confederation shall be bound to the adoption of any principle involved in any resolution, or promulgated by any speaker in the society, or any journal advocating its policy, to which he has not given his special consent, save only the foregoing fundamental principles of the society.'"

But nothing could be more remote from the fact than the assumption that those who supported the Rotunda resolutions were opposed to Mr. Mitchel in principle. If that ground were not expressly repudiated, Mr. Mitchel would have been sustained by a majority of two to one. Every speaker who exercised any influence on the meeting, took occasion emphatically to disclaim it. They did not deprecate the right or the duty of taking up arms against the English Government; but they said: While we approve of the end in view, we condemn the means, and precisely because we think them the most surely calculated of any that could be devised, to frustrate the object. This was the distinct ground, specifically, clearly and unmistakably stated, on which the amendment of Mr. Mitchel was opposed and it was the only ground on which it could be opposed; with sincerity or success. The use, therefore, which was made of the resolutions on Mr. Duffy's trial was false and unsustainable in every point of view.

There is no disposition and no desire to quarrel with the line of defence adopted by Mr. Duffy. It is conceded freely that any defence which his counsel, some of the ablest and most honourable men at the bar in Ireland, or elsewhere recommended was justifiable. But coupling that part of the defence with the evidence given on the same trial, by pensioners and parasites* of the British Government, and with the commentaries that afterwards appeared from the pens of some of Mr. Duffy's friends, the whole was calculated to leave on the public mind an impression, not only utterly inconsistent with the truth, but pernicious and fatal in its influence on the future of the country, if indeed she is ever to have a future.

This impression inevitably would be that Mr. Duffy modelled and moulded the proceedings of the Confederation at his mere pleasure; that Mr. Duffy was not alone averse to revolution, but actually conservatively loyal; and that, in the spirit of that loyalty, he controlled the whole body, and kept an insensate "Jacquerie," which existed within it, in check—that it was only when he was sent to prison this Jacquerie obtained the ascendant, and that Mr. Duffy was the victim of their intemperate folly. However agreeable all this may be to personal vanity, Mr. Duffy must feel compelled to reject it as audacious and unmeaning flattery. There is much more at stake than the estimate of private character—the highest interests of truth. They require that it should be made known and incontestably established that every word of the above—fact and inference—is unfounded. As to the statement that Mr. Duffy was made the victim of others' intemperance, its converse could be much more easily sustained. But it satisfies every requirement of truth simply to state that, morally speaking, Mr. Duffy was equally responsible for the late outbreak, with those who perilled their lives and lost their liberty forever in the struggle.

The *United Irishman* started under auspices more flattering than ever cheered the birth of a similar enterprise. The man in Dublin, who did not read the first number, might indeed be pronounced a bigot or a fool. Every word struck with the force and terror of lightning. So great was the sale of the first number that the press was kept busy for three days and nights. When the second was announced, a guard of police was necessary to keep order and peace among the newsvendors around the office door. In every corner of the island the influence of the *United Irishman* was instant and simultaneous. The letters to the Ulster farmers caused a sensation as universal and profound as the letters to Lord Clarendon excited sentiments of wonder and alarm. Thomas Devin Reilly's powers, too, never before tested in this range of literature, astonished even the warmest admirers of his genius. The journal at once attained a standard of eminence, political, literary and poetical, never accorded to a production of the kind, published in Ireland. For the days in which they were written, the songs and essays of Thomas Davis contained greater depth, and a holier purpose. They seemed to flow, too, from a diviner inspiration; were of a wider, calmer and more generous scope. But the times were different; and it was as if the spirit of fire, burning at the bases of man's social hopes throughout Europe, breathed its prophetic glow on the heart of John Mitchel, conscious that he, of all men, in a prostrate land, could find it befitting utterance. It must not be omitted that the muse of "Mary," of "Eva," and of poor Clarence Mangan, considerably enhanced the high estimate of the *United Irishman.*

In the presence of such an oracle of defiance and vengeance, the Government for a while stood aghast. But the urgency of the times admitted of no temporising policy. Messrs. O'Brien, Meagher and Mitchel, were selected for prosecution; but the latter was honoured with a double suit—one for an article, and the other for a speech. The morning they were called upon to enter into security, all Dublin was startled as if by a spell. The streets were crowded by a dense and anxious mass of men. The police-office in a short time became inaccessible. Mr. O'Connell's two sons, and the staff of the old Association, anticipated the crowd, and occupied the seats around the bench. When Mr. O'Brien was called on, the O'Connells offered to become his security. The fact was trumpeted by the journals, yet living on the garbage of Conciliation Hall. But the offer, if sincere, might then be productive of important consequences. It was not sincere; a fact sufficiently attested by the Messrs. O'Connell's necessary consciousness that Mr. O'Brien would not come without his bail. In truth, it was known to all Dublin that he even found a difficulty in reconciling the conflicting claims of several gentlemen who aspired to that honour. So it was, too, with Mr. Meagher and Mr. Mitchel. All those gentlemen hurried to tender their services, as soon as they heard that bail would be required, the Messrs. O'Connell alone selecting the public court for the display of their magnanimity. It is needless to add that their courtesy was declined; and they must have left the police-office that day in the wake of the crowd, oppressed with the conviction that the confidence of the Irish people had passed for ever from their house.

Thomas Francis Meagher
(A Sketch in May: 1848)

John Martin (About 1865)

This prosecution marked a new epoch in the Irish movement. It was determined at once to meet it boldly—to extenuate nothing, to retract nothing—to take advantage of no legal subterfuge; but dare the issue promptly, openly and fully. Mr. O'Brien at first refused to be defended by counsel. He was with great difficulty prevailed upon to change his determination; and, when it was known that he was willing to accept professional assistance, at least twenty of the ablest young men at the bar volunteered their services; and the traversers saw arrayed at their side an amount of professional ability and chivalry such as was never united on such an occasion. The most respectable solicitors in the profession, too, contended for the honour of being their recorded attorneys. The juries disagreed in both cases; and the charge against Mitchel lapsed into that more formidable prosecution which sealed his fate.

Mitchel's arrest under the Treason Felony Act was not unexpected. But as soon as it was ascertained that he was lodged in Newgate, his fate engaged the entire care of his co-Confederates. The question at once arose whether, if a rescue were attempted, there were resources to ensure even a decent stand. It was ascertained that the supply of arms and ammunition was scanty and imperfect, and the supply of food still scantier. The people had been decimated by three years of famine: and no want could be more appalling than the want of food. On inquiry, it was found that there was not provision for three days in the capital, which depended on daily arrivals for its daily bread. Throughout the country, the supply was even more precarious. The Government had in their own hands the uncontrolled power of preventing the arrival of a single grain of corn; and, if so minded, could starve the island in a fortnight, supposing the people were even able to possess themselves of all the cattle in the country.

These were some of the considerations which influenced the decision of Mr. Mitchel's comrades. Whether the opinion were or were not a correct one, they acted on the conviction that, under all circumstances, any attempt to rescue him would eventuate in a street row which would entail not only defeat but disgrace. If they could but persuade themselves that a blow might be struck, even though defeat and death followed, they most certainly would have attempted it. It was generally understood, on the day before the trial, that the idea of a rescue was abandoned; and the trial commenced amidst gloomy presentiments and blighted hopes. After hours of quibbling and legal fencing, a jury was selected, by the crown, to convict. From the moment they went through the blasphemous process of swearing to give a true verdict, John Mitchel's fate was sealed.

I pass over the details, and come to the last act in the infamous drama, called his trial.

The following account of the closing scene is not mine. Feeling inadequate to describe a scene of which even a distant recollection is exciting, I asked a friend who felt the deepest interest in the trial to describe it. With what he has written I entirely agree, save one sentence. He says that it was owing to the action of the council of the Confederation John Mitchel's personal friends were allowed to be assaulted, with impunity, by the police. I do not think so. With respect to the decision of the council, I feel bound to assume my share of its responsibility, although I yielded to it with the utmost reluctance and regret:—

On the morning of Saturday, the 27th May, 1849, the court was crowded to a greater excess than usual, even in those days. About the empty dock were the personal friends of Mr. Mitchel, those who agreed with him, and those who did not. A little retired on either side sat John Martin, and John Kenyon—in front were William H. Mitchel, brother of the prisoner and his only relative in court, T. Devin Reilly, Thomas F. Meagher, John B. Dillon, Michael Doheny, Richard O'Gorman, Martin O'Flaherty (Mr. Mitchel's attorney), Charles O'Hara and others whom we have forgotten.

A little in advance, on the left of the dock, were the stalls reserved during the sham trial for the counsel for the defence. As yet they were only occupied by the junior advocates, Sir Colman O'Loghlen and John O'Hagan. The benches at the right of the dock, and nearer to the bench, reserved for the Attorney-General and his retainers, were vacant. The Sheriff and his white stick occupied their box, and the galleries to the right and left were crowded with jurymen—those who "had done their business," and those who were eager for employment to do more. The bench of the judges held two empty chairs. And police officers and other mercenaries, dotted thickly over the court, "concluded and set off the arrangements."

An old man, low of stature, and stooped, passed through a side door, and walked slowly and decrepidly into the benches of the prisoner's counsel. Whispers, and then applause from the galleries, were heard and passed by him unheeded. Quietly and unostentatiously he moved to his seat—the junior advocates, and all the Confederates in the body of the court, rising and bowing to him in silence. It was the solitary Republican of the United Irish day, Robert Holmes, coming to discharge his last duty to the great Republican of a younger century.

The applause of the galleries was hushed by the crier's voice—"Silence! take off your hats"; and on the right stalked in the gaunt figure of James Henry Monahan. Triumph, animosity and fear marked his night-bird face. Even yet it was hoped the great opponent of his "government," whom by rascality alone he could convict, would strike his colours, and sue for mercy. Even yet it was feared that a rescue would be attempted. How possible the former was, the reader may judge. The latter was rendered impossible by the council of the Confederation, and the few who cherished the design in the council's despite, had attempted an *emeute* the night previous, and were beaten and placed *hors de combat*. As Monahan and his retainers entered, the red face of Lefroy oozed through the bench curtains, and followed by the pale Moore, "the court was seated."

As yet the dock was empty, save that the jailor of Newgate and his deputy occupied each a corner.

There was a dead silence.

"Jailor, put forward John Mitchel," said the official, whose duty is to make such orders.

A grating of bolts—a rustling of chains, were heard behind. The low door-way at the back of the dock opened, and between turnkeys Mitchel entered.

Ascending the steps to the front of the dock, and lifting, as he advanced, the glazed dark cap he wore during his imprisonment, as gracefully as if he entered a drawing-room, he took his stand in a firm but easy attitude. His appearance was equally removed from bravado and fear. His features, usually placid and pale, had a rigid clearness about them that day we can never forget. They seemed, from their transparency and firmness, like some wondrous imagination of the artist's chisel, in which the marble, fancying itself human, had begun to breathe. The eye was calm and bright—the mouth, the feature round which danger loves to play, though easy, motionless, and with lips apart, had about it an air of

143

immobility and quiet scorn, which was not the effect of muscular action, but of nature in repose. And in his whole appearance, features, attitude and look, there was a conscious pride and superiority over his opponents, which, though unpresuming and urbane, seemed to speak louder than words—"I am the victor here today."

He saluted quietly those friends about the dock he had not that day seen, conversing with one or two, and bowing to those at a distance. He then directed his eyes to the court.

After some preliminary forms, Baron Lefroy commenced operations, by stating that he had called the case the first that morning, in order to give time for any application to be made in court by, or on behalf of, the prisoner of the crown.

Again there was a silence of some minutes. The judges looked at each other inquiringly. The crown prosecutor watched the prisoner's counsel. Upon the prisoner himself all other eyes were fixed.

There was no reply.

"Business proceeded." The "Clerk of the Crown," rising to ask the usual question—"If Mr. Mitchel had anything to say why judgment should not be passed upon him?"

"I *have*," he answered, and after a momentary look at judges, jury-box and sheriff, he slowly continued: "I have to say that I have been tried by a packed jury—by the jury of a partisan sheriff—by a jury not empanelled, even according to the law of England, I have been found guilty by a packed jury obtained by a juggle—a jury not empanelled by a sheriff, but by a juggler."

Here he was interrupted by the sheriff rising, and, in high indignation, claiming the protection of the court.

"That is the reason," continued Mitchel, "that is the reason why I object to the sentence being passed on me."

"That imputation," interrupted Lefroy, "upon the conduct of the sheriff I must pronounce to be most unwarranted and unfounded." And this discriminating judge continued to show that the imputation was so—concluding with the assertion that the sheriff "had done his duty in the case." Then without pausing, he proceeded to the usual lecture, full of hypocritical cant with which British judges usually preface their awards, however infamous. He alluded to the personal condition of Mr. Mitchel, and expressed his regrets that a person of such merits should be in such circumstances, Then having dilated on the enormity of the offence, he assured Mr. Mitchel that he had been found guilty of many heinous charges against the Queen and the Imperial Crown, and among others, of felonious intending to levy war upon that gentlewoman, and that the evidence was furnished by the prisoner's self. "How, therefore," he continued, "you think yourself justified in calling it the verdict of a packed jury, and thus imputing perjury to twelve of your countrymen— deliberate and wilful perjury—"

"No," interrupted the prisoner, "I did not impute perjury to the jury."

"I understood," said the speaker on the bench, "that you had stated, in arrest of judgment, that you had been found guilty by a packed jury."

"I did," was the reply.

Robert Holmes rose, during the judge's speech, and said, "My lords, with the greatest respect, what I said was, that though he might be statutably guilty, he was not, in my opinion, morally guilty. I repeat that opinion now."

This avowal, so boldly and firmly made by the veteran Republican, was answered by all the audience, not pensioned, with plaudits.

Baron Lefroy would say no more on that point, only that the court could not acquiesce in a line of defence "which appeared to it very little short of, or amounting to, as objectionable matter as that for which the prisoner had been found guilty.

"I," replied the aged advocate, "I am answerable for that under your Act of Parliament."

Loud applause followed. "Are there no policemen in court?" shouted Baron Lefroy. The High Sheriff "had given strict orders," he said, "to have all removed who would interrupt." "Make prisoners of them," said the judge. "I wish you to understand," he continued, still excited, and addressing Mr. Mitchel, who during these episodes, stood unmoved, "that we have with the utmost anxiety and with a view to come to a decision upon the measure of punishment which it would be our duty to impose, postponed the passing of sentence on you until this morning." Then, having stated the various considerations which induced him to believe that the punishment should be lenient, and the equally various considerations which induced him to believe the contrary, Lefroy concluded as follows: "We had to consider all this—to look at the magnitude of the crime, and to look also at the consideration, that if this were not the first case brought under the Act, our duty might have obliged us to carry out the penalty it awards to the utmost extent; but, taking into consideration, that this is the first conviction under the Act—though the offence has been as clearly proved as any offence under the Act could be—the sentence of the court is, that you be transported beyond the seas for the term of fourteen years."

The listeners to the hypocritical sentence which concluded Lefroy's speech, heard the sentence with astonishment and indignation. Mr. Mitchel merely asked, apparently without any astonishment, if he might now address some remarks to the court. The leave asked was granted, and a silence still as death awaited the prisoner.

"The law," he said, in his usual manly tone, and unexcited manner, "the law has now done its part, and the Queen of England, her crown and government in Ireland are now secure—'pursuant to Act of Parliament.' I have done my part, also. Three months ago I promised Lord Clarendon and his government in this country, that I would provoke him into his 'courts of justice,' as places of this kind are called, and that I would force him publicly and notoriously to pack a jury against me to convict me, or else that I would walk out a free man from this dock to meet him in another field.

"My lord, I knew I was setting my life on that cast; but I warned him that, in either case, the victory would be with me; and the victory is with me. Neither the jury, nor the judges, nor any other man in this court, presumes to imagine that it is a criminal who stands in this dock."

He was interrupted with the plaudits of the auditory; and again continued:—

"I have kept my word. I have shown what the law is made of in Ireland. I have shown that her majesty's government sustains itself in Ireland by packed juries, by partisan judges, by perjured sheriffs—"

Here he was interrupted by Lefroy, who said, "the court could not sit there to hear him arraign the jurors of the country, the sheriffs of the country, the administration of justice, the tenure by which the crown of England holds that country. The trial was over. Everything the prisoner had to say previous to the judgment, the court was ready to hear, and did hear. They could not suffer him (Mr. Mitchel) to stand at that bar to repeat, very nearly, a repetition of the offence for which he had been sentenced."

"I will not say," Mr. Mitchel continued, "anything more of that kind. But I say this—"

Lefroy again interrupted him, to the effect that, within certain limits the prisoner might proceed.

"I have acted," he then said, "I have acted all through this business, from the first, under a strong sense of duty. I do not regret anything I have done, and I believe that the course which I have opened is only commenced. The Roman," he continued in one of those bursts of eloquence, with which he used to electrify men, stretching forth his clenched hand and arm, "the Roman who saw his hand burning to ashes before the tyrant, promised that three hundred should follow out his enterprise. Can I not promise for one, for two, for three, aye for hundreds?"

Here he pointed to his friends, Reilly, Martin, and Meagher. A burst of wild enthusiasm followed.

"Officer! officer! remove Mr. Mitchel," was heard from Lefroy. A rush was made on the dock, and the foremost ranks sprung from the galleries, with out-stretched arms to vow with him too. The judges rushed in terror from the benches—the turnkeys seized the hero, and in a scene of wild confusion he half walked, and was half forced through the low, dark door-way in the rear, waving his hand in a quiet farewell. The bolts grated, the gate slammed, and he was seen no more.

Men stood in affright, and looked in each others' faces wonderingly. They had seen a Roman sacrifice in this modern world, and they were mute.

An hour elapsed—the excited crowd had passed away; and the partisan judges, nervous and ill at ease, ventured upon the bench again.

They were seated, and seemed to be settling down to get through "business" as well as they could, when Mr. Holmes, whose defence of Mr. Mitchel had been so offensive to them, rose. "My lords," he said, "I think I had a perfect right to use the language I did yesterday. I wish now to state that what I said yesterday as an advocate, I adopt today, as my own opinion. I here avow all I have said; and, perhaps, under this late Act of Parliament, her Majesty's Attorney-General, if I have violated the law, may think it his duty to proceed against me in that way. But if I have violated the law in anything I said, I must, with great respect to the court, assert that I had a perfect right to state what I stated; and now I say in deliberation, that the sentiments I expressed with respect to England, and her treatment of this country, are my sentiments, and I here openly avow them. The Attorney-General is present—I retract nothing—these are my well-judged sentiments—these are my opinions, as to the relative position of England and Ireland, and if I have, as you seem to insinuate, violated the law by stating those opinions, I now deliberately do so again. Let her Majesty's Attorney-General do *his* duty to his government, I have done *mine* to my country."

Such was the conclusion of the trial of John Mitchel. The brother-in-law and friend of Robert Emmet, the republican of our fathers' days, came to attest the justice of the republican of our own, and to vie with him in defying and scorning the infamous laws of England.

It is needless to say that the English officials did not dare accept the challenge so nobly and defiantly flung down before the very dock whence one victim had just been borne.

148

I feel tempted to add a word of a scene that intervened, in which I took a part. When the sheriff recovered his self-possession, he ordered several to be arrested; among others, Mr. Meagher. The officer who seized him acted rudely and violently, which led to further confusion, and the exchange of blows. At last Mr. Meagher and myself were secured and removed to prison. When order was restored, we were brought out before the court, and asked for an expression of regret. I answered, that having heard Mr. Mitchel express, in the dock, sentiments in which I entirely concurred, I took immediate occasion to mark my most distinct and emphatic approval. In doing this I had no intention of an affront to the court. But as to retract, or regret, no punishment in the power of that or any other court to inflict, would compel me to do either one or the other.

Mr. Meagher repeated the same thing. We were then reprimanded and sent back. Soon after we were recalled, and upon motion of Mr. Dillon and Sir Colman O'Loghlen, on behalf of Mr. Meagher, who stated that he would express his regret for the contempt of court, but nothing else, we were both released, although I persisted in refusing even to join in the expression of regret made *for* but not *by* Mr. Meagher.

On the same day on which the above scene took place, John Mitchel was borne in irons from the land of his love, the wife of his bosom, and the children of his heart.

Immediately after, the council of the Confederation was reduced to twenty-one; and everything wore a sterner aspect, as if, whether they willed it or no, an imperious obligation required fulfilment at their hands. The slight disunion, which the fate of John Mitchel created, between those who favoured and opposed his rescue, quickly disappeared, and both parties only emulated each other in the activity and earnestness of preparation. Among the agencies of progress, suggested by the crisis, were two new journals—the *Felon*, edited by John Martin and T.D. Reilly, assisted by Mr. Brenan, and the *Tribune*, edited by Richard Dalton Williams and Kevin Izod O'Doherty, of which Mr. Savage and Dr. Antisell were joint proprietors, and to which they were joint contributors, with S.J.

Meany and myself. The great object of the first was to follow in the footsteps of the *United Irishman*, and that of the latter was to urge the same principles upon a more republican basis. The *Felon* soon acquired additional interest from the daring principles and extraordinary ability of Mr. James F. Lalor, who had become a joint contributor with the recognised editors. Of the *Tribune* it would not become me to speak; perhaps no more is needed than that in the race to doom it was not outsped.

On the 8th of July, John Martin surrendered. Messrs. Duffy and O'Doherty were arrested on the same evening, and Mr. Williams on the following morning.

Although the trials that followed did not take place until long after the events which form the principal subject of this narrative, a brief account of them will not be inappropriate here.

Mr. O'Doherty was the first placed on his trial. The jury was of the stamp usual in such cases in Ireland. But a point of great importance was raised by his counsel, as to the publisher's *intention* to commit the felony, which they insisted should be proved, to bring his case within the provision of the Treason Felony Act. The court, composed of Chief Baron Pigot and Baron Pennefather, gave an opinion favourable to this construction, and the jury refused to convict, for which the Castle Organ did not hesitate to pronounce them perjurers. Every one supposed and rejoiced that Mr. O'Doherty had escaped; but the vengeance of the Attorney-General was far from satisfied, and he had ample satisfaction on a future day.

On the 16th of August, John Martin was placed at the bar, before the same judges. The instincts of the official, exasperated by defeat, exercised a keener vigilance in selecting a jury; and one was finally sworn that did not disappoint his sagacity. They found a verdict of guilty without hesitation; but recommended the prisoner to mercy, which in that case was a distinct contradiction of their oaths. The composition of the jury, and the character of the prosecution, will be best understood by a perusal of the subjoined speech. No higher proof could be given of his purity of purpose, elevation of sentiment, and goodness of heart. On the 19th of August he was called up to receive sentence He stood in the spot hallowed by the footprints of Robert Emmet and John Mitchel; nor was the heart he brought to the same sacrifice less worthy than theirs. Upon his benevolent countenance or stout heart, the appliances of terror around him had no effect. He stood unmoved and unawed, in the glorious consciousness that he had fulfilled his duty to his friend and to his country.

When asked what he had to say why sentence should not be passed upon him, he replied:—

"MY LORDS: I have no imputation to cast upon the bench, neither have I anything of unfairness toward myself to charge the jury with. I think the judges desired to do their duty fairly, as upright judges and men, and that the twelve men who were put into the box, not to try, but to convict me, voted honestly according to their prejudices. I have no personal enmity against the sheriff, sub-sheriff, or any other gentleman connected with the arrangements of the jury panel, nor against the Attorney-General, or any other person engaged in the proceedings called my trial. But, my lords, I consider *I have not yet been tried!* There have been certain formalities carried on here for three days, *but I have not been put upon my country, according to the constitution said to exist in Ireland!*

"Twelve of my countrymen, 'indifferently chosen,' have not been put into the jury-box to try me, but twelve men, who, I believe, have been selected by the parties who represent the crown, for the purpose of *convicting,* and not of *trying* me.

"Every person knows that what I have stated is the fact; and I would represent to the judges, most respectfully, that they, as honourable judges, and as upright citizens, ought to see that the administration of justice in this country is above suspicion. I have nothing more to say with regard to the trial; but I would be thankful to the court for permission to say a few words after sentence is passed."

Chief Baron and Baron Pennefather: "No. We cannot hear anything from you after sentence is pronounced."

"Then, my lords, permit me to say, that admitting the narrow and confined constitutional doctrines, which I have heard preached in this court, to be right, *I am not guilty of the charge according to this Act!* In the article of mine, on which the jury framed their verdict, which was written in prison, and published in the last number of my paper, what I desired to do was this, to advise and encourage my countrymen to keep their arms; because that is their inalienable right, which no Act of Parliament, no proclamation can take away from them. It is, I repeat, their inalienable right. I advised them to keep their arms; and further, I advised them to use their arms in their own defence against all assailants—even assailants that might come to attack them unconstitutionally and improperly, using the Queen's name as their sanction.

"My object in all my proceeding has been simply to establish the independence of Ireland for the benefit of all the people of Ireland—noblemen, clergymen, judges, professional men—in fact, all Irishmen. I sought that object first, because I thought it was our right; because I thought, and think still, national independence was the right of the people of this country. And secondly, I admit, that being a man who loves retirement, I never would have engaged in politics did I not think it necessary to do all in my power to make an end of the horrible scenes the country presents—the pauperism, and starvation, and crime, and vice, and the hatred of all classes against each other. I thought there should be an end to that horrible system, which while it lasted, gave me no peace of mind, for I could not enjoy anything in my country, so long as I saw my countrymen forced to be vicious, forced to hate each other, and degraded to the level of paupers and brutes. This is the reason I engaged in politics.

Kevin Izod O'Doherty

"I acknowledge, as the Solicitor-General has said, that I was but a weak assailant of the English power. I am not a good writer, and I am no orator. I had only two weeks' experience in conducting a newspaper until I was put into jail. But I am satisfied to direct the attention of my countrymen to everything I have ever written, and to rest my character on a fair examination of what I have put forward as my opinions. I shall say nothing in vindication of my motives but this, that every fair and honest man, no matter how prejudiced he may be, if he calmly considers what I have written and said, will be satisfied that my motives were pure and honourable. I have nothing more to say."

The Chief Baron, in passing sentence, alluded to the jury's "recommendation to mercy."

Mr. Martin: "I cannot condescend to accept mercy where I believe I have been morally right. I want justice, not mercy."

He was then sentenced to ten years' transportation.

On two successive occasions, the jury empanelled by the Government, and carefully packed to serve their end, refused to convict Mr. O'Doherty. He was placed on his trial, a third time, on the 30th of October, prosecuted with the same enduring malignity, and a verdict of guilty, suspected to be the result of a fraud practised on the jury, was returned. Mr. Williams, who was joint proprietor of the *Tribune*, and jointly responsible, was acquitted after a protracted trial on the 3rd of November, the jury being of opinion that although the articles given in evidence were felonious, there was no proof to satisfy them that the proprietors, when publishing them, did so with a felonious intent. This distinction arose in consequence of the fair and candid construction of the Felony Act, given by Chief Baron Pigot and Baron Pennefather, on Mr. O'Doherty's first trial, to the effect that the jury should be satisfied of the publisher's felonious intent; a construction which the present judges 'Crampton and Torrens' would not dare to contradict.

Notwithstanding this, just as the words, "Not guilty," were pronounced by the jury, in Mr. Williams' case, despite the most flagrant and audacious bullying of the bench, Mr. O'Doherty was called up for judgment. Among all the martyr-band whom this year consigned to doom, not one behaved himself with truer or nobler heroism; not one, either, whose fate commands a deeper sympathy. Under thirty years of age, largely gifted, with most respectable connections, a high place in society, brilliant prospects, and so unostentatious in his enthusiasm that it was only then his country heard of his devotion, and learned his worth; there he stood with as lofty consciousness and as brave a heart as ever consecrated the scaffold or the battle-plain.

Judge Crampton pronounced the sentence. Nature has supplied his lordship with characteristics of countenance admirably befitting such a scene. Had he been only elevated to the kindred office of actual executioner, he would have been spared the expense of a mask; for without it, no one could look into his eyes. Of course, he was teeming with compassion and regret, which jointly resulted in a sentence of transportation for TEN YEARS. Mr. O'Doherty, who stood unmoved, after a few preliminary observations in reference to the unfairness of his trial, spoke as follows:—

"I would feel much obliged if your lordship would permit me to mention a few more words with reference to my motives throughout this affair. I had but one object and purpose in view. I did feel deeply for the sufferings and privations endured by my fellow-countrymen. I did wish, by all means, consistent with a manly and honourable resistance, to assist in putting an end to that suffering. It is very true, and I will confess it, that I desired an open resistance of the people to that government, which, in my judgment, entailed these sufferings upon them. I have used the words open and honourable resistance in order that I might refer to one of the articles brought in evidence against me, in which the writer suggests such things as flinging burning hoops on the soldiery. My lords, these are no sentiments of mine. I did not write that article. I did not see it or know of it until I read it when published in the paper. But I did not bring the writer of it here on the table. Why? I knew that if I were to do so, it would be only handing him over at the court-house doors to what one of

155

the witnesses has very properly called the fangs of the Attorney-General. With respect to myself I have no fears. I trust I will be enabled to bear my sentence with all the forbearance due to what I believe to be the opinion of twelve conscientious enemies to me, and I will bear with due patience the wrath of the Government whose mouthpiece they were; but I will never cease to deplore the destiny that gave me birth in this unhappy country, and compelled me, as an Irishman, to receive at your hands a felon's doom for discharging what I conceived, and what I still conceive, to be my duty."

Mr. Duffy's trial was postponed. His final escape is known to most of my readers; but as I cannot approve of the character of his defence, I prefer saying no more of it in this place.

It is here needful to refer to myself, a topic always disagreeable to others, but painfully so on this occasion to me. The proposal to form a league with the remaining members of the Association originated with certain gentlemen, among whom the Rev. Mr. Miley held a prominent place, who personally waited on Mr. O'Brien to testify their abhorrence of the outrages offered to him in Limerick. Some very questionable politicians, who watched with the eye of traffic the current of public opinion, and sought to make the same profit of the reflux they had formerly made of its unimpeded tide, attended on those occasions. Others, of purer motives, and loftier patriotism, joined in these interviews, and contrived to have them repeated. Among these were the poet, Samuel Ferguson, and Richard Ireland, two recent and brilliant converts to the cause of nationality. There were others, whom I need not name, of equally unquestionable purity. But for several weeks, while these interviews were held, there was no exact delegation from either the Confederation or Association. I am not, indeed, aware whether any such delegation was ever formally given or assumed. However, negotiations proceeded, and though they were never brought to a satisfactory adjustment, the dissolution of the Confederation was formally proposed and adopted. On that day the greatest hope of Ireland perished.

The generosity of the suicide on the part of the Confederation was met by a new chicane. Though every member, whose character and talents could for a moment redeem the deformity, dulness and decrepitude of the Repeal Association, had passed from its ranks and enrolled themselves in the new League, it resolved to struggle on, acting as a check and a stain by its anility and crookedness, on the rising hopes of the country. During the discussions that led to the formation of the league, it was emphatically announced by certain members of the Confederation that on no ground and for no purpose would they abjure one principle they ever announced. Above all, they avowed their purpose to urge on the country the duty of armed resistance whenever its success appeared probable. The Government heard of these avowals, and the time spent in captious discussions about moral nonentities and legal quibbles, when the stake was a nation's death or life, was diligently employed by the Government in accumulating means of defence.

The motives of the principal promoters of the league are by no means questioned here. On the contrary, it is freely admitted their convictions were as sincere as they were fatal. The due appreciation of that movement requires that a few leading facts and inferences upon which it was based should be calmly considered. The first and most important is the great change which had taken place in the feelings of the country. The vast majority of the thinking population were ranged at the side of the Confederation. So, too, was that of the people of the rural districts. The intellectual leaders of the great Protestant party had actually identified themselves with it, and a reconciliation with the entire body of the Orangemen had been nearly effected. Most of the men whose integrity and ability had preserved the lingering existence of the Association, openly avowed their approval of its principles, and such of them whose hearts were not mere empty sounds, would join its members at a crisis.

Thus stood the facts. The considerations in favour of the junction were these: Certain men of influence, who, contrary to their own convictions, adhered to the Association, in the commencement through fear, and still adhered to it through an unintelligible hankering after consistency, pressed for an opportunity where they might abandon their former associates without the appearance of abandoning their old principles. There were others who followed a middle course, and were always with the greater crowd and the more intense enthusiasm, who demanded the same means of escape.

There was a consideration of some weight which no doubt influenced the decision of the Confederates. It was this: the Roman Catholic clergymen had given unmitigated opposition to the Confederation. Their hostility had been the most formidable obstacle in its way; and it was assumed that the presence of some leading churchmen among the Confederates, would remove the distrust which the former opposition of the priesthood had mainly tended to create.

These were the chief considerations at the affirmative side. On a less pressing occasion, and at a former period, they might have been forcible, nay, even conclusive. But the issue had been then narrowed to one of actual force. John Mitchel was transported, and the most trusted of his comrades had pledged their lives to redeem their brother felon at any cost. Every consideration connected with the question should be examined and determined on in reference to that position and that pledge. Tested by them, the first above presented would thus resolve itself: either these men whose characteristic had been indecision, were sincere in seeking for an opportunity to redeem their patriotism by their blood, or they were not. If they were, they would never be restrained by the miserable fear of being charged with inconsistency. If they were not, the cause would be cursed by their adhesion. The same argument would apply to the priesthood with still more imperious force; such of them as were actually sincere would be found at their post at the hour of trial, in obedience to no form, but influenced by their own conscientiousness. Such of them as were insincere would be true to no obligation imposed by conventionality. Untrue to their convictions, they could not be faithful to their words. And finally—an argument which appears unanswerable and insuperable—Mr. John O'Connell and his immediate followers had so solemnly abjured, denounced and cursed the principles of the great majority with whom they were asked to league, that they could not comply without such a debasement of character as to compel the scorn of all men, not only to themselves, but all those with whom they were united. It could not fail to strike any ordinary observer that materials so incongruous and repulsive were incapable of cohesion; and the consequence must be the distrust of the more ardent of their followers at both sides.

These were my opinions. I pressed them at the time as strongly as I could, and perhaps more urgently than I ought. But I was absent from Dublin, and my remonstrances were vain. I would have retired in despair had I not been too deeply engaged. The Rev. John Kenyon did actually retire, influenced by the same motives which I refused to yield to, solely because retirement would brand me with an imputation of cowardice, which no explanation could ever efface. I refused all connection with the League, but continued to act in concert with my confederates, in establishing clubs and training the manhood of the country for the stern trial before it. My position rendered bold, undisguised and explicit language indispensable. This led to prosecution and arrest. The charge was supposed to be high treason and Mr. Richard O'Gorman wrote to me to inquire what I wished to have done in my behalf. My answer was a distinct refusal to accept any aid from a body whose constitution I could not approve. This circumstance is mentioned, not because it deserves distinct attention, or even a place in this narrative, but to prove that my objections to the dissolution of the Confederation, and my feeling that it was a fatal step, are not of recent growth, or founded on ex-post facto opinions. I feel bound to add, however, that I stood alone, or almost alone, as far as I have been able to hear. I dismiss the subject now, anxious to claim no praise, and ready to submit to the blame that may attach to my course, such as it was. I am only desirous, that in whatever memory of me my country may preserve, the truth alone should determine the public estimation of my conduct and character.

The League met, resolutions were adopted, and speeches made that meant nothing. New men came together, looked each other in the face, and turned away as if at the heart of each there was something with which he could not trust the other. There was a short, feeble and false flourish, and no more. Those who augured so sanguinely for its action and effect were disappointed. But they shamed openly to relinquish a project for sake of which they had made such sacrifices. By degrees, however, they sought to rekindle the embers of that fire which with thoughtless hand they aided to extinguish. The Government availing themselves of the inactivity that prevailed, and acting on the information they received, resolved to strike a second blow. Charles Duffy was arrested for an article which the Castle Organ branded as shrinking and cowardly, and which evidently lacked the burning spirit of the time. Immediately the clubs, which continued a precarious and unintelligible existence, came together and elected a directory of five from among their own members. This directory consisted of Messrs. Dillon, Meagher, O'Gorman, Reilly, and M'Gee. What their exact duty was does not sufficiently appear. But I believe the fact to be that they never took counsel together.

Mr. Meagher and Mr. O'Gorman left town immediately. About that time I was actively engaged in Tipperary. On the same day and hour Mr. Meagher was arrested in Waterford and I in Cashel. An attempt was made to rescue both of us, and by us both the effort was checked. I knew nothing of what had occurred. I had been acting since the formation of the League on my own judgment and responsibility. Independent of the fact that the harvest was yet remote, and that we were tacitly pledged to await its coming, my experience for the previous month satisfied me that the people were far from being prepared; and I could not allow any personal considerations to influence the country at such a crisis. Mr. Meagher was governed by similar motives. It might have been better had we acted otherwise, but with our then convictions, the least risk on our own account would have been selfish and criminal; and rather than be guilty of it we yielded to our fate. At the time each of us thought the charge against him was at least felony. It turned out otherwise, and though the magistrates who arrested and committed us refused to entertain the question whether or not the offence was bailable, and though we were both paraded through the country under an escort of several hundred men, the Government directed we should be admitted to bail. Mr. Meagher proceeded from Dublin to Limerick, where the indictment against him was found; and on the same day I was liberated from Nenagh Jail. Previous to my arrest, I had arranged to hold a meeting on the summit of Slievenamon mountain. It was fixed for the day after that on which I was liberated at Nenagh, which is at least fifty miles from the place of meeting. I was not liberated until late in the evening; but I resolved to be present at the meeting, and immediately proceeded on my journey. I travelled all night, partly on horseback and partly on foot, arriving at Cashel early in the morning. I there learned that Mr. Meagher and some friends of his from Limerick had also arrived with the same object as myself. We rode together to the mountain, followed by several thousands, a distance of twenty miles. Fifty thousand men at least clambered that steep mountain side, under a scorching July sun. Four times as many would have been there to meet us, but it had been widely rumoured none of us would be there; and in fact most of those who came believed we were both in our prison-cells. Besides this, efforts were made by men high in the confidence of the leaders and the country to prevent the meeting altogether. To fix their motives was difficult, but it would be hazardous to attribute to them any but the best. Facts have since proved, however, that their patriotism had even then begun to halt. The Rev. Mr. Byrne, of whom much shall be said, hereafter, was foremost in this endeavour, and actually dissuaded the people of Waterford, Carrick and Wexford from proceeding to the mountain. These people all remained in Carrick, and Mr. Meagher was informed that they were in a state of extreme excitement. This intelligence determined him to leave the mountain suddenly and proceed to meet his fellow-townsmen. Had all these been allowed to attend the meeting, our resolution might have been very different from what it was. But we were, in fact, disappointed and chagrined. The mountain-top had been selected for many reasons. Principal among them were these: Public meetings in Ireland had actually become a farce. We determined to hold one from which all senseless and idle brawlers would be excluded. The difficulty of ascending the hill would, we thought, sufficiently test the courage and sincerity of our followers. Secondly, we wished for a spot not accessible to her majesty's troops, so as to avoid a chance of a collision. Thirdly, we thought it would be a precaution against detectives; and finally, it was possible we might determine on some bolder step when we saw our strength. The excitement in Carrick had nearly become uncontrollable, when Mr. Meagher arrived there, and it was deemed advisable to lead the people out of the town. The distance to Waterford is twelve Irish miles, over the entire of which the procession stretched; and so dense was the crowd that Mr. Meagher did not arrive in Waterford sooner than three o'clock, next morning. It may well be supposed that such a scene of excitement, heat and tumult, afforded but little opportunity for deliberation. I was able to speak with my friend only in brief snatches; and I did not afterward see him until it was too late to take counsel for the future.

The meeting on that day, the evening scene at Carrick, and the arrival in Waterford, were relied on by the English minister, as a perfect justification for the suspension of the Habeas Corpus Act. Others and more powerful ones influenced the Cabinet; and foremost among these was the great meeting at New York, which too clearly evidenced the purpose of America, should the struggle proceed. I had no communication, directly or indirectly, with any of my comrades after that day, save one letter from Mr. O'Brien. This letter had reference solely to my approaching trial, which he signified his wish to be present at. To this letter I replied, informing him that it had been intimated to me that a number of men would assemble, armed, near Nenagh, during the trial; and I besought him to be there for the purpose of preventing an outbreak, which I regarded as disastrous, unprepared as the people then were. Neither the trial nor the meeting took place, and other events shaped our destiny.[9] A few days after the Slievenamon meeting, it was intimated to me that I was to be arrested on a second charge, the exact nature of which was not stated. I could not doubt the accuracy of my information, and being fully determined to preserve my liberty for the coming struggle, which under any circumstances could not be long delayed, I left home on the 22nd day of July, and proceeded through the country to the foot of Slievenamon. Here I took up my quarters at a farmer's house, where I remained two days and nights, in total ignorance of the circumstances then rapidly hurrying the crisis wherein our fondly cherished hopes were blasted.

FOOTNOTES:

8   From the position in which Mr. Carleton is now placed, it may be necessary to say that I do not allude to him.

9   Since the above was written, I have heard it said that a report, current about the time of Mr. O'Brien's conviction, had been recently received here. The report was, that I promised Mr. O'Brien to have 50,000 men to meet him; which was his principal inducement to act as he did; and that I not only had not one man, but was myself absent when he came. The absurdity of the rumour was sufficiently proved by the fact that Mr. O'Brien did not come to me, or my part of the country, in the first instance. The real truth is that I never directly or indirectly, by word or letter, counselled the outbreak. Nay, more: I was as ignorant of Mr. O'Brien's purpose as the President of these States. At the time of Mr. Mitchel's trial, I believe I expressed a very strong opinion in favour of rescuing him; and that opinion was grounded on the belief that the whole people would rise up *en masse*, and in one wild burst of vengeance, sweep their oppressors from the land. But neither then nor afterwards, did Mr. O'Brien give me the least reason to believe that he was prepared to resist the government in arms, save as far as he concurred in acts which had a tendency to that end.

When first the report above referred to was circulated, I wrote the strongest contradiction of it, and Mr. Meagher, with Mr. O'Brien's sanction, addressed the following note to the editor of the Tipperary *Vindicator*. I am sorry it should be in any way necessary to produce it here; but as this is the last time I shall ever refer to this subject, I thought it best to add this testimony to my own.

CLONMEL GAOL

"MR. MEAGHER fully authorises his friend, Mr. Lenihan, to state that the exculpation which appeared in a recent number of his paper, from Mr. Doheny, is the perfect truth.

"Mr. Meagher is most anxious to have this stated, for he has felt for a long time deeply pained at many of the false reports that have appeared against his friend—his dear and trusted friend, Michael Doheny.

"One of the most grievous of these reports has been that very false one, charging Mr. Doheny with having invited Mr. Smith O'Brien to the county Tipperary. Nothing could have been more false than this.

"Mr. Doheny, so far from inviting Mr. O'Brien to Tipperary, did not, in fact, know of his being in the county at all, until Mr. Meagher told him, and that was on Tuesday, July 25th.

(Signed) "THOMAS FRANCIS MEAGHER.
"Written a few hours after the passing of the sentence of death.
"*October 23, 1848.*"

CHAPTER VII

THE OUTBREAK.—MR. O'BRIEN IN CARRICK.—CASHEL.—
KILLENAULE.—MULLINAHONE.—BALLINGARRY.—
AFFAIR AT KILLENAULE.—DEFEAT OF MR. O'BRIEN'S
PARTY AT THE COMMON.—PERSONAL ADVENTURES OF
THE WRITER AND HIS COMRADE, UP TO THE DATE OF
MR. O'BRIEN'S ARREST

On the night of the 24th of July, I was awakened, where I was
staying, by a rapping at my window. I recognised the voice of my
sister-in-law, and learned from her, in a few seconds, how matters
stood. Her information, in brief, was this that: Messrs. O'Brien,
Dillon and Meagher had left Dublin on learning that the Habeas
Corpus Act was suspended; and that it was supposed their object was
to throw themselves on the courage of the country. This intelligence
rested on the authority of two trusted members of the council of the
Confederation, Messrs. James Cantwell, and P.J. Smyth. The fact was
all which I then cared to know. I parted from my sister in half-an-hour,
and rode off in the direction of Carrick-on-Suir, where I was certain
Mr. O'Brien would direct his way, whether he came alone or followed
by his countrymen in arms. 'Mid the lone silence of that journey,
while there was leisure to revolve all the difficulties and hazards of
the future, the idea never once occurred to me that, supposing my
information correct, the step was rashly taken. On such occasions,
when centuries gather into moments, some one overmastering feeling,
hope or passion absorbs and controls the whole understanding. That

which was then present to my mind, and occupied all its faculties, was the hope of satisfaction, or vengeance, if you will, for so many ages of guilty tyranny. The tears, the burning and blood of nearly one thousand years seemed to letter the eastern sky, as day dawned upon my way. Apprehension, I had none. From earliest childhood to that hour, I never met one Irishman whose hope of hope it was not to deliver the country forever from English thrall. I had lived amidst all ranks (at least in their characters of politicians), had known the sentiments of all, from the most ignorant peasant to the very highest official of government; and then or now, I would find it difficult to say where hatred to English domination—English power in Ireland is neither government nor dominion—reigned the most intensely. Some men there are by nature cowards, and they would shrink from the perils of national deliverance; but if any sentiment could be said to live in natures so grovelling, the grudge against England, even though too craven to make itself audible, constitutes the essence of their mental vitality. Some there are, too, so selfish as to sell their own and their families' honour for gold; but as they count their sordid gains, if they fall short by a scruple, whether in fact or in anticipation, the deficiency becomes a heap of hoarded spite against England. One man of that class, whom I had known, will furnish a conclusive example. Trusted and paid by the Whigs, he was a supreme West Briton, who saw in his country but a prey for meaner cormorants; distrusted and dismissed by the Tories, he would storm the Castle, even with the baton of the English office from which, he had been discarded. Others, also, of a loftier stamp, were reined in, in the path of allegiance, by considerations more justifiable, yet more or less cowardly in character.

Ballingarry, Slievenamon in the distance, 1848

Some doubted the ability of their country to effect her redemption. Some doubted the capacity, and perhaps the sincerity, of the chiefs. Some were schooled in duplicity, and under the ermine, or under the privy councillor's robe, carried fierce hearts, benumbed by mendicancy and seared by shame. But the first flash of their country's liberty would see them ranged at that country's side, repaying with the fiercest hate the beggar crumbs which England had flung from the fragments of her overloaded table. It is true enough that a long course of corruption, beginning with the perjured peer and ending with the tidewaiter, had created a class of conditional loyalists, with nine-tenths of which the condition is always unfulfilled; while, in its very fulfilment, the other one-tenth has found but bitterness, the "sauce piquante" of their daily bread. But as a general rule, such a thing as a pure Irish loyalist does not exist. Its possible existence presupposes an absurdity in nature. An Irishman cannot become loyal to English domination, without divesting himself of the last attribute of his nature, not as an Irishman, but as a man.

The knowledge of this fact was my "base of operations." Ten thousand armed men successful against a garrison of five hundred would produce a more abundant crop of avenging warriors than the fabled dragon's teeth, and that simultaneously through every square mile of the island. In ten days there would be two millions of Irishmen in arms. It may well be asked, what arms? But even instinct will reply, what arms would be needed? England had in Ireland less than forty thousand men, and, without hazarding the question, how many of them could she rely on, it requires no consummate military genius to suggest how they could be dealt with by a simultaneous rising of the country. The arms of her enemies would then be hers. She would have time to form a regular army to aid her undisciplined strength. England's position at home, where she had not a soldier to spare; her condition abroad, where she was beaten to the wall; and her relations with foreign powers would achieve the rest. To a successful Irish revolution, a *coup-de-main* is indispensable; and a *coup-de-main* would be incompatible with any organised plan other than existed. It will be seen at once that for this place details are unfit. The above sketch rather comprehends the bolder outlines of an insurrection in action, and they suggest nothing to warn the enemy as to future operations. The prospect they presented to me—a prospect which long contemplation seemed to have realised into fact—excluded from my mind the preliminary and intermediate considerations of time, place, and other circumstances. There was but one of any importance, the success of the commencement; and that seemed beyond all question if, as I hoped, the neighbourhood of Carrick-on-Suir were selected. As I approached that town in the grey of morning, and the past and the future in burning recollection thronged on my brain, I envied the destiny which God had awarded to its inhabitants, in breaking the first link of the slavery of nearly twenty generations. This, alas, was a dream. The people of Carrick had already, with shrinking hand, marred their own immortal lot.

Arriving at the house of John O'Mahony, one of the truest of living Irishmen, I heard what follows. On the previous day Messrs. O'Brien, Dillon and Meagher had arrived at Carrick. Their arrival was unexpected, sudden and startling. They had apprised no one of their approach; and no counsel had been taken or decision come to. It is needless to say that the crowd which gathered to see them, when the intelligence of their arrival spread, came unarmed and unprepared. The speeches addressed to them were brief, determined, and to this effect: "We learned," said the chiefs, "that an act was passed authorising the Irish Government to seize our persons without even the imputation of a crime. You have vowed to strive with us in every extremity, and die with us if need be. We are here to demand the redemption of your pledge, in the name of your enslaved country. The hour has come when the truth of that country is to be tested; and first among her children the trust of her honour is committed to you." How much more might have been said, and how far short of the passionate appeal made by the most gifted of men the above language may fall, this is not the place to inquire. The crowd answered with a loud shout. With the leaders of that crowd other thoughts were busy. Some of them waited on the "Traitors"; others, and the most influential, absented themselves. Among the latter was the Rev. Mr. Byrne, who, up to that hour, had taken an advanced position among those who were most forward in the cause of the country. Not a fortnight before, he delivered a speech to nearly one hundred thousand persons in the town of Carrick, pre-eminently insurrectionary in its tendency; and he had acted more than once as controller and regulator of the violent passions his own vehemence aroused. For this duty, which he effectively discharged because of his known disloyalty, he received the public approval of England's Prime Minister. From all these circumstances, the responsibilities of his position were such as it would require great hardihood of character to shrink from. It was reported at the time that he did not rest content with abandoning a post which he had attained with intense ambition, but exerted his utmost influence with the people against an enterprise which he designated as rash, ill-designed, and fraught with ruin to the town. This report has been repeated as a fact by the present writer, and has not been contradicted by the Rev. Mr. Byrne. But it is right to add that a very respectable gentleman, a witness of that day's proceedings, has distinctly contradicted it. He added that the Rev. Mr. Byrne remained a passive spectator; and he defended the conduct of those who really influenced the people, on the ground that the preparations seemed of their very nature to preclude the possibility of success; and that it was the sacred duty of every man capable of appreciating the position and resources of the people, the difficulties of the enterprise and the consequences of failure, not alone to Carrick but the entire island, at all hazards to prevent a useless wreck and slaughter. The great argument relied upon by every one was, why should Carrick be selected? The same question would apply everywhere else; and if the consideration it involves were to avail, there never could be a revolution. However, in Carrick it seems to have prevailed. Other arguments, no doubt, were urged, such as want of provisions, want of arms and want of ammunition. The moment of indecision is the harvest of evil passions—avarice, selfishness, cowardice cloud the intellect, and blast the destiny of man. There is some doubt as to who principally superinduced this indecision and the judgment which here ranks it with a faulty weakness and a fearful fatality refuses to question the motives upon which it was based.

One singular fact, attested by all, deserves particular notice. It is this: The other Roman Catholic clergymen of Carrick did not then interfere. They had been always opposed, on other grounds, to the Irish Confederation; but in that hour of fate they were silent.

Mr. O'Brien and his comrades left the town deeply disappointed, if not in actual disgust and despair. They were ignorant of my absence from Cashel and determined to join me there. When I had learned this, I was thirty miles from that town and knew that they had arrived there during the night, and had, long before then, taken some decisive course. My hope was that the town was in their hands. But, before I could decide on what it became me to do, a messenger arrived from Cashel, directing me to remain where I was, and conveying an assurance that Cashel was by that time captured. Mr. Meagher immediately followed, confirming the intelligence. He was on his way to Waterford. We immediately determined on scouring the country along the bases of Slievenamon and the Slatequarry hills, which stretch into the county Kilkenny. During that journey the enthusiasm of the people was measureless. At every forge, pikes were manufactured, the carpenter was at work fitting the handles, and the very women were employed in polishing and sharpening these weapons on the rough mountain stones. We called at several villages, and were surrounded by the young men and the aged, by matron and maid, and from no lips did one sound of complaint, or discouragement, or fear fall. Everywhere hope and resolution and courage lit up the hearts and eyes of young and old. We rode, at least a distance of twenty miles, and returned assured that there was not one man within that district who was not then prepared and would not be armed ere night came. We appointed the chapel of Ballyneal, within two miles of Carrick, as the place of rendezvous, determined to act according to the intelligence which we might receive from Cashel. Meantime deputations from Carrick waited upon us, to assure us the people there would follow us notwithstanding any advice they might have received. We agreed that we would not attack the town, and required five hundred men for another enterprise. A short time afterwards some directions were required, and I wrote one or two sentences on a scrap of paper which was taken from the messenger by the Rev. Mr. Byrne and torn. What his influencing motives might have been I know not, nor do I care to inquire. My first impulse was immediately to appear in the town and throw myself on the protection of the people. My friend dissuaded me from this attempt and proposed to go into town himself, which he could do without danger, to ascertain what would be the probability of my proposal's success. After two or three anxious hours, he returned, impressed with the conviction that such an attempt would be fatal.

By this time crowds began to assemble at the place of rendezvous before alluded to, and word was brought us that the Reverend Mr. Morrissey, the parish priest of that place, was endeavouring to disperse them. Owing to his character, there was not much to be apprehended from his influence with the people. His associations had been with the aristocracy, and most of his friendships and sympathies contracted at the fox-covert, or on the "Stand House." This is mentioned, not in disparagement of the man, but for the purpose of rescuing his Order from imputations attaching to his conduct alone. The very fact of his interference would suggest the conclusion that the course he recommended was opposed to the general sentiments of his brethren; so we felt at this time. But we mistook his influence with the people. It was reported to us that he used certain arguments, incredible, because blasphemous. But the argument which succeeded, and which all alike attested, was this, "that he would put himself at the head of the people if they but waited three weeks."

Influenced by this promise, the people had dispersed before my friend arrived at the place of rendezvous. He returned to me sadly discouraged, after a day and night of labour and agitation as intense as ever strained the energies of man. I then determined to ride on to Cashel, to learn the fate of Mr. O'Brien and his comrades. I was accompanied by two young farmers, well armed. We arrived about midnight at Brookhill, where I was made acquainted with all that had occurred at Cashel.

The history was more melancholy than our own. My absence was used as an argument, sincere or pretended, against any effort in that town. Mr. O'Brien, in ignorance of whom to apply to, took counsel with one man at least, since accused of the darkest treachery. Others, from whom I had different hopes, shrank from an encounter which, at other times, they seemed to long for as the dearest blessing Heaven could bestow. There no clergymen interfered—the people were left to act for themselves; but it must be admitted that the actual people never had an opportunity of proving their courage. A young friend of mine, who had all my trust, and justified it by unshaken fidelity through many a trial, was despatched to the country to procure assistance, but he applied to the wrong source, and, deluded by the character of him to whom he had spoken, returned under the mistaken conviction that from the country nothing was to be expected.

This decided Mr. O'Brien and his friends. He had been joined at Cashel by P.J. Smyth, and James Cantwell, now in the United States, by James Stephens, now at Paris, and by Patrick O'Donohoe, now sharing the doom of his chief. As an episode in this history, the fate of Mr. O'Donohoe is singular and startling. He was much relied on by his friends in the Confederation, and was entrusted with the dispatches to Mr. O'Brien. He proceeded on his mission to Kilkenny, and there applied to one of the clubs. He was known to none of the members, and became at once the object of suspicion. It was, accordingly, determined to send him for the rest of the journey, under arrest, and Stephens and another member were appointed to that duty. They proceeded in execution of their mission to Cashel, where Mr. O'Donohoe was warmly welcomed by Mr. O'Brien, whose fate he thenceforth determined to share. Mr. Stephens came to the same resolution; but the other guard of Mr. O'Donohoe, refused to commit himself to fortunes which appeared so desperate. With Messrs. Stephens and O'Donohoe, their very desperation acted as the most ennobling and irresistible inducement. They clung to him to the last with a fidelity the more untiring in proportion as his circumstances portended imminent disaster and ruin.

Their departure from Cashel compelled a feeling of gloomier forebodings and deeper despair than they had yet experienced. The darkest consciousness that ever clouded the hopes of man began to darken upon them. Where they expected that every man would make a fortress for them in his very heart, they were almost abandoned. But their resolution remained unchanged. They, therefore, resolved as a final resource to take up their position in the most inaccessible part of the country. As they proceeded through the hilly grounds, skirting the Tipperary collieries, a crowd began to gather around them, and they saw what they hoped would form the nucleus of an army. Braver hearts never beat beneath a cuirass, but they were not armed, disciplined or even taught. On that day they took the road to the village of Mullinahone, situate about seventeen miles south-east of Cashel. As they entered Mullinahone, the chapel bell was rung, and a crowd of some thousands collected.

Mr. O'Brien addressed them with the same brevity and force as at Carrick-on-Suir, where his hopes were far brighter. The two clergymen, Rev. Mr. Corcoran and Rev. Mr. Cahill, appeared by his side, and openly resisted his advice. But, with the people, their influence totally failed. Three thousand persons at least formed their bivouac that night. Mr. O'Brien remained up with them most of the night. Notwithstanding the disappointments of former trials, he once more entertained most sanguine hopes of his country's resurrection. But, ere morning, the counsels of the clergymen prevailed so far as to introduce discussion and disunion; and next day he was abandoned by more than half his followers. Once more the priests interfered and openly remonstrated against the course Mr. O'Brien had proposed. They tried every means, entreaty, expostulation, remonstrance, menace, but without any considerable effect; and Mr. O'Brien left the town with a large multitude, directing his way to Ballingarry. The village of Ballingarry is about four miles distant from Mullinahone; and the inhabitants of the latter accompanied Mr. O'Brien to the boundaries of the former parish, whose inhabitants in turn assumed the duty of his escort and, if need be, of his defence. When the cavalcade reached the village, they took up their position in the chapel-yard, and summoned the neighbouring people by the ringing of the chapel bell. A great number of people answered the signal, and Mr. O'Brien explained to them his purpose and his hopes. He did not then propose any plan of immediate offensive operations, but stated in general terms that his object was to protect himself from arrest, while the country would be engaged in organisation, and the crop coming to maturity. An idea prevailed among the people that he only wished to be protected for a time, and they seemed incapable of appreciating either his object or his motives. I reached the spot as the assembly was breaking up and the people retiring in small groups to their respective districts, some four or five hundred who were partially armed, remaining in the village. I was accompanied by Thos. D. Reilly, who made his way to me on that morning. We had entered into arrangements with certain men whom we met in the morning as to a joint movement, for which the followers of Mr. O'Brien seemed but ill-adapted and prepared. Our first care was to take counsel as to the future. We detailed mutually to each other the respective circumstances which had shaped our movements so far, and with which it was our duty then to contend. But one thing seemed quite clear; namely, that the country demanded a delay of at least a month. Although the sincerity of the motive on which this demand was founded seemed questionable to many, there was no way of counteracting its effect or denying its universality. The question then was, how was the demand to be complied with without compromising our liberty or the position we occupied? It was argued that the necessity of our condition would justify any act which would reassure the minds of the people in reference to the apprehension of starvation, which was so sedulously inculcated, and that a proclamation should forthwith be published confiscating the landed property of the country, and offering it as the gage of battle and reward of victory, and another proclamation directing the people to live at the expense of the enemy. This proposal was resisted on the ground that it required an aggressive act on the part of the Government to justify so sweeping a proceeding, which, if attempted by us in our then position, would be regarded as an act of mere plunder, unredeemed by any of the stern necessities of war. So decided the majority. It was then proposed that we should scatter, and take shelter individually as best we could until harvest time. But Mr. O'Brien refused to hear counsel which involved, as its first principle, the idea of becoming fugitives. A middle course was therefore decided on. It could not fairly be said that the country had been tested, and we were not, at the time, aware how far people at a distance were prepared to second our efforts. The strength of the Government, too, seemed paralysed. For miles on miles around, one solitary soldier or policeman was not to be found. The small garrisons had been withdrawn, and all the available forces stationed in the county had been concentrated in the large towns. The idea of maintaining our position for a few weeks seemed not at all improbable; and, meantime, we would have an opportunity of organising the distant parts of the country, and of preparing those then around us for active service. When men differ, a compromise is sure to prevail. It did so on that occasion, and it was accordingly resolved, that we should return to the neighbourhood of Carrick, wait the arrival of the expected assistance from Waterford, and keep the neighbouring garrison of Clonmel in awe, by signal-fires by night and scattered parties by day. We immediately returned and rode most part of the night on our way back. We slept a few hours at Brookhill and had interviews next morning with men who, on the previous day, were in high heart and hopes. We at once saw the effect that delay and indecision had produced on their minds. Reports, the most contradictory and false, respecting what Mr. O'Brien proposed and stated, had found their way among them, and it took hours to reassure them. They again promised us to be ready, however, and we proceeded across Slievenamon. On our journey we had interviews with the leaders of clubs and of other bodies, and at each step we found the difficulties of our position and the weakness of public confidence fearfully increased. We still hoped that the arrival of assistance which we expected from Waterford would restore unanimity and confidence.

When we reached Kilcash, at the southern base of Slievenamon, we learned that all hope of the expected assistance was at an end. Mr. Meagher had returned; and having despatched O'Mahony to Mr. O'Brien, to request he would once more return to the neighbourhood of the mountain, where he either could be more safely concealed for a time, or a last desperate effort could be made under better auspices, he waited several hours after the time appointed for his return, and then departed towards the direction of Borrisoleigh, in the northern riding of Tipperary, accompanied by Mr. Maurice Leyne, with whom unhappily he fell in, and to whose weak counsel, according to the information I received, much of his subsequent ill fate was owing. The distance to Borrisoleigh could not be less than forty miles. Mr. Meagher must have been persuaded by O'Mahony's delay, that Mr. O'Brien had been driven from his position, and perhaps captured, or he would not have undertaken so long a journey, the sole motive of which could only be the hope of rousing, with the aid of the Rev. Mr. Kenyon, that district of the country, so as to rescue his chief or avenge him. It was then apparent that our position had become desperate. We instantly proceeded to the house of our friend, who recounted the particulars of his visit to Ballingarry, and its results. He agreed in the propriety of going a second time to meet Mr. O'Brien, and urging upon him the necessity of some decisive course. The startling events of the two preceding days too clearly proved that his position was not tenable, and that whatever might be resolved on, it was indispensable to remove from Ballingarry. It was then night, and we were all sorely taxed by long riding and want of rest. Not one of us was able to mount, so we placed hay in a car on which we flung ourselves, and trusted to the guidance of the boy who led the horse. We travelled about nine miles in this way, one endeavouring to act as sentinel while the others were asleep; but we found that unless we trusted to blind chance, we could not continue our journey. So, half by force and half by persuasion, we obtained liberty to stretch on a pallet in an empty room. Mr. O'Brien was then snatching a little broken rest in a field, not four miles away from us, without our being aware of the fact. In the morning we learned that he remained there only while a car was procured at Mullinahone, and then returned to the neighbourhood of the collieries. He left Ballingarry on the advice contained in Mr. Meagher's message, and, accompanied by some hundreds of his followers, proceeded towards Carrick through the town of Mullinahone where for the third time he had to encounter the open hostility of the Catholic clergymen, who on this occasion had recourse to

177

threats and even blows. Owing to their interference, one-fourth of those who followed him so far, did not accompany him outside the town. He was nearly deserted, when he changed his resolution of falling back on his former position. When the car arrived he proceeded directly to the town of Killenaule, which might be said to be the head-quarters of the colliery. There he and his companions entered the hotel, where they remained till morning. Early that day the chapel bell was rung, and a great multitude flocked into the town. They were, as usual in that quarter, miserably armed. But they were enthusiastic, and the Catholic priests did not interfere. While the bell was tolling, intelligence was received that a troop of dragoons was approaching. The people immediately erected a barricade at the farthest extremity of the principal street. It was constructed of empty carts and baulks of timber. The moment the troop entered the street, a similar barricade was constructed in the rear. The hotel was situated between the two barricades. The officer in command made no demonstration of active resistance; and as he approached the last barricade he was surrounded by a great multitude. A few of the people were armed with rifles and muskets, others with pitchforks, scythes and slanes, and others had no weapons but stones. John Dillon stood at the barricade. The officer asked why his passage was interrupted, and stated he was only on an ordinary march. Mr. Dillon demanded whether his object was to arrest Smith O'Brien? He said emphatically, No. Mr. Dillon then asked if he would pledge his honour as a soldier, that he had no intention of arresting Mr. O'Brien, adding, that if he did so, the troop would be allowed to pass unmolested. He unhesitatingly pledged his honour, and immediately the barricade was partially removed. Mr. Dillon took his horse by the bridle and led him out of the town.

We were approaching Killenaule by another route when Mr. O'Brien and his party left it by the high road to the collieries. We followed, and after a race of some ten miles overtook them near Lisnabrock. Thence we proceeded in cars to Boulagh, and thence to the Commons. This was on Friday evening, the 28th day of July. We retired to an upper room in a publichouse. There were then present Mr. O'Brien, Mr. Dillon, Mr. Stephens, Mr. Cantwell, Mr. Meagher, Mr. O'Donohoe, Mr. Maurice Leyne, Mr. Reilly, Mr O'Mahony and myself, with others whose names I cannot mention, fourteen, as well as I remember, in all.[10] The same questions that were discussed on the former day were again revived, and we, who felt the necessity of the bold course we recommended then, were much more convinced of it under the altered circumstances of our position.

The debate was long and warm, but Mr. O'Brien's objections were even more immovable than ever. It will not be expected that all the proposals of that evening should be reproduced here. Suffice it, therefore, to add that as far as the principles by which Mr. O'Brien's conduct was guided, he adhered to them the more steadfastly in proportion as ruin became more inevitable. Many calumnies have been circulated respecting that meeting. It has been said that the discussion was acrimonious and the separation final. The truth is, there was not one word, even, of an angry tone, and we separated just as on the former occasion, determined to cope as best we could with a doom we were unable to avert. Often afterwards it was a source of melancholy pleasure to some of his comrades that he had not been induced to incur what he regarded as guilt. The lofty consciousness of unerring rectitude which sustained his fortitude could not fail to be chequered by the recollection of acts which in his own estimation were not purely blameless. Had success attended the suggested proposals, they would receive the world's unqualified approval; while failure, explained through the medium of a malicious law, and a warped and cowardly public opinion, would brand them as iniquitous. But Mr. O'Brien's scrupulous sense of honour escaped the hazards of such feeble probabilities; and in the hour of deepest gloom his own unsullied conscience shed peace, light and glory on his fate.

A Street in Ballingarry, 1848

Some of his companions exulted in the morning scene at Killenaule. To *seem* able to capture a troop of her majesty's dragoons, they regarded as a victory. But others, more thoughtful and correct, mourned over the escape of the military, which was only to be justified on the ground that the incongruous force around the feeble barricades, would be unequal to the task. It is a singular thing that while Captain Longmore utterly despaired of forcing his way, Mr. Dillon was fully conscious of his inability to resist him. The latter assumed a superiority he was unable to sustain, the former abjured a design which it was criminal according to the civil, and cowardly according to the military code, not to attempt the execution of Mr. Dillon, who led his horse, was a proclaimed "traitor." So was Mr. O'Brien, whose presence was avowed; by virtue of his allegiance, and still more, by virtue of his commission he was bound to arrest them. To neglect it was cowardice, cognisable by a court-martial and punishable by death. There could be but one justification—utter inability to effect the service. The evidence, then, that could alone satisfy a court-martial must directly contradict that which Captain Longmore offered at the trial in Clonmel. But while Mr. O'Brien viewed the conduct of Captain Longmore as cowardly submission, it would be unjust to conclude that it imparted a single shade of inflexibility to his principles or purpose. On the contrary, they assumed their attributes of most rigid sternness as his fortunes became clouded by a deeper gloom. He was averse to everything which bore the stamp of desperation, or could possibly imply a shrinking from fate.

Of those who took part in the deliberations of that evening, Messrs. Dillon, Stephens, MacManus and O'Donohoe resolved to continue with Mr. O'Brien. There seemed a possibility, though a desperate one, that they could baffle the enemy for the time the country required, and maintain their position of open defiance, whilst we, in different parts of the country, should keep up an appearance of force, so as to distract attention and check any attempt to despatch a force from the garrison of Clonmel. Meantime we were to endeavour to organise a force, and, if strong enough, act on our own responsibilities and according to our own principles. We left him about nine o'clock in the evening, after the best dispositions available out of the number with us were made to prevent surprise during the night. Soon after our departure he strongly advised Mr. Dillon to leave for another part of the country. I proposed to take up my post on Slievenamon, where I would be in the best position to fulfil Mr. O'Brien's wishes; where, at all events, I could escape arrest, in spite of any efforts to capture me, and where I expected, in a few days, to rally a considerable force. Mr. Meagher said he would take his stand on the Comeragh mountains, in the county of Waterford, with similar views and purposes. Mr. Meagher and Mr. Leyne, with three or four others, travelled together on a car. We dismissed ours, and crossed the country. Next day we arrived once more at Brookhill, which is within about one mile of Fethard, where we were able to procure a car that brought Mr. Reilly as far as Kilkenny. The first care of us who remained was to fulfil the commission assigned us. A young friend, of whom mention has been already made, joined me that evening. He had been two days in search of me, and was greatly exhausted by anxiety and fatigue. Rumours of various kinds were rife. But, what was most disheartening was that the courage of the people was fast subsiding. Men who were most eager for deeds of any daring two days previously, began to exhibit symptoms of hesitation, doubt, and even indifference. But a far sadder disaster had elsewhere befallen. Mr. O'Brien, after a night of anxious care, was still full of hope. He was even then engaged in drawing up a manifesto, embracing, as far as possible in such a document, the motives and causes which suggested and justified an armed revolt, and the principles upon which it was to be conducted. Whether the draft was destroyed or fell into the hands of the Government, is not now clear, save in as far as the non-production of the paper at his trial, is evidence that it never reached his persecutors. The leading principle of his entire conduct was, that the property, the liberty, the destiny of the island belonged to the entire people, and that the institutions which guaranteed them should be the calm embodiment of the nation's deliberate judgment, ascertained through the medium of a free assembly, deriving its authority from universal suffrage. This was one potent reason why he refused to assume, either as military leader, or as the chief of a provisional government, the responsibility of an act which could be regarded as the basis of the future government of Ireland. He was scrupulously anxious that the great principles upon which the future liberty of Ireland was to be based, should emanate from the free will of the people, uncontrolled by dictatorial power or personal prestige.

But Mr. O'Brien was not destined to accomplish the object of his solicitude. About twelve o'clock on the morning of Saturday, the 29th day of July, he was apprised of the approach of a body of police, under command of Captain Trant. Simultaneously with the appearance of the police, an indiscriminate crowd, composed for the most part of women and boys with a few armed men, ranged themselves around him. They occupied an eminence in front of the road by which the police approached. Another road crossed this at right angles, and Captain Trant, instead of leading his men directly against Mr. O'Brien's position, denied along the cross-road to the right hand—that which led to the Widow M'Cormick's. The motive of this manoeuvre was obvious. Either from personal cowardice, or from cool judgment, he determined to await further reinforcements, and, meantime, to secure some place of shelter and defence. The crowd, with Mr. O'Brien, immediately rushed from their position and hung fiercely on the policemen's rear. Captain Trant ordered a retreat, or those under his command adopted that precaution without his authority. The armed leaders among the people, Messrs. MacManus, Stephens and Cavanagh, hesitated to fire on troops flying for their lives. But they urged the pursuit so rapidly, that, by the time the police took shelter in Mrs. M'Cormick's house, they were hot upon their track. The crowd surrounded the house, and Mr. O'Brien, approaching one of the front windows, called on Captain Trant to surrender. The latter demanded half an hour to consider, which Mr. O'Brien unhappily granted. Pending the half hour, the crowd became furious and began to fling stones in through the windows. Some of the men inside were knocked down by the stones, and the officer hurt. Seeing that their own leaders could no longer control the people, and believing the destruction of himself and his party to be inevitable, Captain Trant gave orders to his men to fire, which presented his only chance of escape. Mr. O'Brien immediately rushed between the people and the window, on one of which he jumped up, and once more demanded the officer to surrender. But the order to fire had been given and executed with deadly effect. Two men fell dead, and several were badly wounded. The crowd fell back; but Mr. O'Brien remained still in front of the house. There were several windows in front and two small ones only in the rear; parallel with the rear was a barn, in which there were two still smaller windows. Messrs. Stephens and MacManus took possession of this house, and, placing three or four sure marksmen inside for the purpose of taking down any of the police who should appear at the back windows, they proposed to burn the house in which the police took shelter. They carried bundles of hay and placed them against the back door and roof. The police seized on

Mrs. M'Cormick's children, and held them up to the windows, to terrify or appease the people. At this juncture the Catholic clergymen appeared on the scene. Either, being appalled by the scene of death before them, or being personally cowardly, or feeling that to continue the conflict would be productive of useless slaughter, they exerted themselves to the utmost to disperse the crowd. Whatever may have been their motives, it is certain that, although Mr. O'Brien was in the neighbourhood since the previous Wednesday, they had not in any way interfered, and only came upon the scene to attend to the dying and the dead. Mr. O'Brien and his comrades, finding themselves beset by this unexpected difficulty, retired a short distance, to consider what was best to be done. The people were again quickly forming around them, and all were hurriedly preparing to storm the house, when a fresh body of police was seen approaching from the opposite direction. This force consisted of sixty men; the first only amounted to forty-five. Constable Carroll rode on considerably in advance of his party. He found himself suddenly surrounded, and was forced to surrender and dismount. He and two others of the advance-guard were removed. But the main body continued to approach rapidly; and Mr. O'Brien was not in a position and had not strength to intercept their junction with the other body. His friends pressed Mr. O'Brien to retreat, which he refused. Admitting, fully, his inability to cope with these forces, he declined to avail himself of the means of escape at his disposal. His comrades impressed on him that his life belonged to the country; that another effort was yet within the range of possibility, and that it was incumbent on him to save himself for the final issue. By long and passionate entreaty, they induced him to mount the police-officer's horse and retire. When he had left, Messrs. Stephens and MacManus led off the remainder of their party, without being pursued or molested.

After a short consultation, they determined to separate. Mr. Stephens proposed to go on to Urlingford, where a large force was collecting, and MacManus accepted the duty of bearing to us the intelligence of the disaster, and taking chance with us for the future. He came up with Mr.

Meagher, Mr. O'Donohoe, and Mr. Leyne, who were then on their way to the Comeragh mountains, but changed their purpose on hearing this sad intelligence. They remained that night at the house of a man named Hanrahan, near Nine-mile House, a small village on the high road from Kilkenny to Cork.

I was all this time ignorant of what occurred. After Mr. Reilly had left me, and I was joined by the young friend already mentioned, I summoned as many of the farmers of the neighbourhood as I could collect, and it was agreed that ten of them, who would represent each one hundred men, should meet me next day, after divine service, at the wood of Keilavalla, situate near the western base of Slievenamon. We were to be joined by two others from the neighbourhood of Carrick-on Suir, from which we were distant about ten miles. On that morning the news of Mr. O'Brien's disaster spread far, and was, of course, exaggerated. I had slept the previous night not far from the mountain, where I was watched by two brothers named Walsh, who lived at Brookhill, but have since removed to the United States. I gladly avail myself of this occasion to attest their fidelity and bravery. At the time appointed, my friend and I proceeded to the place of rendezvous. We remained for hours, and remained in vain. At last one only of the ten arrived. He told us that at the chapel the Rev. Patrick Laffan read the names of the proscribed traitors for whose persons a reward was offered . . .

We continued on the mountain during the remainder of the day; and toward evening about fifty men came up to us, who, one and all, expressed the utmost indignation at what had happened. Once more our hopes revived. If Mr. O'Brien could avoid arrest for a few weeks only, we expected that a sense of shame would sting the country to desperate exertion.

After night-fall we descended, and slept at a farmer's house at the southern base of the mountain, where we were most kindly entertained and sedulously guarded. We there heard of the Ballingarry disaster. Next morning we once more ascended Slievenamon, where we endeavoured to dissipate the heavy hours and the still heavier consciousness at our own hearts by firing at a mark. The day suddenly darkened, and we had to seek shelter under rocks from a pitiless mountain shower. We had dispatched a messenger to O'Mahony to demand an interview that evening; and, after he had returned, we were invited to partake of some new potatoes (then beginning to exhibit the blight), milk, eggs and butter. I remember lying down in a bed, and getting so feverish that I believed my doom was sealed. My noble young friend sat at my bedside, with a rifle and two pistols, prepared to defend my rest with his life. The illness was, however, but trifling and temporary, and the necessity of acting enabled me at once to shake it off. After nightfall, we proceeded to the appointed interview. We travelled in a common car, accompanied by four others, all armed. Our haunt was a poor cabin on the roadside, near a place called Moloch, in the neighbourhood of Carrick. There I bid my faithful young friend good night, but was doomed not to see him afterwards. Mr. O'Mahony and myself slept on some straw, but we had scarcely closed our eyes when we learned that the cabin was surrounded by the military and police. We were apprised of our perilous position just in time to escape: this we effected, after a struggle, aided by extreme darkness. We spent the remainder of the night in a field, where I slept very soundly. At break of day we retired to a farmer's house near the Suir, where, after partaking of some refreshments, we went to bed, and slept, one or two hours. The breakfast scene of that morning is not easily forgotten. Perhaps there is no place in the world where a more substantial breakfast can be produced than at a comfortable Irish farmer's. On this occasion the silent, watchful, anxious grace of our young hostess, in her attentions, enhanced the flavour of the repast. It is only by those who have partaken of such hospitality that the speechless tenderness of the females among that class of farmers can be appreciated. But on the occasion to which I refer, there was added to the customary delicacy a deep anxiety for our fate. Save hushed words of pressing and eloquent looks of sympathy, the meal passed off without conversation; and we rose from the table to depart, as if conscious we had exchanged our last earthly greeting. It was not so, however, and our hostess shared much of our after fortune, and now shares our exile. Her fate, too, is harder than ours. We are occasionally cheered by public approval, by the sympathy and admiration of every lover of liberty, whereas her name is never spoken. She has fallen from a position of comparative affluence, lost her independence (I use the word in its practical worldly sense), and is doomed to toil for her daily bread. Of all the vicissitudes of fortune in which the attempt of which I write resulted, there is not one that has given me more pain than that of Margaret Quinlan, the lady (who has higher claims to that title?) to whom I have alluded.

FOOTNOTES:

10   The other four were Terence Bellew MacManus, John Cavanagh, J.D. Wright (a T.C.D. student, afterwards a lawyer in America), and D.P. Cunningham, afterwards a journalist in New York.—Ed.

CHAPTER VIII

ARREST OF MR. O'BRIEN, OF MESSRS. MEAGHER AND O'DONOHOE.—ARREST OF TERENCE BELLEW MACMANUS.—CLONMEL SPECIAL COMMISSION.—TRIAL, CONVICTION, SPEECHES AND SENTENCE OF THE REBELS.—WRIT OF ERROR.—COMMUTATION OF SENTENCE.—TRANSPORTATION OF THE HEROES.

Before proceeding further with the details of my own wanderings, I wish to follow out to its conclusion the fate of those whom we parted with at Ballingarry, and were destined to see no more, though, in doing so, I must anticipate the order of time, in which the events took place. My task here is more difficult and painful than any detail of facts, however gloomy. There are always in the reverses of the brave, some glimpses of glory to reconcile us to the dark disasters on our way; but when calumny pursues their path, gnawing, with ceaseless tooth, the priceless jewel of their character, the historian must shudder to find his labour beset by the filth and rubbish the viper has left behind. In this instance, that lesson of Mr. O'Connell's which was the most fatal in its influence, found many believers. It was said, and said unscrupulously, that Mr. O'Brien and his followers were actual agents of the British Government, suborned to precipitate the country into revolution, for which they were to receive large possessions and lucrative employment beyond the sea. It was the constant habit of Mr. O'Connell, when any one proposed a course bolder than his own, to suggest that he was doing the business of the enemy. He may have adopted this course in his self-assumed character of Dictator, as the surest and speediest means of clearing all obstructions out of his way. Whatever his motive, it was an unworthy resource; for it supplied the meanest minds with an example and a pretext for the gratification of their own vile propensities. Their voice was heard, amid the silence of mourning and death, when in an hour of universal dismay, John Mitchel was borne from his loved fatherland; and still more audibly when the dungeon closed on Smith O'Brien and his illustrious comrades. In the latter instance, slander availed itself of an incident connected with their arrest to justify its infamous conclusions. "If," it croaked, "they were in earnest, why suffer themselves to be arrested so easily?—Why come to the railway terminus?—Why parade on the high road in front of a police barrack? In effect, why surrender?" But in Ireland this was little heeded; nor should I deem it worthy of the least notice, if it were not revived in the new world, under circumstances calculated to give it credence and durability. At one time it is insinuated that they "surrendered," such as "it was said they gave themselves up," and immediately afterwards, in reference to the period or the fact, is to be found "at the time of Mr. O'Brien's surrender." And again, in the same breath, it is positively stated as a mere matter of course.

The propagator of this malignity knows it to be false. He knows also that it serves the purpose of those who would charge the country's truest and bravest with vilest treachery.

I shall pursue the theme no further. The truth is, Mr. O'Brien remained among a people who were sorely stricken by terror. Their friends were dead or scattered; and rumour, with a thousand tongues, multiplied the most awful horrors which were said to be approaching them. Although they received and sheltered Mr. O'Brien, he evidently saw that their generosity cost them dearly, and that they were in the utmost alarm. His own privations he could endure; but not the fear and suffering his presence caused to others. This, and this only, determined him in the first instance. He might also have hoped that if he could reach the neighbourhood of his own home, he would be defended with desperate fidelity. He was aware that Mr. Richard O'Gorman was in that district, and he had been informed that he was followed by thousands. That he did not seek to reach the county Limerick by some other means of conveyance—by a car, on foot, or on horseback—may be a mistake of judgment; but none would be free from peril: and had he escaped detection at Thurles, there would not be the least danger, until he reached Cahermoyle, as the rest of the journey would be entirely by night. His sagacity may be questioned, perhaps, but it is extreme villainy to question his purpose. He took that course only and solely because he thought it the safest; and he had no more intention of surrendering than I had when I crossed by the packet to Boulogne.

Mr. Meagher and Mr. O'Donohoe were arrested under circumstances over which they had still less control. They were utterly unacquainted with the country, and did not know, if they left the high road, but the first house they might approach would be a police barrack. They had made every attempt desperation could suggest to rouse the people, but in vain. They were opposed by some, shunned by some, and from some they received false counsel. They had exhausted the welcome of all who were inclined to receive them, and they knew not one step of their way. Previously, too, Mr. Meagher had peremptorily refused to avail himself of a mode of escape provided for him and he equally peremptorily refused to listen to any terms from Government, which did not include all his comrades. His object, on the night he was arrested, was to make another trial at Cashel, which he designed to approach by a circuitous route.

The 6th day of August was the date of Mr. O'Brien's arrest; the 13th of August that of Messrs. Meagher and O'Donohoe, and the 7th of September that of Mr. MacManus. Mr. O'Brien was taken at the Thurles railway station; Messrs. Meagher and O'Donohoe, near Rathgannon, on the road between Clonoulty and Holycross, about five miles from Thurles, and Mr. MacManus on board the ship *N.D. Chase*, in the bay of Cove, on the 7th of September. They were each conveyed to Kilmainham Jail, in the first instance, where they remained until within a few days

190

of the opening of the special commission at Clonmel. This took place on Thursday, the 21st of Sept., when the bills were found, but six days were allowed to Mr. O'Brien and the rest of the prisoners to peruse the indictment, with copies of which they were respectively furnished. On Thursday, the 28th, the trial of Mr. O'Brien commenced; that of Mr. MacManus on the 9th of October; that of Mr. O'Donohoe on the 13th, and that of Mr. Meagher on the 16th.

Juries were empanelled in each case, from whose prejudice and bad faith verdicts for high treason were expected, even though the evidence only sustained a charge of common assault. Roman Catholics were, in the first instance, scrupulously excluded; but after the first two verdicts one or two were admitted, upon whose weakness of character, or genteel aspirations, the Government might safely rely. It is but justice to say that, according to the law expounded by the Bench, and the evidence given on the table, any other verdict was not to be expected. But a jury differently composed, a jury of Englishmen, with their country, their liberties and their lives perilled to the last extremity by misgovernment and maladministration of law, would have spurned the law and the evidence, and relied on the great fundamental rights of humanity so flagrantly outraged by the Government that then appeared as prosecutors.

The scene presented by Clonmel excited much public surprise. Newspaper correspondents magnified the sullen gloom that prevailed into popular apathy or national cowardice, as suited the bent or purpose of their employers. The truth was, the people exhibited during the trial a decent and respectful forbearance. Empty parade or vociferous sorrow would only mock the lofty purpose of the sufferers; and besides, the mortification which rankled in the public heart was too deep for utterance. The hopes of the people had been dashed, and they were stunned and stupefied by their fall. But so far from being apathetic, nightly assemblages were held to consider if, even in that extremity, something was not yet possible to be done.

But, if there were a show of popular indifference on the streets, the courthouse presented a very different spectacle. There everything manifested an intense bitterness of purpose; the court, composed of the two most unscrupulous partisans, Chief Justices Blackbourne and Doherty, and the weakest or falsest political convert, Mr. Justice Moore, simulated the uncontrollable emotions which an overweening loyalty awoke in the bosom of the Catholic Attorney-General. So far were their lordships swayed by the spirit of imitativeness, that the most polished speakers, mistaking the incoherent jargon of the official for the broken utterance of overwrought zeal and shocked loyalty, mimicked his distempered language as the only befitting medium of expression for disturbed feelings such as theirs. The simplest and most usual facilities accorded to murderers and pickpockets on their trial were rudely denied the counsel for the defence. The principles of law, recognised in England as sacred, were scouted from the bench, and the farce of trial proceeded through its different stages to the final *denouement* with perfect regularity, every one performing the part assigned him with unerring accuracy.

Of the intrepid ability which struggled against this fearful combination of bigotry, prejudice and passion, at the bar, on the bench and in the box, I do not purpose to speak here. But I would be unfaithful to my trust, and unjust to the rarest heroism, if I did not record the fortitude and fidelity of O'Donnell, from whom the menaces of the crown, or the frown of the bench, could not wring one word of evidence. In an ordinary man, this would be singular intrepidity; but circumstanced as O'Donnell was, it amounted to a Roman virtue. One brother of his, a doctor, was in jail at Liverpool, charged with political felony; another was hunted through the country, and another was in irons, involved in the same charge as the illustrious accused; for them all he could command his own terms, for much depended on his testimony; but though doom were upon them, and a word of his could avert it, he refused to speak. Honour be his. His integrity almost cancelled the shame and darkness of those disastrous times.

The Widow McCormack's House, near Ballingarry

I can add nothing to the testimony that established the fortitude, manliness and dignity of the prisoners, as beyond precedent or example. That their bearing, one and all, was truly noble, friends and foes took pride in attesting.[11] It was a solemn and a glorious sight; and men, through all time, will turn to that Clonmel dock to learn the inestimable and imperishable value of sincere and lofty convictions and a truly heroic soul.

Of the speeches that follow, it will be observed that Mr. O'Brien's was delivered before the fate of his comrades was known. No man had ever greater need of vindicating others if not himself. No man ever possessed in a higher degree the capacity and strength to do so. He was satisfied it was the last opportunity he would ever have on earth for explanation. Yet, lest any sentiment of his might injuriously affect those that were then, or might thereafter be on their trial, he forebore to assert the principles of which he was there the martyr, and of which he was more than ever proud. It was to the same unselfish sentiment he yielded, when consenting to say, "Not guilty," to a charge he would have felt the greatest glory in avowing.

I despair of conveying to my readers an adequate idea of the gloom and horror of the scene in which those immortal words were spoken. Death, near and terrible, was in the future. The recollection of ten days' infamy peopled the present with ghastly images of evil. Vindictiveness inexorable glared from the bench. The dust around the feet of the speakers was laden with guilt. It would not rise to the briskest breeze, beneath the clearest sky, in light summer air, so heavy had the tread of murder been upon it. And oh, to think when they closed their eyes upon this world, what deeper death they left their country . . . Will no day of vengeance come, O God! . . .

One of those benefits of the British constitution, which excites the mortal envy of benighted "surrounding nations," is this, that the law lies to the face of death, in the usual question addressed to the condemned: "Whether he had anything to say why sentence of death and execution should not be passed upon him?" when the most conclusive reasons that ever innocence had to offer would be worse than vain. On the morning of the 9th of October, 1848, this barbarous mockery was addressed to William Smith O'Brien, and he answered thus:—

MR. O'BRIEN.—"My lords, it is not my intention to enter into any vindication of my conduct, however much I might have desired to avail myself of this opportunity of so doing. I am perfectly satisfied with the consciousness that I have performed my duty to my country—that I have done only that which, in my opinion, it was the duty of every Irishman to have done, and I am now prepared to abide the consequences of having performed

194

my duty to my native land. Proceed with your sentence." (Cheers in the gallery.)

On the morning of the 23rd of the same month, the same formula was repeated to Terence Bellew MacManus, Patrick O'Donohoe, and Thomas Francis Meagher, who replied respectively as follows:—

MR. M'MANUS.—"My lords, I trust I am enough of a Christian and enough of a man to understand the awful responsibility of the question that has been put to me. My lords, standing on this my native soil—standing in an Irish court of justice, and before the Irish nation—I have much to say why the sentence of death, or the sentence of the law, should not be passed upon me. But, my lords, on entering this court, I placed my life, and what is of much more importance to me—my honour—in the hands of two advocates; and, my lords, if I had ten thousand lives, and ten thousand honours, I would be content to place them under the watchful and the glorious genius of the one and the high legal ability of the other. My lords, I am content. In that regard I have nothing to say. But I have a word to say, which no advocate, however anxious, can utter for me. I have this to say, my lords, that whatever part I may have taken through any struggle for my country's independence—whatever part I may have acted in that short career—I stand before your lordships now with a free heart, and with a light conscience, ready to abide the issue of your sentences. And now, my lords, perhaps this is the fittest time that I might put one sentiment on record, and it is this: Standing as I do between this dock and the scaffold; it may be now, or tomorrow, or it may be never; but whatever the result may be, I have this sentiment to put on record. That in any part I have taken, I have not been actuated by animosity to Englishmen. For I have spent some of the happiest and most prosperous days of my life in

England; and in no part of my career have I been actuated by enmity to Englishmen, however much I may have felt the injustice of English rule on this island. My lords, I have nothing more to say. It is not for having loved England less, but for having loved Ireland more, that I stand now before you."

Mr. O'Donohoe confined himself to a few words concerning his trial.

MR. MEAGHER.—"My lords, it is my intention to say a few words only. I desire that the last act of a proceeding which has occupied so much of the public time should be of short duration. Nor have I the indelicate wish to close the dreary ceremony of a State prosecution with a vain display of words. Did I fear that hereafter when I shall be no more the country I have tried to serve would think ill of me, I might, indeed, avail myself of this solemn moment to vindicate my sentiments and my conduct. But I have no such fear. The country will judge of those sentiments and that conduct in a light far different from that in which the jury by which I have been convicted have viewed them; and by the country, the sentence which you, my lords, are about to pronounce, will be remembered only as the severe and solemn attestation of my rectitude and truth. Whatever be the language in which that sentence be spoken, I know that my fate will meet with sympathy, and that my memory will be honoured. In speaking thus, accuse me not, my lords, of an indecorous presumption. To the efforts I have made in a just and noble cause, I ascribe no vain importance—nor do I claim for those efforts any high reward. But it so happens, and it will ever happen so, that they who have tried to serve their country, no matter how weak the effort may have been, are sure to receive the thanks and the blessings of its people. With my country, then, I leave my memory—my sentiments—my

196

acts—proudly feeling that they require no vindication from me this day. A jury of my countrymen, it is true, have found me guilty of the crime of which I stood indicted. For this I entertain not the slightest feeling of resentment toward them. Influenced as they must have been by the charge of the Lord Chief Justice, they could have found no other verdict. What of that charge? Any strong observations on it, I feel sincerely, would ill befit the solemnity of this scene; but I would earnestly beseech of you, my lord—you, who preside on that bench—when the passions and the prejudices of this hour have passed away to appeal to your conscience, and ask of it was your charge as it ought to have been, impartial and indifferent between the subject and the Crown. My lords, you may deem this language unbecoming in me, and perhaps it may seal my fate. But I am here to speak the truth, whatever it may cost. I am here to regret nothing I have ever done—to retract nothing I have ever said. I am here to crave with no lying-lip the life I consecrate to the liberty of my country. Far from it: even here—here, where the thief, the libertine, the murderer, have left their footprints in the dust; here, on this spot, where the shadows of death surround me, and from which I see my early grave in an unanointed soil opened to receive me—even here, encircled by these terrors, the hope which has beckoned me to the perilous sea upon which I have been wrecked, still consoles, animates, enraptures me. No I do not despair of my poor old country, her peace her liberty, her glory. For that country I can do no more than bid her hope. To lift up this island—to make her a benefactor to humanity, instead of being the meanest beggar in the world—to restore to her her native Powers and her ancient constitution—this has been my ambition, and this ambition has been my crime. Judged by the law of England, I know this crime entails the Penalty of death; but the history of Ireland explains this crime, and justifies it. Judged by that history, I am no criminal—

you (addressing Mr. MacManus) are no criminal—you (addressing Mr O'Donohoe) are no criminal—I deserve no punishment—we deserve no punishment. Judged by that history the treason of which I stand convicted loses all its guilt, is sanctified as a duty, will be ennobled as a sacrifice. With these sentiments, my lord I await the sentence of the court. Having done what I felt to be my duty—having spoken what I felt to be the truth, as I have done on every other occasion of my short career, I now bid farewell to the country of my birth, my passion and my death—the country whose misfortunes have invoked my sympathies—whose factions I have sought to still—whose intellect I have prompted to a lofty aim—whose freedom has been my fatal dream. I offer to that country, as a proof of the love I bear her, and the sincerity with which I thought, and spoke, and struggled for her freedom— the life of a young heart, and with that life, all the hopes, the honours, the endearments, of a happy and an honourable home. Pronounce then, my lords, the sentence which the law directs, and I will be prepared to hear it. I trust I shall be prepared to meet its execution. I hope to be able, with a pure heart and perfect composure, to appear before a higher Tribunal—a tribunal where a Judge of infinite goodness, as well as of justice will preside, and where, my lords, many—many of the judgments of this world will be reversed."

The sentence of the court was then pronounced, as it had been previously on Mr. O'Brien. It was in the following words:—

"That sentence is, that you Terence Bellew MacManus, you Patrick O'Donohoe, and you Thomas Francis Meagher, be taken hence to the place from whence you came, and be thence drawn on a hurdle to the place of execution; that each of you be there hanged by the neck until you are dead, and that afterward the head of each of you shall be severed from the body, and the body of each divided into four quarters, to be disposed of as her Majesty may think fit. And may Almighty God have mercy upon your souls."

A writ of error was sued out principally on the ground that the principles of constitutional law were violated. The House of Lords finally quashed the error and confirmed the judgment. Meantime, the country, or a great portion of the people, took the last step in the direction of debasement by praying the Queen and the Lord Lieutenant for a free pardon. The petitions were spurned; but her Majesty, yielding to the powerful sentiment of abhorrence against the punishment of death for political offences, commuted the sentence into transportation for life. This final sentence was carried into effect on the 9th day of July, 1849, when the ship of war *Swift* spread her sails and hoisted her felon flag, bearing out to sea, and having on board the four illustrious exiles.

Martin and O'Doherty had been conveyed to Cork on board the *Triton*, on the 16th of June, whence they were sent to herd with common malefactors on board the *Mount Stewart Elphinstone*—at the time infested with the plague. This vessel remained off Spike Island while the cholera was doing its ravages among her passengers, and finally put to sea, with the patriots and pestilence, a few days before the departure of the *Swift*.

FOOTNOTES:

11   The following is from the *Freeman's Journal:*—An eminent Queen's counsel, who was present during the awful ordeal, was heard to give utterance to a sentiment so truthfully graphic that we record it in full:—"Well," said he, his eyes full and his countenance flushed with emotion, "never was there such a scene—never such true heroism displayed before. Emmet and Fitzgerald, and all combined did not come up to that—so dignified, so calm, so heroic. HE *is* a hero."

CHAPTER IX

CONTINUATION OF PERSONAL WANDERINGS.—
DUNGARVAN.—THE COMERAGHS.—MOUNT MELLARY.—
KILWORTH.—CROSS. DUNMANWAY.—GOUGANE BARRA.—
BANTRY BAY.—THE PRIEST'S LEAP.—KENMARE.—THE
REEKS.—KILLARNEY.—TEMPLENOE.—DEPARTURE.—
CORK.—BRISTOL.—LONDON.—PARIS.

After leaving Quinlan's, as detailed in a former chapter, O'Mahony and myself agreed to separate for a few days. No reward had then been offered for him, and my presence only impeded his movements. We crossed the river Suir, and remained most of the day in Coolnamuck wood. Toward evening I was conducted far into the county Waterford, where I was to remain until I heard what progress he was able to make. My host was the chief of one of the fierce factions of county Waterford, and bore many a mark of desperate fray. I do not remember having met any man, before or since, who felt so acutely the fate of the country. He procured the best fare he could, and prepared my bed with his own hands. After I retired to rest, he continued pacing the room for several hours, sometimes sighing deeply, sometimes muttering curses between his clenched teeth, and sometimes suggesting plans which he thought might be even then available and efficient to redeem the past. These plans were all of a character more or less desperate; but some were exceedingly ingenious. A truer type of a Celt could not easily be found; his very caution was stamped with vehemence.

Next day but one I proceeded to meet O'Mahony, to learn his success in his nocturnal interviews. I was unable to meet him; but encountered a faithful follower of Thomas Francis Meagher, who was the bearer of a message to the effect that if he could be prevailed upon to attempt escaping, means could be procured for him. I expressed at once my entire concurrence, and desired the messenger should return to say that on condition the same means would be made available for those who were not yet arrested, we would all gladly accept of them. I ventured into a house, where, in early life, I spent many a happy day. Those of the family whom I had known and loved, had passed out of the world. They were a brother and sister, the former educated for the Church, and the latter highly gifted and educated far above her condition. I never knew a woman, in any rank of life, of nobler character or a more heroic nature. She had the richest store of womanly tenderness and kindly affections. She took the veil at the Dungarvan Convent in very early youth, where she died two years afterwards. I asked for some food, and while it was being prepared I wrote the following lines on a blank leaf of a book belonging to my dead friend:—

Bliss to thy spirit, gentlest maid,
Fond, faithful and beloved; how oft,
Within the circle of this glowing glade,
Our mingling souls had soared aloft;
And wooed the knowledge of our destiny—
What is it? I a fugitive, and thou on high.

Yet hopeless of the land I'd save,
Nay, spurned by those for whom I'd die,
Unknown where your fond welcome gave,
There's still a throb of ecstasy.
Even though the latest I may feel on earth.
In lingering o'er the scene where thou hadst birth.

Where wrapt by evening's crimson flush,
We hoped, and felt, and breathed together,

Beside the broad Suir's silent gush,
Or resting on yon mountain heather;
And dared to look beyond the narrow span,
That circumscribed the hope of man.

How sweet, if from the blessed spheres,
Thou didst bestow one look of love,
To cheer the hearts and dry the tears
Of those whose only hope's above;
And win, beloved one, from the throne of light,
One saving ray for our long slavery's night.

Or if this may not be, and yet
Her old doom clings unto the land;
If on her brow the brand be set,
And she must bear the chastening hand
For longer years, O grant, sweet saint, to me,
To die as if my arm had made her free.

GLENN, *August 3, 1848.*

I left Glenn next morning, with still some hope remaining, and sought out my friend to learn his success and prospects. He came, according to appointment, to a farmer's house in the direction of Rathgormack, bringing with him James Stephens, who was destined to be thenceforth the companion of my wanderings, privations and dangers. He detailed to us, nearly as I have repeated it, the affair at Ballingarry. When he reached the village of Urlingford, he found some difficulty in escaping from the very men he hoped to lead back to the conflict. After vainly making every effort first to urge them on, and secondly to satisfy them of his own identity, he travelled a distance of thirty miles, and took shelter in the house of a private friend, where he hoped he could remain until something definite would be known of his comrades' fate. That his stay was not of long duration, his appearance with us on Thursday, forty miles from the place of his concealment, amply testifies. That distance he travelled on foot on the preceding day, after having slept a night with a drunken man in a brake. He was even more averse than we were to giving up the struggle, and it was agreed on finally that he should be allowed to rest in a place of safety; that the messenger who had come from Mr. Meagher's friend should be despatched with my proposal, and meantime, that I should betake me to the Comeragh mountains in search of Mr. Meagher, while our other comrade should make a final effort to rally the remaining strength of the people. We would then be in a position to determine finally what we should do. Stephens and myself proceeded together as far as my former host's in the mountains, where I left him, and continued my route as far as the Comeraghs, I rested that evening at a place called Sradavalla, and early next day recommenced my search around and over the mountains. After crossing several minor hills, I ascended the summit of the Comeragh, called Cuimshinane, which commands a prospect of nearly the whole counties of Waterford and Kilkenny, with a great part of Tipperary. That prospect was at once grand, beautiful and mournful. The corn crop began to be tinged with coming ripeness; but the potato was blighted, and presented a spectacle as black and dismal as the country's hopes. This widespread ruin was the dread work of an hour. On the morning, when Mr. O'Brien appeared in Carrick, that crop was the most abundant, promising and healthy that had been seen for years. Then it appeared from sea to sea one mass of unvaried rottenness and decay. Notwithstanding this, I spent hours looking down on the landscape, and mourning more over the mental and moral blight, which shed its influence on the public heart, than the plague spot whose dark circumference embraced the circle of the island. From heat, fatigue and the effects of weak food, I discharged my stomach more than once, while descending the ranges of the Comeraghs. I again took up my station for the night at the village of Sradavalla. It was deemed prudent I should not sleep in the same house as on the previous night, and about eleven o'clock, accompanied by five or six men of the village, I proceeded to a house farther up the mountain. Here the accommodation was not such as we expected, and we were forced to return. On our arrival, I found my sister-in-law who was escorted by two boatmen from Carrick-on-Suir, and who reached this wild sequestered and almost inaccessible mountain village, after a journey of fifty miles. A sad change had come over our circumstances since last we parted. My hopes were then nearly a conviction, and I went on my way not alone without remonstrance or regret on her part, but with intense encouragement. She had heard of Mr. O'Brien's disaster, and a rumour of his arrest, had witnessed the prostration of the people, had heard I had means of escape proposed for me, and came with what money could be provided. We spent that night together at the house of a woman who had been lately confined. She endeavoured to provide tea and eggs, and we enjoyed our supper with as keen a relish and as high a zest as possible. I learned that Meagher was in the other extremity of the county Tipperary, and she undertook to convey my message to his friend a second time, while his faithful scout would endeavour to discover his retreat, and induce him to join us. She departed on her mission, having to walk ten miles over the mountain roads. I returned to the place where I parted from Stephens, whom I found greatly recovered. We remained that night at the house of his entertainer, where we were joined the following morning by O'Mahony. We spent the three succeeding days in and about the woods at Coolnamuck. Three more anxious days and nights never darkened the destiny of baffled rebels. Every morning arose upon a new hope which was blasted ere night came on by some sad intelligence. The news that reached us was partly true and partly false: of the former character was the account of our beloved chief's arrest, which took place on the evening of Sunday, the 6th of August. In proportion as it nerved our purpose and urged us to desperation, did that fatal information scatter the agencies on which we were to depend. The most desperate hazards would be readily undertaken in that hour of gloom. One more effort we decided on, and the experiment was to be tried the next night. We heard Mr. Meagher also was arrested, and we resolved, in order to satisfy ourselves of the correctness of this and other reports, to put ourselves in direct communication with some person in the town of Clonmel. We accordingly proceeded to the neighbourhood of that town, within a mile of which, at the Waterford side, we established ourselves, and remained two days. Each day we sent in a messenger who brought us correct intelligence of what occurred; and satisfied us not alone that Mr. O'Brien was then in gaol, but that he was allowed to be torn from the midst of a people for whom he had perilled his life, without a hand being raised in his defence. We then returned to the scene of our former meetings, and met, for the last time, beside a little brook near the Waterford slate-quarries. My ambassadress had also returned, and there were present three or four others. The reunion was gloomy. But one question remained for discussion: Was there any hope left? The message I received as to the means of escape was dark and discouraging. Nothing remained but the hazards of some desperate enterprise. What had chiefly animated our hopes for the few days was the knowledge that disaffection and conspiracy existed in the ranks of the British army. But among other intelligence of evil omen that reached us was this, that the conspiracy had been discovered. Whether this were true or not, our means of communication were suspended; and, unable to learn what had occurred, we naturally concluded it was the worst. It is not quite correct to say, *we*, as far as the proceedings of these days in that neighbourhood were concerned. Neither Stephens nor myself was in communication with more than the one friend, to whose honour and heroism we would commit the liberty of the world. Never yet lived a man of more sanguine hope or intense patriotism. All the vigour of a gigantic intellect, aided by the endurance of great physical strength was tasked to the uttermost in attempting to rouse the broken energies of the country. He generally spent his nights in interviews with the chief men of the surrounding districts, while his duty by day was to communicate the result to us, and secure a place of safety for the ensuing night. Our last conference was of course the longest and most anxious. There was no chance within the range of possibility we did not discuss. Of the intensity of our feelings, some idea may be formed by the fact, that the one woman who was of the party, whose sole stay on this earth I was, as well as the sole stay of her sister and a most helpless little family, never uttered one word of remonstrance against any project, however desperate, which was proposed. We concluded an interview of several hours, by referring the entire question to the sole decision of our friend. After a short silence, during which the agony of his mind was extreme, he solemnly advised and adjured us to provide as best we could for our own safety, while he, who was not so deeply compromised, would maintain his position, and still struggle against our common destiny. If he succeeded, and that we had not left the country, we could return. But to advise us to continue in our then position where an iron circle was closing around us, relying on the slender chances that then presented themselves, involved a responsibility which would be no longer endurable. We then partook of a comfortable dinner which he had provided, and parted with sad hearts.

The Knockmeldown Mountains from Ardfinan

The place which, as far as we could form an opinion, presented the greatest facilities for escape, was the town and neighbourhood of Dungarvan. Thither we resolved to repair; and about three o'clock, on the 13th day of August, we set off across the nearest range of the Comeraghs—Stephens and myself, accompanied by my sister-in-law, whom we hoped to employ in negotiating for a passage to France. A farmer and two women of the place undertook to conduct us the shortest way across the mountains, and provide us an asylum for the night, which we reached after a forced journey of six hours. We there parted from our guides; and the people to whom they recommended us were exceedingly kind, and much more hospitable than their means would permit. On the following day our host became our guide for several miles across the declining Comeraghs, until we came in view of Dungarvan. We purchased some bread, eggs and tea at a village called Tubbernaheena; but while in the village we learned that the military and police were scouring the country far and wide, in search of arms, which compelled us to change our route and take an easterly direction. We crossed several miles of bog, and had to pass many a ravine; but the worst trial was before us. We applied in several houses for the means of preparing our dinner, having travelled at least twenty miles over moor and mountain. We applied in twenty places in vain. At last, half by force and half by entreaty, we prevailed on a woman, whose circumstances seemed comfortable. We were, of course, unknown; and though we met many a rebuff, we determined to endure them, rather than reveal our names and character. During the progress of our meal we established ourselves in the good graces of the housewife, but she obstinately refused to allow us to remain for the night. She directed us to a publichouse, where, on our arrival, we found a proclamation menacing any one who entertained, harboured or assisted us, with the direst punishment. In answer to our inquiry the owner, who was a woman, pointed to the proclamation, as an argument against which all remonstrance was vain. We made three or four other attempts equally fruitless; and when the night had closed around us, on a bleak, desolate road, I determined to call on the Roman Catholic priest, and state who we were; for while, if alone, we would infinitely prefer taking such rest as we could in the nearest brake, or under shelter of a wall, we could not think of submitting our delicate companion to the trials of a night in the open air, during an exceedingly inclement season. With some hesitation and great alarm, he procured a lodging for us at a farmer's house in the neighbourhood. We saw him next morning, and his most earnest injunction was that we should leave the locality, which, according to him, was altogether unsafe. To escape arrest there for twelve hours was, he said, impossible. Similar advice was pressed on us afterwards in many a safer asylum; but we learned to mock at others' fears, whereas, on this occasion, we yielded to an impression we felt to be sincere.

Before venturing nearer to Dungarvan, we determined to bespeak the services of another clergyman, who lived a distance of six or seven miles in the direction of Waterford. A ridge of the Comeraghs lay between us and his lonely dwelling. Along this ridge lay a winding bridle-road, skirted by patches of green sward, and occasionally crossed by a sparkling mountain rill. Above us, on the hill-side, was a considerable bog, where crowds of country people were collecting to their daily toil. A merry laugh or boisterous joke occasionally rang clear in the morning air. The mirth went heavily to our hearts. The snatch of song, the unrestrained laugh, the merry glee, broke upon the ear of the wayfarers like the mocking of demons. The consciousness that they then sped, without a beacon or a guide, over the flinty path of flight, to end perhaps at the gibbet, imparted to the voice of mirth the sound of ingratitude. However, the day was brilliant; above us the clear, blue, unfathomable sky; around us the bracing mountain air, laden with the breath of hare-bell and heather, and far below the calm sea, sleeping in the morning light; and weariness, hunger and apprehension yielded to the influence of the scene. Many a time, ere passed the sunny noon, did we sit down to enjoy the glad prospect, unconscious, for a moment, of the fate that tracked our footsteps. At length we descended the eastern slope of the hill; and after proceeding some distance, through cornfields and meadows, we reached the mansion of the clergyman, wayworn and half-famished. He, whom we sought, had won a character for truth, manliness and courage, and we calculated upon his unrestrained sympathies, if not generous hospitality. He was absent from his house, which is situate in a lonely gorge of the Comeraghs.

We waited his arrival for more than an hour, and, through delicacy for his position, we remained concealed in a grove some distance from the door. He at length appeared, and I proceeded alone to meet him and make known my name. He started involuntarily and retreated a few paces from me. After repeating my name for a few seconds, he said, "Surely you are not so unmanly as to compromise me?" I replied, that so sensible was I of the danger of committing him, that I refused to enter his house, though we all, and particularly my female companion, sadly needed rest and shelter. After some time, he began to pace up and down in front of his door, repeating at every turn that it was indiscreet and dishonourable to compromise him. Among the many trials to which fate had doomed me, through hours of gloom, of peril and disaster, and even during reveries of still darker chances, which fear or fancy often evoked, I never felt a pang so keen as that which those unfeeling words sent through my heart. For a while I was unable to articulate, but at length I said: "You are one of those who urged us to this fate. You gave us every assurance that, in any crisis, you would be at our side. We made the desperate trial which you recommended. We have failed, because we were abandoned by those who were foremost in urging us on; and even now—here, where God alone sees us—you meet with reproaches one who has sacrificed his all on earth in a cause you pretended to bless. Is not that fate worse than defeat—than flight—than death?" "'Tis a sad fate, no doubt," said he. My object, I said, was to escape to France, and I called on him, believing he could assist me, as he must be acquainted with the boatmen around that part of the coast. He answered it was possible he could, but not then; asked how he could communicate with me; pointed to a shorter route across the mountains than that by which we had descended, and turned in to his dinner, which was just announced.

* * * * *

We faced towards the mountain, hungry and exhausted, without being asked to taste food or drink. It need not be detailed how sore at heart we felt as we recommenced our dreary journey. It was already evening. Censer masses of fog had gathered on the hill, and lurid streaks spreading far out on the sea, portended a night of storm and gloom. However, we had no resource but to regain the house where we had slept two nights before, which we supposed might be distant about seven miles; and by gaining the summit of the hill before dark, we hoped to make our way easily down the other side. To obtain some food, of whatever kind, was an indispensable preliminary. The house nearest to the mountain appeared to be that of a comfortable farmer. We entered it trembling, and found our expectations not disappointed. But the housewife peremptorily refused our first request, evidently suspecting there was something wrong, and unable to reconcile our appearance with the idea of hunger or distress. She bestowed a peculiarly sinister scrutiny on my poor sister. After some parley, we said we should have something to eat, either for love or money, and while saying so, we began to examine the locks of our pistols. Either admonished by these stern intercessors, or by a look of compassion from her beautiful daughter, who stood at some distance, she replied we should have what we asked for, but only for love. Her daughters, of whom there were two, busied themselves in producing new barley bread and skimmed milk, of which we partook immoderately. We parted on better terms, and my friend Stephens was greeted with a smile from each of the lovely girls, which so influenced him that he insisted upon revealing our character and asking their hospitality for the night. After a good deal of discussion it was agreed he should make the experiment alone. He returned and produced the military cap which he always wore inside his shirt. This at once produced the desired effect, and one of the young girls came bounding up the hill to invite us to return. It was arranged, however, that we should remain on a hay-loft until quite dusk, which we gladly agreed to. The host entered with us, and stayed until we were admitted to the dwelling-house. To me, at least, that hay-loft imparted a sense of unutterable enjoyment. I was there enabled to support the drooping head of my sister, as overcharged with weariness and pain of mind, she sank into unconscious sleep.

As night fell, we were introduced into a comfortable parlour. There we had tea and eggs, with some punch. The family felt the warmest interest in us; but at the same time they occasionally manifested evident alarm. The utmost precaution was observed so as to prevent our being noticed, and we only retired to bed when the hour of midnight had struck, and the house was sunk in silence and solitude. During all that night the storm roared pitilessly and the rain fell heavily. Had it surprised us on the bleak hill, our wandering had that night ended, and the ravens of Cumshinane had feasted on our flesh. Next day the storm did not cease to howl nor the rain to sweep on the angry winds. About five o'clock, during a brief pause of the rain, preparations were made which significantly intimated that we were expected to leave. Our host was well acquainted with the fishermen of Dungarvan and he solemnly warned us against treating with any of them. Betrayal, he said, would be certain. But he promised to accompany my sister next day to the town, where he would make every inquiry; and if he failed, as he anticipated, would see her away on the car; in which case we were to try another and a far remote sea-board. A certain newspaper of high Liberal character, affected to bestow upon us intense consideration and deep compassion. It had a guard of mobile reporters, some of whom contrived to be everywhere and hear everything—especially what did not occur. One of them, with a keener scent than his fellows, discovered my sister's track—made himself familiar with her person and apparel—and announced her movements with a mournful accuracy. He conjectured, not unjustly, that my haunts must be near the scene of her wanderings. Completely absorbed by the one idea of gratifying the curiosity of his readers, he seemed indifferent to the conclusion, which, to a mind less engaged, would appear palpable, and inevitable—namely, that what was information to our anxious friends would equally serve the purpose of our watchful pursuers.

It became, therefore, dangerous to have her continue any longer with or near us. A hasty dinner was prepared, and we arranged to meet our host next day within a mile of Dungarvan. Never did parting look more like a last one than mine with my sister, on that occasion. For some time I thought she would be the first victim of our hard destiny. She seemed incapable of withstanding the agony that shook her frame. While sharing in the hardships and the hazards of my struggle for life, her heart, sustained by its own deep enthusiasm, triumphed over every obstacle. But she was returning to a house of mourning and of woe, where life would be one blank of desolation and stupor, to be wakened to bitter consciousness by intelligence of our doom. The sense of my responsibility, the full appreciation of the living death which, through my agency, had fallen upon a home as hallowed as ever love and joy consecrated to happiness, had burned up my eyeballs and my brain. I went forth into the recommencing storm, utterly unconscious of its rage and equally indifferent to fate. My comrade, who had no life to lose but his own, and who of that was recklessly prodigal, provided he could dispose of it to good account, stepped blithely along and uttered no complaint, although he left behind him traces marked with blood. His terrible indifference soon restored my self-possession, and we found shelter for the night in a house near the spot designated for the next day's interview. Just as we arrived there, the chief magistrate and police had completed a search of the house. We entered as they retired, told who we were, and claimed hospitality, which we readily obtained. The night passed as many a similar one did afterwards. Let our hardships be what they might during the day, we invariably enjoyed ourselves at night, and went to bed without a fear. On the following morning we sent our hostess into the town for shoes and other matters which were indispensable to our further progress. She returned, evidently alarmed to death, having read on the walls the viceregal threats against all who harboured the "traitors." She scarcely allowed us to remain until the time appointed for the interview, which was of short duration. We were informed that there was no hope from that quarter, and that our safety for one hour was extremely precarious. This intelligence and a copy of the *World* newspaper, completed the information communicated by our former host.

Having laughed heartily over the *World*, and no less heartily at the alarm of our host and hostess, we set out on our long journey, about four o'clock in the evening, under very heavy rain. Our first effort was at the publichouse, already mentioned, where we again failed. We had some bread and punch, while drying our clothes at the fire. My comrade became very ill; but even this did not overcome the obstinate repugnance of the hostess to receive us. We were compelled to leave at about nine o'clock; and having travelled some miles, 'midst cold and rain, my comrade shivering from fever and suffering, we determined to sleep in freshly-saved hay. While making ourselves a resting-place in the hay, we were surprised by some countrymen, who recognised us as the persons who dined on a former evening, but were coldly received and rudely expelled. Upon consulting with the women, who had seen us, they conjectured we were some of the fugitives, and followed for the purpose of inviting us to the hospitalities of their home. We accepted the offer gladly, and were received by our friends of the former evening with the warmest welcome. The principal apartment contained two beds, one of which was usually occupied by the man and his wife, and the other by their grown daughters. They gave both up to us, treated us most kindly, and the whole family, men, women and children, watched over our sleep until morning. The eldest son displayed considerable information and still greater energy of character. He evinced the deepest interest in our fate, and accompanied us for several miles next morning. It was Sunday; the cold and wet of the previous evening had given way to calm and sunshine;

and we made rapid way along the slopes of the Comeraghs—thence to the Knockmeldown mountains, having one main object in view—to place the greatest distance possible between where we were to rest that night and where we had last slept. The greatest difficulty we experienced was in passing deep ravines. The steep ascent and descent were usually wooded and covered with furze and briars. Far below gurgled a rapid and swollen mountain stream, which we crossed without undressing, and always experienced the greatest relief from the cold running water. But toiling our upward way, through trees and thorny shrubs, was excessively fatiguing. About three o'clock in the evening we reached the picturesque grounds of Mountmellary Abbey. We had then travelled thirty miles of mountain without any refreshments. The well-known hospitality of the good brothers was a great temptation to men in our situation, pressed by toil and hunger. But we felt that we possibly might compromise the Abbot and the brethren, and determined on not making ourselves known. We entered the beautiful chapel of the Abbey, and ascended the gallery while vespers were sung. We were alone on the gallery, and had an opportunity of changing our stockings and wiping the blood from our feet. We remained upwards of an hour, and then set out, but little refreshed. We hoped to find refreshments in a small publichouse, on the road leading from Clogheen to Lismore. I entered the house rather hurriedly, and the first object that met my view was a policeman. I turned quickly round and disappeared. The rapidity of my movement attracted his attention, and, calling to his comrades and some countrymen who were in the house, they commenced a pursuit. At first they appeared little concerned, but walked quickly. We accordingly quickened our pace, and they, in turn, began to run, when it became a regular chase, which continued four miles, until we disappeared in the blue mists of the Mitchelstown mountains, as night was falling around us. When we saw our pursuers retiring, we ventured to descend, and entered a cabin where we found a few cold half-formed new potatoes and some sour milk which we ravenously devoured. I do not remember ever enjoying a dinner as I did this. My comrade, who had suffered much from illness, was unable to eat with the same relish. It was night when we finished our repast, and we set off in search of some place to lay our heads. We met several refusals, and succeeded, with great difficulty at last, in a very poor cabin. We saw a lone hen on a cross-beam, which we proposed to purchase, and bought at last for two shillings. In less than an hour she was disposed of; and, as was invariably the case, we got the only bed in the house, where we slept a long and dreamless sleep. It rained incessantly the next day, and we were forced repeatedly to take shelter in cabins by the wayside. But, being excessively anxious to get as far as possible beyond the circle enclosed by our foes, we descended several miles along the Kilworth mountains. Towards the close of evening we crossed the River Funcheon, near Kilworth, by means of a fir-tree, the roots of which had been undermined by the rapid flood. We had spent the whole day in wet clothes. We mounted this tree, Indian-like, in the midst of rain, and dropped in the shallow part of the river from the branches. We were unable to procure lodgings afterwards until nearly eleven o'clock, and then not without difficulty. We succeeded, at length, within about a quarter of a mile of Kilworth, whence we were able to procure bread, tea and beefsteaks. We were very kindly treated, and next day accompanied to the Blackwater, at Castle Hyde, by the eldest brother of the family.

I shall not easily forget the delicacy with which this young man requested, if we thought it compatible with our safety, to tell him our names. There are few requests which either of us would feel greater reluctance in refusing. He saw our evident struggle, and said he would be satisfied with a promise that when our fate would be decided one way or the other, we would write to him; a promise which I redeemed the day after I reached Paris.

This day I think, August the 20th, we travelled over forty miles, along bog and mountain, passed within a few miles of the city of Cork, and then, taking a north-western direction, proceeded to the village of Blarney; where we slept on a loft with a number of carmen who were on their way to Cork with corn.

It is known to most people, at all familiar with the traditions of Ireland, that this village is one of her most classic spots. There is deposited the celebrated Blarney stone, a touch of which imparts to the tongue of the pilgrim the gift of persuasion. So famous has this stone become, not only in Ireland but in England, that the most plausible fluency is characterised by its name, which at once confers on such oratory the stamp of unapproachable eloquence. It must be confessed, however, that in many instances "Blarney" conveys doubts of the speaker's sincerity, as well as admiration for his capacity. To see this talisman would be with me, on another occasion, an object of deep anxiety and most eager curiosity. But I was compelled to forego the pleasure, by the fact that a police-barrack loomed in its immediate vicinity, and at the other side was posted a proclamation offering a reward for my person. We could scarcely sleep, owing to the noise and bustle of the carmen, as they came and went, and loudly snored in various parts of our dormitory. But we were allowed to rest until seven in the morning, when we took a hasty breakfast and departed. It was a point with us never to walk along a road, and never to ask our way. We were now travelling through an open corn country, and our progress was accordingly slow. We felt, too, the necessity of not departing far from our intended route, and accordingly we called in occasionally to national schools to make the necessary observations on the maps. Sometimes we examined the children, and sometimes the master; generally one of us was so employed while the other was noting down carelessly on the map the points of observation to direct our path. We crossed the Lee undressed, near the village of "Cross," and slept soundly in a churchyard on a neighbouring hill the name of which has passed from my memory. We then directed our footsteps to a small village called Crookstown, situated in a romantic spot on a branch of the Lee. We experienced much difficulty, and narrowly escaped detection, in entering this village, which is surrounded by beautiful country seats, through the grounds of some of which we were obliged to grope our way. We obtained lodgings, after one or two fruitless trials, in a very comfortable house kept by a farmer. The young family seemed to be rather tastefully educated, and we soon became fast friends. We passed as whimsical tourists, and delighted our entertainers with glowing accounts of the scenery of Connemara, Wicklow and Kerry. We remained with them two nights, on pretence of being engaged in sketching the enchanting views in the neighbourhood; and left, promising, that if we returned by the same road, we would delay a week. Our destination was Dunmanway, near which a friend of mine lived, in whose house I hoped we might remain concealed, while means of escape would be procured somewhere among the western headlands. A short journey brought us to this house. My friend was absent, but daughters of his, whom I had not seen since childhood, recognised and welcomed us. We had then travelled 150 miles, and fancied that, as no one could think of our making such a journey without walking one half-mile of road, we would be safe there for many days. In this we were disappointed. It was communicated to us next morning early that our persons were recognised, and that half the inhabitants of Dunmanway were by that time aware of our whereabouts. It was added, that the people were venal and treacherous; a character which the inhabitants of that region of Cork invariably attribute to each other. We remained a second and most of a third day, notwithstanding, and enjoyed ourselves heartily, although our little festivities had all the air of a wake. We set out at length on the evening of the third day, having made one glorious friend, whose exertions afterwards tended mainly to secure my escape. We had expected letters from home before we reached Dunmanway, and received them there on the day after. They contained the concentrated and compressed agony of weeks, but no word of complaint or regret. They also confirmed the intelligence which we had heard ere we set out, namely, that all our comrades were arrested, except Dillon, O'Gorman, and a few others, of whose fate we remained uncertain. Certain friends of the family undertook to communicate with clergymen, near the seashore, who were supposed to be in a position to facilitate our escape, while we proposed to visit Gougane Barra and

Ceimeneagh, and, if practicable, Killarney, before we returned to learn the success of their applications. We followed the stream that passes Dunmanway for several miles through an almost inaccessible valley, until we reached the southwestern base of Shehigh, the highest mountain in the range which stretches between Mallow and Cape Clear.

Here we purchased some good new potatoes, butter, eggs and milk, on which we dined satisfactorily. We then faced the mountain which we crossed near the summit, being desirous to gain Gougane Barra by the shortest possible route. A steep ascent gives the traveller fresh impulses and an irrepressible desire to bound down at the other side. It seems to spring from that principle of action and reaction pervading all nature. At the northern base of Shehigh, after traversing some miles of bog, we found ourselves entering the pass of Ceimenagh. Though that Pass had been recently immortalised in the unequalled verses of Denis Florence M'Carthy,[12] and I had learned to love a spot where echoes of minstrelsy so soft and passionate had found a "local habitation," I was ignorant of its locality and entirely unprepared for the surpassing grandeur of the scene, which, in the full blaze of a harvest moon burst upon my view. My comrade was even more startled than I, and we paused at every turn of that enchanting passage to gaze upon the masses of rock projecting over our heads hundreds of feet in the air, and casting their dark rude outlines upon the clear autumn sky. The pass is a mile long, while in no one spot can many yards' distance be seen on either side. The road seems to lose itself every moment in the bowels of the mountain, but as you proceed, you find a new avenue of escape, and a more fantastic group of impending rocks of a yet more entrancing beauty than that you had left behind. In such a scene one could have no feeling of weariness and no sense of fear. Neither could he doubt man's truth any more than God's omnipotence. We lingered in the solitude and drank the moonbeams as they strayed through disjointed rocks and fell silvery and glowing on our path. Our reverie ended in a mistake, for we unconsciously passed the point where we should turn to Gougane Barra, then the scene of a ceremony, half

218

religious, half superstitious, as it has been during the autumn season from time immemorial. People come great distances to perform "stations" on the ruins of a very ancient church on poor Callanan's "green little island." We were advised against returning, but told to seek shelter in a publichouse at a place called Ballingeary, on the banks of Lough Lua through which the infant Lee runs. We found the house quite full, in consequence of a fair which was to be held the Monday following at Bantry. We were accordingly refused; but we insisted on remaining in the house. We had some milk and whisky, in which we asked the host to join us, and after one or two potations, he and his wife offered to give us their own bed and remain up. We thankfully and gladly accepted the offer. I know not whether they recognised us, and if not, it is not easy to account for the generous kindness that prompted such a sacrifice. The next day being Sunday, we proposed to spend it wandering about the lovely lake in the bosom of the hill, and to return in the evening to dinner. The day was an anxious one; but we left no spot on the island or near the lake which we did not explore.

Dunmanway from the Bridge on the Cork Road, 1848

The "Green Little Island," is surpassingly romantic. The old ruin of a monastery, God knows how old, gigantic forest trees, bowing their aged limbs into the clear water, the shadows of the frowning mountain thrown fantastically on the bosom of the lake, form a *tout ensemble* of lonely loveliness rarely equalled. Then the play of

> "The thousand wild fountains
> Rushing down to that lake from their home in the mountains,"

the scream of the eagle on the crags of Mailoc, far, far on high, all justify Callanan's preference for the spot which was meetest for the bard. We endeavoured to recall his tender strains, and thought mournfully of his sad prophecy—alas! when shall it be fulfilled?

> I too shall be gone, but my name shall be spoken,
> When Erin awakes and her fetters are broken
> Some minstrel shall come in the summer's eve gleaming,
> When Freedom's young light on his spirit is beaming,
> And bend o'er my grave with a tear of emotion,
> Where calm Avonbui seeks the kisses of ocean,
> Or plant a wild wreath from the banks of that river,
> O'er the heart and the harp that are sleeping for ever.

We saw at a short distance, the pass which so enraptured us the night before, but we resisted the temptation to revisit it, lest the glare of light might disenchant us of those sublime impressions of beauty it had made on our minds.

We found a most comfortable dinner on our arrival, for which we could not account. In the course of the evening we learned casually from our host that he had spent several years of his life where it was impossible he should not have seen and known me. This was a disturbing conviction wherewith to retire to rest, but we trusted to our propitious

220

stars, in which we had begun to feel a superstitious confidence. We were not disappointed then or afterwards, and next morning we slept in unquestioning security. We rose late and reluctantly, and left a scene where we enjoyed more undisturbed rest and real comfort than had fallen to our lot for weeks before. The day became dark and showery. Crossing the bogs in the recesses of Shehigh, we were overtaken by a storm, from which we took shelter in some hay gathered on the bleak moor, where I wrote the following:—

Hurrah for the outlaw's life!
Hurrah for the felon's doom!
Hurrah for the last death-strife!
Hurrah for an exile's tomb!
Come life or death, 'tis still the same,
So we preserve our stainless name
From losel of the coward's shame.
Hurrah for the mountain side!
Hurrah for the bivouac!
Hurrah for the heaving tide!
If rocking the felon's track.

Hurrah for the scanty meal!
If served by th' ungrudging hand,
Hurrah for the hearts of steel,
Still true to this fallen land!
Still true, though every hazard brings
Some new disaster on its wings,
Which o'er her last faint hope it flings.
Hurrah, etc.

Hurrah; though the gibbet loom!
Hurrah; though the brave be low!

221

Hurrah; though a villain doom!
The true to the headsman's blow.
As long as one life-throb remain,
We'll spurn the tyrant's gyve and chain
On gallows-tree or bloody plain.
Hurrah, etc.

Hurrah for that smile of light,
Which like a prophetic star,
Illumined the long, lone night
Of the wanderers from afar.
Give us for resting-place the rath,
Give us to brave the foeman's wrath,
So that dear smile be o'er our path.
Hurrah for the mountain side!
Hurrah for the bivouac!
Hurrah for the heaving tide!
If rocking the felon's track.

Being apprehensive that our former retreat near Dunmanway was discovered, and that we would be looked for there, we determined to try another district, from which we might be able to communicate with her who had evinced such sympathy for us. We sought the house of a friend of hers, but found him so terrified that we could not think of forcing ourselves on his hospitality. He promised, however, to call on her and learn if she had any letters or other information for us. On our return, next day, he was somewhat reassured. He brought us a note from her, and letters from home. My comrade's was a sad, sad blow. Where he had most trusted on earth, his application had been coldly received, and his most unlimited confidence utterly disappointed. Money was forwarded to him from other sources; but the spirit that braved every disaster up to that, broke under disappointed affection and blighted love. For some time he refused to take another step, but yielding himself up to the agony of shattered feelings, he ardently desired to abandon a struggle involving nothing but the life he no longer desired to save. From my knowledge of the country, and other resources, he regarded my chances of escape as favourable, and his own presence as an impediment and a check. He was therefore anxious to relieve me of a burden, at the same time that he would free himself from a weight still more intolerable. In that he was mistaken. His imperturbable equanimity, and ever daring hope, had sustained me in moments of perplexity and alarm when no other resource could have availed. During the whole time which we spent, as it were, in the shadow of the gibbet, his courage never faltered, and his temper never once ruffled. The arrival of our enthusiastic friend, who had stolen to see us, revived his spirits, and her persuasions reassured his resolution. We drove for some time in her car, and after nightfall returned to the house where we had slept on the previous night. A practice which prevailed in that part of the county Cork greatly facilitated our efforts. It was this: in the vicinity of the great routes of travel, the farmers are in the habit of giving lodgings for payment, the amount of which generally depends on the traveller's ability to pay. As our means, for purposes of at least this kind were not stinted, we were sure of welcome a second time. But this fact had a tendency to frustrate our aim in another point of view; for it always excited curiosity, so that it was doubtful whether we would not be safer with persons who would provide for us at the cost of their last morsel, by confiding to them who and what we were. But in this district of Cork, the centre of which is the notorious town of Bandon, were scattered several families of Orangemen, who were intensely inimical to the cause and people of Ireland. In this very instance we lodged with one of those families. A letter that I tore near the house was picked up, put together, and read, so as to lead to suspicion, which was immediately communicated to the magistrate. This caused the most vigilant surveillance to be exercised over the homes and persons of our friends. But before the discovery was made we were far beyond the reach of our pursuers. We had learned that the efforts made for our escape were unsuccessful, and that time would be required to effect anything, so as not to arouse the suspicion of those who guarded the coast; and we agreed to conceal ourselves as best we could in some distant part of the country, for three weeks, and then return or communicate with our friend, who promised, meantime, to leave no effort untried on our behalf. A second time, we set out by the same route. When we found ourselves on a hill-top, far from human haunts, we sat down as was our wont, to consider our future course. We determined to visit some obscure watering-place in the vicinity of Cape Clear. With that view we skirted the picturesque mountains that surround Dunmanway. These mountains present features to which the eye of one living in the inland country is little accustomed. The mountains of the midland and eastern counties are generally enormous clumps with little inequality of surface, and covered over with heath and weeds. Here, on the contrary, the mountains seemed to be carved out into the most fantastic shapes, covered with white granite stones, whose reflections in the watery surface gave the scene an appearance of singular beauty. However strange it may appear, we lingered over these picturesque scenes in intense delight; the more so because there seemed no limit to our journey, and no definite aim to which our efforts led. And a mountain-top has always an assurance of safety stamped upon it. There we could indulge our admiration for the beautiful; there we could snatch an hour of fearless and unbroken sleep.

But elements of danger began to lower over our loved haunts. The grouse season had just set in, and occasionally the report of a musket broke our reverie, or startled our deepest sleep. Yet, even from this cup of bitterness did we derive some sparkles of happiness. We could easily avoid the sportsman's eye; and when we wanted anything from the lower regions, the vicinity of the mountains, and the business of the fowler, accounted for our presence and our wants, and readily gained us a supply. But the potato crop had failed, and the disease had already destroyed all the tubers which had approached maturity. This rendered it necessary to look to other resources, and we contrived to procure bread and sometimes meat, which we were able to get prepared easily under pretence of being catering for shooting parties.

On the first day we made this experiment, we found ourselves descending into that dreary plain that stretches out to the doomed district of Skibbereen. Under cover of night we sought to penetrate this desolate region in the remotest direction of the sea, where we hoped we might remain unnoticed as country bathers. We obtained shelter at a small farmers, and made a great many inquiries concerning the neighbouring watering-places, whither we said we were going for the benefit of our health. There were two young girls, the confidence of one of whom my comrade contrived to win during the evening. She told him that her sister had a courtship with the sergeant of police, who usually visited there every day. This hastened our departure next morning. We set out in the grey dawn, and once again reascended the mountain, to rest and take thought. The communication of the young girl; the sister's long delay, when she went to procure refreshments at the village, where the police-sergeant was stationed; the father's pursuits, and other circumstances, induced us to believe that to follow the plan which, to a certain extent, we had unfolded, would be dangerous. We therefore determined to change our course. We were then about fifteen miles south-southwest of Dunmanway. Adhering to our resolution of settling for a few weeks in some village on the seaside, we purposed to substitute the Kerry side of Bantry Bay for the district we had at first fixed on. The distance was about fifty miles, and we had to cross a plain several miles wide. We swept over this plain with a rapidity that taxed severely our exhausted energies, and lay down to sleep on the first patch of heath we gained on the Bantry mountains.

We bathed our feet in a mountain stream, and having partaken of a slight meal, resumed our weary journey. Night fell on us in the midst of a desolate bog on a mountain top. We travelled several miles in search of shelter, first in cabins and next in haycocks. It was a dark, gloomy and threatening night. After lying for some time on the roadside, where alone a dry spot was to be found, I forced Stephens to consent to make a trial of the town of Bantry, then a mile distant. The darkness and gloom were favourable to the experiment. We entered the town, and traversed one or two streets, we knew not in what direction. On inquiring for a lodging-house, we were directed to the house of Mrs. Barry, who kept a large grocery establishment. We found accommodation and comfort. Next day, having made some small purchases through the agency of the servant, and posted some letters, we deliberately walked out of Bantry, by the road which seemed to lead the most directly to the country. The day was miserable, and we found our journey through the mountains, which overhang the beautiful bay, very unpleasant. We determined to reach a place called the Priest's Leap, which is consecrated by a holy tradition in the estimation of the people. They tell that in the times of persecution a priest was set and sold in these fastnesses. Having discovered that he was betrayed, he effected his escape through a circle of enclosing pursuers, which it was deemed impossible to break through; the country people believed that he floated invisibly through the air, and alighted on the deck of a Spanish frigate then coasting these shores.

An impenetrable fog descended the mountain, and the rain deepened into a torrent. Moored in the bay were two war-steamers, with screw propellers; but they had all their sails unfurled, and swung uneasily to and fro. We, who were ignorant of their character, frequently paused to regard them, utterly unable to account for their extraordinary movements. Believing them American packets, which had put in through stress of weather, we would have given worlds even for an opportunity of swimming to them through the waters of the bay. But the coast was strictly guarded by police and revenue officers. Notwithstanding this the vessels had for us an irresistible attraction, and we entered a mountain cabin, where we learned their real character. A second attempt to reach the Priest's Leap, of whose exact bearing we were ignorant, involved us in deeper mist and a heavier shower, from which we took shelter in a wretched hut, directly over the bay, and within about one mile of an hotel of great fame, frequented by travellers who are attracted to these districts to view the magnificent bay and the singular beauty of Glengarriff. Here we spent the remainder of the day. Eggs and potatoes were provided for us; and when, as evening approached, we prepared to depart to the hotel, the woman pressed us to remain, and produced clean sheets, telling us they would give up their bed, and adding that she would be satisfied with the fifth of what we should pay in the hotel, where, she slyly hinted, our reception would be very doubtful in our then trim. We readily consented to her arrangement; and it was further agreed that her husband should go to the hotel and provide some bacon, bread, tea, and whisky.

We had not, during our wanderings, met two such characters as this man and woman, nor had we taken shelter in so extraordinary an abode. They had a single child, a girl about four years of age, whose dark eyes and compressed lip Akkad evidenced the presence of those terrible passions which had burned deep channels along the brow and cheek of her mother. The cabin was ten feet square, with no window and no chimney. The floor, except where the bed was propped in a corner, was composed of a sloping mountain rock, somewhat polished by human feet and the constant tread of sheep, which were always shut up with the inmates at night. The fire, which could be said to burn and smoke, but not to light, consisted of heath sods, dug fresh from the mountain. A splinter of bog-wood, lurid through the smoke, supplied us with light for our nightly meal. The tea was drawn in a broken pot, and drunk from wooden vessels, while the sheep chewed the cud in calm and happy indifference. They were about twelve in number, and occupied the whole space of the cabin between the bed and the fire-place.

In that singular picture, the figure of the woman stood out bold, prominent and alone, absorbing, in its originality, every character of the entire. Neither she nor her husband could be said to wear any dress. Neither wore shoes or stockings, or any covering whatever on the head; shreds of flannel, which might once have borne the shape of drawers, a tattered shirt of unbleached linen, with an old blanket drawn uncouthly around his waist and shoulders, completed the costume of the man. His wife's was equally scant and rude, but so arranged as to present the idea that even in her breast the sense of fitness, the last feeling of froward womanhood, was not quite extinguished. The squalid rags and matted hair, by a single touch of the hand, a gesture, or a shake of the head, assumed such shape as she fancied would display to greatest advantage what remained of a coarse and masculine beauty. The consciousness that she once possessed such beauty fired at once her heart and eye. Her foot and ankle, which had been rudely tested by flinty rocks and many a winter's frost, were faultless; her step was firm; her form erect and tall; her hair black as ebony; her features coarse, but regular; her brow lofty, but furrowed and wrinkled; and her terrible eyes dilated with pride, passion and disdain. Her lip's slight curl, or a shade of crimson suddenly suffusing her dark complexion, bespoke her feelings towards her husband. He was her drudge, her slave, her horror and her convenience. Her ruling idea was a wish to have it understood that the match was ill-assorted and compelled by necessity; though the last idea bespoke a youth of shame. The child alone was dressed, and with some care, as if she wished to assert its claim to a superior paternity or better destiny. Among the predominant passions which swayed her, avarice seemed uppermost; and she scowled ominously on her stupid husband, whose rigid impassable stolidity seemed impervious to all prospects and chances of pleasure and of gain.

The rain continued to pour without abatement during the whole night and until sunset the succeeding day. The next night passed nearly in the same way as the first, save that I could not rest from a vague sense of apprehension with which this woman inspired me. Both the people of the house slept on the hearth-stone, without any bed, or, as far as I know, any covering, save their rags. I had an opportunity of overhearing their connubial colloquy, which was in Irish, and had reference solely to conjectures respecting us, our character, our object and our money.

It convinced me that our safety would be compromised by any longer delay. During the pauses of their conversation, I endeavoured to string together a rough draft of the stanzas that follow, or a considerable part of them. I give them here, with the accompanying notes, as they were published in the *People* newspaper. In the notes or in the text, there is nothing I wish to alter.

Air: "*Gradh mo Chroidhe.*"

* * * * *

The long, long-wished for hour had come,
 Yet came, mo stór, in vain,
And left thee but the wailing hum
 Of sorrow and of pain.
My light of life, my lonely love,
 Thy portion sure must be,
Man's scorn below, God's wrath above
 A Chuisle geal mo chroidhe.

'Twas told of thee, the world around,
 'Twas hoped from thee by all,
That, with one gallant sunward bound,
 Thou'dst burst long ages thrall.
Thy faith was tried, alas! and those
 Who perilled all for thee,
Were cursed, and branded as thy foes;
 A Chuisle geal mo chroidhe.

What fate is thine, unhappy isle,
 That even the trusted few[13]
Should pay thee back with hate and guile,

When most they should be true?
'Twas not thy strength or spirit failed;
And those that bleed for thee,
And love thee truly, have not quailed;
A Chuisle geal mo chroidhe.

I've given thee manhood's early prime,
And manhood's waning years;
I've blest thee in thy sunniest time,
And shed with thee my tears;
And mother, though thou'st cast away
The child who'd die for thee,
My latest accents still shall pray
For Chuisle geal mo chroidhe.

I've tracked for thee the mountain sides,
And slept within the brake,
More lonely than the swan that glides
O'er Lua's fairy lake.[14]
The rich have spurned me from their door,
Because I'd set thee free;
Yet do I love thee more and more,
A Chuisle geal mo chroidhe.

I've run the outlaw's brief career,
And borne his load of ill,
His troubled rest, his ceaseless fear,
With fixed sustaining will;
And should his last dark chance befall,
E'en that shall welcome be,
In death, I'll love thee, most of all,
A Chuisle geal mo chroidhe.

I was awakened next morning by a strange voice, with an accent, as I thought, different from that which we had been accustomed to. Our immediate conclusion was that we were betrayed. But a short time convinced us that our visitor had come to warn us that if we remained many hours where we were, our fate would be sealed. He represented "Finey" (as our hostess was familiarly called, in derision of her affected pride) in colours not very flattering to her virtue. He said he could positively furnish us with the means of escape; described his resources as unlimited, and his interest in us as paramount to every consideration he had on earth. He was an ecclesiastical student, and had left college to take part in the struggle of his country. He bitterly lamented that Dillon and O'Gorman were not in the way, that he might have the happiness of assisting in saving them also. Agreeably to his advice, we left our den and proceeded up the mountain. It was Sunday morning, and there was not a cloud darkening the azure sky. Below us slept the waters of the bay, reflecting, in their crystal depths, the superincumbent mountains and overarching sky. The sun rose majestically, broad, unclouded, full of effulgence, and shed his yellow beams, on a scene as lovely as ever met his burning eye. The mountains around the bay form very nearly a complete circle; the numerous peaks, from south to north, range at an average height of about 500 feet above the water's level, while a few ascend as high as 1,000. We stood on the loftiest of all. Immediately below us, a little to the right, embosomed in the mountains, lay the unmatched beauties of Glengarriff. There are few spots on earth of wilder attractions. The hills around form a complete amphitheatre. On an island in the centre of the valley is the cottage of the noble proprietor, accessible only by one narrow pathway which winds through hillocks and passes various rivulets on rustic bridges. The grounds about the cottages are tastefully laid out in shrubberies, flower-knots, green pastures, and artificial lakes. That which constitutes the chief feature of beauty in other landscapes, namely, an extensive prospect, is wanting here. From the cottage, or any part of the grounds, you can only command a view of the limited demesne, and the craggy and bleak mountain rising almost perpendicularly from its outskirts. But the view is unique, and the contrast exquisite between the rich green of the arbutus, amidst clumps of which sparkle the impeded mountain waters, and the barren hill-sides whose blue summits seem blended with the skies giving to the scene such an air of calm serenity and soft repose as to leave the beholder almost without a wish to look beyond.

Market Day in Thurles, August, 1848

By this time we had learned to lose all consciousness of our own fate in contemplating lines of beauty such as then marked the outline and radiated through every minor detail of mountain, ocean, and cosy lawn. We dwelt on the scene with enraptured eye and heart, and scarcely felt the time glide by, which was to bring us our promised deliverer. He was with us at the appointed moment, and only preceded his sisters by about half an hour. They came, three in number, and toiled up to the summit under a hot sun, bringing each a basket with abundant and delicate provisions for a picnic. They were joined soon after by two other brothers, who kept watch while we enjoyed the delicacies of our meal, which we finished with some bottles of excellent claret. While we were thus engaged, Lord Bantry was at the cabin we had left, gnashing his teeth at the misfortune of missing such a prey. My comrade sang the newly-composed verses and others of more exquisite melody and far higher sentiment, within less than half a mile of the frowning and fuming lord. At four o'clock we took leave of our kind entertainers, the student promising to use the coming night in efforts to secure our flight, and a younger brother undertaking to act as our guide across the mountain and round the base of the Glengarriff ridge of hills to a dark gorge, at the County Kerry side. This was a most trying journey, at least twenty miles long, over precipitous mountains, and performed, for the most part, during night. It was necessary that we should not rest until we travelled far out of range of the locality where our persons had been known and our retreat discovered. Our young guide left us with friends or dependents of his family, and returned to be in readiness to communicate any tidings from his brother. Those tidings came fast on our footsteps; but the message was to warn us that we were not even there safe; for that Lord Bantry had all his tenantry engaged in searching for us. The despatch added that, if able, we were to be at the "Priest's Leap" at a certain hour in the evening, where we would hear the result of the efforts made for us. The tone of the letter left us nothing to hope; still we determined to test the doubtful promise to the last. Accordingly we set out for the new rendezvous. The distance was very long unless we crossed through Glengarriff. This we determined to do, feeling satisfied that the last place we would be looked for would be his lordship's pleasure-grounds. We paused to examine more minutely the exquisite serenity of that scene, and learned from a game-keeper several matters illustrative of our pursuer's character, while his adherents were tracking our supposed footsteps, over moor and mountain, far away. Arrived at our destination, we had to wait several hours, during which we were amused by our guide claiming fraternity with us, on the ground of being banned by the law, in consequence of a suspicion (a false one, he averred) of having mistaken another man's sheep for his own. He had an idea that we, too, must have infringed the law, but in what particular he did not concern himself to inquire. The fact sufficed for the establishment of a good understanding between us.

We at last saw our female friends approach. They brought us another excellent dinner, for which we had a still more excellent appetite. During the time we dined, they informed us that everything was proceeding as favourably as we could expect, and that they had no doubt of success. When taking leave of us, however, one of them pressed a little note into my hand, and they disappeared in the darkness. I burned to learn what the note contained. With the assistance of our new friend we found lodgings in the neighbourhood, where I read that the student failing in his enterprise, and being afraid to compromise himself further, left that very night for college. He had to consult a clergyman, a very near friend of his, and we made no doubt the present step resulted from his considerate advice.

This is written here, not for the purpose of disparaging the clergyman's counsel or the student's resolution. On the contrary, no doubt was then entertained of the sincerity of either, nor has there ever since been. There could be no one more disposed to make allowance for the difficult position in which both were placed, as well as all others who ventured to serve us: nor could we blame men for shrinking from peril, which at the best, presented no rational chance for us, while the effort involved those who made it in almost certain ruin. I had other opportunities of satisfying myself afterward that this clergyman, who visited us in the mountains, never relaxed in his exertions to save us.

We found ourselves next morning in an exceedingly romantic valley to the north of the "Priest's Leap," the property of Lord Lansdowne, where there are many comfortable farmers' houses, and many others, whose showy exterior is sadly belied by the filth and discomfort of the inside. We spent the day with the man of the sheep, who promised to obtain lodgings for us at a publichouse, where he was refused. But during our stay there we met a farmer's son, who took us home and travelled with us the whole of the next day. We proposed to him and his sister to accompany us to the United States, having for some time entertained seriously a project of trying our chances to escape as emigrants. He consented to be of the party, although we fully explained to him the risk of being taken in our company. He guessed from this that we were engaged in the attempted outbreak, and being sent in to the town of Kenmare to make some purchases, he could not conceal so important a secret, but sought out a friend, a true man, to whom he unburdened himself. We had appointed to meet him at a place called Cross, about two miles from Kenmare. We were repairing thither at the appointed hour, and were met, not by our trusty messenger, but the friend to whom he had revealed his important secret. This friend, alarmed at our temerity in approaching so near the town, had come to forewarn us. His advances were met by distrust and menace, which pained him deeply. He remonstrated and referred to the fact of coming to meet us alone, when if he meant us injury he could easily secure us. Satisfied, at length, that his friendship was sincere, we consented to accompany him to meet another friend who had taken a different road in the direction of the mountain. He was known to us by character, but that knowledge, with me at least, tended to increase rather than to allay distrust. I had formed an idea of the man from reading speeches of his which appeared of an unscrupulously partisan character. I was very soon disabused, but not however until I communicated to him my feelings in his regard. The best proof of my mistake is furnished by the fact that my unnecessary frankness did not in the least check the enthusiasm with which he was prepared to risk fortune, liberty and life in our service. Our interview was short. We dismissed the ambassador who had acquired for us these new allies. They, or rather he, of whom I have last spoken offered us money which we declined. In opposition to his remonstrance, we insisted on remaining for the night at a publichouse in the village of Cross. He, to whom peril was new, could not understand our "audacity." But we who had experienced the disadvantages of asking for entertainment in quarters where such things were unusual, preferred the chance of escaping unobserved among crowds of persons similar in appearance and, applying only for ordinary accommodation. In this and many such instances we determined aright. We obtained a comfortable bed and passed unnoticed. Next morning we set out for the southern slope of the Killarney mountains. As soon as we attained a safe elevation, we took a western direction, skirting those mountains and crossing the road which leads from Killarney to Kenmare, about five miles from the latter town. We then kept a westerly direction, and turned round the vast bog situated at the western side of the road. This bog contains several thousand acres, and seems quite susceptible of reclamation and improvement. We ascended the steep hill at the north-western boundary where we slept for an hour or so, and then resumed our journey in the direction of the Reeks. We purposed ascending the loftiest of these mountains, and not wishing to take the route by the Gap of Dunloe, we crossed the intermediate valley and began to ascend the mountain to the north, believing it to be that which we had determined to climb. After having toiled to the summit, we discovered in the distance the peak we were in search of, its wonderful elevation leaving no manner of doubt as to its identity. Between us and its base lay another broad valley. Before attempting the ascent, we secured a lodging at the foot, and leaving our coats behind, we began our task about four o'clock in the evening, having then travelled upwards of twenty miles and crossed two large mountains. The southern acclivity is more steep than the northern, and we lost much by our ignorance of the best routes; but we reached Carn-Tuathail, far the highest spot in Ireland, about sunset. The view that presents itself from that peak is of the most extraordinary character. Stretching out into the sea a distance of thirty miles, is a jumble of mountains tossed together in the wildest confusion, and exhibiting no definite outline. At the east, far inland, lay the long ridge of which Mangerton is the loftiest point. At the north alone could we discern an extensive view, where a rich and well cultivated valley extended along Dingle Bay as far as Ballyheige. But the grandeur of the scene lay at our feet. Beneath us yawned at every side chasms of seemingly unfathomable depth, whose darkness it was impossible to penetrate, as the sun was sinking in the Atlantic. It was really a spectacle full of grandeur and of awe, and we remained enjoying it till the last ray of the sun ceased to glimmer on the distant waters.

At that hour, we were well assured, many a brain was busy, and many an eye set to discover our retreat. By the side of the public thoroughfares, on great bridges, and frequented cross-roads, detective vigilance kept sleepless watch, and fancied in every approaching form, the doomed victims, who were at once to satisfy the angry gallows and its own excited avarice. Equally well assured were we that the most inventive and hazardous scrutiny would never track our footsteps to the dizzy height of Carn-Tuathail. One motive with us was to baffle all calculation on the part of our pursuers. When we found we were tracked and discovered, our first care was to consider how our enemies would be likely to judge respecting our future movements. If we had reason to suspect that we were recognised on a mountain, we sought shelter in or near a town, and after we appeared in public places for a day or an hour, we kept the mountain-side for a week following.

We had, too, another, and it must needs be confessed, a more powerful motive. In either alternative which our fate presented, there was no hope of ever beholding these scenes again, and we could not omit this last opportunity of minutely examining and enjoying what was grandest and loveliest in our native land. We resolved, therefore, to leave no glorious spot unvisited, whatever toil it cost, or risk it exposed us to. Mountains, indeed, never did involve a risk, but the Lakes of Killarney, which were much frequented at the time, could not be seen without imminent danger, unless by overcoming great physical difficulties. After we descended from Carn-Tuathail, we were so utterly exhausted as to be obliged to lie down in hay, within one field of the cabin where we were to sleep, from which nothing could tempt us to stir for the night; but we were assailed by swarms of small flies of the mosquito species, that stung us to further exertion. Although the owners of the cabin gave us their only bed, and provided the best supper for us, we were so persecuted by these flies, that we were forced to quit our bed before day dawned, and endeavour to shake off our tormentors by rolling in the dew and shaking our shirts in the wind. We set out early, finding the place utterly intolerable, owing to these terrible tormentors, although we had resolved the evening before, to remain a few days fishing in the lovely lakes collected in the gorges of the reeks. The day was misty and wet. This, we hoped, would afford us a good opportunity of seeing the lakes unobserved; for such weather would necessarily confine the tourists to their hotels. We accordingly directed our way to the Upper Lake, along ledges of rocks covered with tall wet grass, wading or swimming through outlets of the lake. We obtained a tolerable view of the Upper Lake, and minutely examined the several accesses to it through the wood on the southern side. After spending most of the fore-noon in this wood, we attempted to cross the upper neck of the lake for the purpose of skirting the base of Mangerton and gaining the summit of Turc Mountain, from which are to be seen the Middle and Lower Lake in their most varied and seductive loveliness. Few travellers ever see the lakes from this point, because it is difficult to attain; but I had been there, and knowing its superiority over every other, I wished to give my comrade a taste of the exquisite pleasure derivable from a scene of beauty unsurpassed in the world. There is no spot, in or near Killarney, from which its wonderful scenery can be seen to such advantage. On the water, at Ross Island, at Mucross or Glena, the view is

238

confined to the scenery immediately around, with an occasional glimpse of the nearer mountains, which indeed may well satisfy the most exacting curiosity and fastidious taste, while from the summit of Mangerton (the great mountain attraction of travellers) but miniature forms of beauty present themselves, the great distance and height contracting the circle of beauty, and depriving every object of its fulness and natural proportions. From Turc mountain, on the other hand, you see the lake at your feet—all its islets, curls, cascades are within ken, entrancing your senses. Standing on that green hill, it is impossible to divest the mind of the idea, that the scene is one of pure enchantment.

But we were destined not to realise it. There was a police-station immediately on our way. In our first effort to avoid it, we found ourselves, after much trouble, within one field of the door. We then made a still wider circuit, keeping, as we thought, far clear of it; but following a valley which led round a clump of hill, we once more very nearly stepped into its back yard. To avoid similar mistakes we ventured along the public road direct towards Kenmare; but when we were clear of the police-barrack, we had to travel several miles of mountain to gain the intended spot. Our feet were all cut and bleeding, and we lay down on a rock in our wet clothes, where we slept soundly, and I suppose sweetly, until near sunset. When we awoke we were obliged, from the lateness of the hour, to abandon our project.

During our stay near Killarney, we fondly indulged the last dream for our country. In the remote regions of the counties of Cork and Kerry, the people seemed possessed of no political information. They had a vague notion that an effort was made to free the country from foreign thrall, and that the patriots and their cause were lost through the Catholic priests. It was easy to perceive, by the bitterness with which they cursed, that they—although never reached by a speech of Mr. O'Connell's, or an article or song of the *Nation's*—had cherished in their hearts the same imperishable purpose and hope of overturning the dominion of the stranger. We calculated on collecting between fifty and one hundred of the hardiest and most desperate mountaineers, whom we could easily place in ambush near the lakes, to seize on Lord John Russell, who was at the time announced as a visitor to Killarney. Once in our possession, we could have him conveyed to some inaccessible fastness where we could dictate terms to him concerning our imprisoned comrades. We had scarcely a doubt of putting our plan into execution, and our sojourn near Killarney was prolonged for the purpose of becoming more familiar with the pathways whereby to escape to the mountains with our prisoner. How success in that enterprise might have suggested or shaped a further course of aggression, it is now bootless to conjecture. The project was marred by the Premier's abandonment of his intention.

Having appointed to meet a person this evening, near Kenmare, who was to bring us the latest papers and otherwise inform us of his lordship's movements, we proceeded in that direction, determined to return to Killarney next day to prosecute our examination of the locality. But the current news informed us that Lord John Russell had left for Scotland.

We remained several days in the neighbourhood of Kenmare, where we had daily interviews with the friend to whom I have already alluded. He spent all his time in endeavouring to devise some means of escape, and intermediately provided resting-places for us at various distances. We had the guidance of a young country lad of fine intelligence and true fidelity, who was acquainted with every foot of bog and mountain for miles around. We spent several days rather agreeably, perambulating the ranges of hills between Kilfademore and Templenoe, embracing a district about fifteen miles square. One night we slept in an empty cabin within a field of Kilfademore House, a fine old mansion, belonging to the father of Christabel,[15] the mountain poetess, which is now only inhabited by the tenant of the farm, while the whole available military and police force of the district were drawing their lines of circumvallation around this old house, which, as soon as they made the proper dispositions to prevent our escape, they burst into with the stealth and precipitancy of a robber band.

We were most kindly received and cared for wherever our friend or his guide bespoke a night's hospitality. But although we unquestioningly reposed on the truth of all to whom our safety was committed, we felt the circle of our armed foes was closing and contracting around us, and it became indispensable to break through it. It was clear that our steps were tracked, for every night a search was made for us in one or other of the houses over which the influence of our friend extended. But our information respecting their arrangements was always earlier and surer than theirs concerning our movements. During this interval when, although we travelled an average of fifteen miles a day, we considered ourselves resting, we received the kindest attentions everywhere; frequently finding a rude mountain cabin furnished with excellent beds and every delicacy. But we pined to be more at large. We had interviews with clergymen and others, who discussed various projects of escape. Among the rest, it was proposed to my comrade to accompany a lady—who was about leaving for London—in the dress and character of a servant-maid. He was well fitted for such disguise, being extremely young and having very delicate features. Besides this, he was supposed to be dead, having received a slight wound in the skirmish at Ballingarry. He obstinately refused to adopt the disguise, but consented to that of a servant boy. When the matter was finally arranged, it was proposed to us to sleep at Templenoe, on the north side of Kenmare Bay, where he was to be furnished with suitable clothes. Since the commencement, I did not feel the same sense of desolation as when these arrangements were completed, and an hour was appointed for his departure next morning. It was on the evening of the 23rd of September. We spent the day with one of the noblest of fellows. He had beds brought far into the neighbouring mountains, where he remained with us for the night. A cloud of sadness, and I believe chagrin, enveloped all my senses. I could not help feeling myself utterly abandoned. It seemed fated that even from the most kindly efforts my unfortunate position utterly excluded me. Stephens sang as usual, and endeavoured to rally me; but my mind had set in impenetrable gloom. One idea was uppermost with me, namely, that within the circle that was then drawn around me, there was no further possible safety. We parted before daylight, and I immediately determined on my own course. It was this: to assume the disguise of a clergyman and attempt to cross to France. The trials at Clonmel were approaching, and I concluded that they would engross the entire attention of Government, and would even require the presence of the whole corps of detectives who were acquainted with my person and were then on my track. I communicated my intention to the friend to whose hospitality I was then indebted. He combatted it with great earnestness, and could not be persuaded of its practicability. I, however, persevered, and he offered to place a horse, upon which he set great value, at my disposal. Just as we made our final arrangements and had despatched a messenger to Kenmare to provide the disguise, Stephens returned, wet, weary and hungry. He was in the worst spirits: but the case admitted of no delay. The lady with whom he was to travel had to stay one day in Cork, and to overtake her there was the only chance left. There was only one possible way to effect this—to give him the horse and let him ride on to Cork. I at once agreed, and he immediately set off. The loss of the horse imposed on me the difficulty of a journey on foot to Cork, and this rendered the assistance of a man to carry my disguise—who would take a different route from myself—indispensable. Our friend who, in giving his favourite horse to Stephens, told him to try and sell him in Cork and put the money in his pocket, provided me with another horse and car, by which my baggage was to be brought about forty miles. Having settled all preliminaries, he conveyed me to a cabin on the hills, where he provided an excellent dinner, and left me to my musings.

They were, it may be well conceived, not of the gayest character. The responsibility and hazards of the attempt before me, narrowed the chances of my destiny to the one alternative, and I could not shake off gloomy phantoms which represented every phase of the last bloody drama which was to close the career of those who loved, too dearly, our ill-fated land. But, come what might, my purpose was definitely fixed. I spent the evening in the deepest gloom, which I endeavoured to dissipate by composing the following stanzas, suggested at the time by involuntary visions of my wife and children at the foot of the gallows:—

THE OUTLAW'S WIFE

Sadly silent she sits, with her head on her hand,
    While she prays, in her heart, to the Ruler above,
To protect, and to guide to some happier land,
    The joy of her soul and the spouse of her love:
And she marks by her pulses, so wild in their play,
    The slow progress of time, as it straggles along;
And she lists to the wind, as 'tis moaning away,
    And she deems it the chaunt of some funeral song.

Then anon does she start in her struggles with fear,
    And she strains at the whispers of every one round,
While she brushes away, half indignant, the tear,
    That will gush, tho' unbidden, at every fresh sound;
And she strives to conceal—oh! how idle the task—
    The deep lines in her cheek, and the rent in her heart;
But her neighbours grow pale as they gaze on the mask,
    And more lowly and slowly they talk, as they part.

When her babes are at rest will she breathe to their breath,
    And keep vigil, how wistfully, over their sleep,
As it mirrors, poor mourner, the stillness of death,
    And she stirs them, and calls, for she deems it too deep;
But again does she hush them, first telling them pray,
    Till at length overcharged by the tears yet unshed,
Will she sink, and as consciousness passes away,
    O'er her pale furrowed cheek, see the hectic o'erspread.

Slowly thus, day by day, does the fever-fire trace
    Its incessant course down her fast-withering cheek,
Till the smile that made light in the glow of her face,
    But the faint, fading glimpses of vigour bespeak,
And her reason will fitfully pass into night—
    Into night even deeper than that of the blind,
As the shade of the gibbet-tree looms in her sight.
    And she fancies a death-scream in th' echoing wind.

In the house where I slept—as indeed in every house of the same character in the county—the whole stock of the family, consisting chiefly of cows and sheep, were locked in at night. Such was the extreme poverty of the people that they would not be otherwise safe. The weather was excessively wet, and, for the season, cold. There was a slight partition between the room where my bed was and the kitchen, where there were three cows, a man, his wife and four children. It is impossible to convey any idea of the sensations which crowd upon one in such a scene. I fell asleep at last, lulled by the heavy breathing and monotonous ruminating of the cows. Never was deeper sleep. On being awakened next morning by my watchful friend, it required some time before I could satisfy myself of my position. An excellent breakfast was provided for me, and I parted from my stout-hearted and magnanimous ally. He had sent my baggage, and also provided me with a guide who would lead me across the mountains. He taught me the password of his clan, which I was to use on certain contingencies. The morning was fearfully wet, and we did not travel many miles before we were wet to the skin. The circumstance was the most auspicious that could occur, as it enabled us to pass unobserved.

James Stephens (Circa 1867)

John O'Mahony (Circa 1868)

Besides this, it facilitated the task of crossing streams, which we always did precisely as if they were dry land. One river only opposed a serious barrier to us—that, which enters Kenmare Bay. It was greatly swollen, and rushed fiercely over precipitous rocks. At the same time, even in the rain and tempest, to cross the bridge was not to be thought of. The guide pointed out a house belonging to one of our friend's clan who immediately provided a horse and accompanied us to a ford. When we reached the ford he hesitated to cross, so deep and rapid was the flood. No persuasion could induce him to make the experiment. I had no choice left but to trust myself to chance. I faced the animal against the current, and forcing him to make his best efforts to mount the stream, we were carried directly across. The owner of the horse said he would come back of his own accord. I turned him into the stream, and when half way across, he was borne headlong over a precipice, where I concluded he was dashed to pieces. Another horse was immediately procured, by a man who had no fears, to bring the guide across; but the latter was so terrified that he made himself drunk ere he attempted the dangerous passage. As he was essential to me in consequence of the arrangements made about my luggage, I endeavoured to rouse him. He staggered on for several miles, but seemed utterly unconscious where he was going. When I found him incapable of directing me, I endeavoured to procure some food for him, and with that view proceeded to a mountain hut, but before I reached it, he sank down utterly exhausted and powerless. He was unable even to articulate the name of the man to whose house he was directed to take me, or the locality where he lived. It was only from circumstances and a dim recollection of the name that I was able to apprise the owner of the cabin whither I was bound; and after all, much remained for the exercise of his sagacity, which was not long at fault. We brought my old guide to the cabin, thrown across a pony, and I set out anew, guided by the dweller on the hills. He forced me to mount the pony, and led the way over the crags. He bounded from rock to rock with the agility of a deer, though the stones were sharp as flint, and he barefooted. He was a man of powerful proportions and extreme activity. My pony, on the other hand, crept his way through narrow pathways, worn by the rain. In this way we crossed two considerable mountains, and, leaving the pony at the summit of the last, I pursued my companion's flight down the slope with the best speed my stiffened limbs could be forced to. Arriving over a valley which is called, I think, Branlieu, situated in a western direction from Gougane Barra, he pointed to a lone house at the extremity of the valley, as my destination. It was about four o'clock, but the rays of the sun had ceased to irradiate this gloomy valley, over which hung the shades of night. At the western side the mountain was steep as a wall, and down from the summit dashed headlong torrents, swelled by the morning's rain. The waters gleamed like sheeted ice through the haze, and their roar fell upon the ear with a dull sense of loneliness and pain. On the eastern slope wound a new road, one of those heartless experiments which the inventive genius of the Board of Works in Ireland substituted for the exploded trial of prolonging beggars' lives by Soyer soup and chained spoons. On these roads the people were to perform the greatest possible amount of work, and live on the least possible quantity of food. But, although these operations cost much waste of blood, the roads opened no new and fruitful sources of industry in these mountain valleys, only frequented by the footsteps of the sportsman, or scanned by the eye of the votaries of pleasure. The house where I called was intended for my guide. However, I found my claim for hospitality at once recognised on pronouncing the password of my host by the sea. The cabin—it was literally such—was in the most filthy state. The dung of the cattle had not been removed for days, and half-naked children squatted in it as joyously as if they rolled on richest carpets. The housewife merely replied to my question in the affirmative. But she immediately proceeded, with the help of two little girls, to remove the filth. I was so fatigued and hungry that I could willingly postpone the process of cleaning for the sake of providing any sort of food. I was doomed to disappointment. No appearance of supper interrupted the busy operation, until the dung was removed, and the floor drained. I retired, and endeavoured to ascend the eastern hill, to a point where I could catch a glimpse of the setting sun.

On my return I found the owner of the house, a man of giant frame and noble features. His dress bespoke a taste or pursuit incompatible with the wild mountain destiny stamped upon the external aspect of his home and family. His wife spoke a few words in Irish, explaining my presence, to which he answered that I was welcome. Supper was at length prepared, when he drew from a basket a few of the finest trout I ever saw. He cleaned and fried them with his own hands, as if the operation were above the capacity of his wife, who performed the other culinary duties with silent assiduity. It might be owing to hunger, it might be owing to the actual superiority of the fish, or it might be owing to the mode of cooking, but it seemed to me as if I never tasted anything of equal flavour to those trout. The entertainment was ended with some boiled new milk, slightly curdled, a delicacy little known in the circle of fashion, but never surpassed either in that or any other. Some fresh hay was procured and strewn on an article of furniture common in the houses of the Kerry peasantry, called a "settle." It is a sort of a rude sofa, made of common deal timber. On this "settle" my host prepared my bed of new-mown hay, barricaded with old chairs and a table against the assaults of the hungry animals. I had not long lain down when a man entered (the door consisted of a pair of tongs, so placed as to prevent the egress of the cattle), lay at full length on the table, and fell fast asleep. In an hour or so afterwards, there came another, who groped his way over the cattle, and, sweeping the fire from the hearth, lay down to sleep in peace. This man slept uneasily, and groaned heavily, as if some terrible sense of guilt or fear pressed against his heart.

I had a vague feeling of uneasiness, not free from alarm, but the hearty snoring of the one, and the fitful complaints of the other of my bedfellows died away on my ear, and I, too, shared their unconsciousness in deep sleep. The man who brought my baggage arrived early next morning. My host soon provided a good substantial breakfast—excellent new potatoes, which had escaped the blight, butter, new milk, and a slice of the flesh of fried badger. He then proposed to accompany us with his son, aged about thirteen, who by some inexplicable privilege seemed exempt from any portion of the drudgery which was the lot of the family.

The other man who brought the baggage was persuaded to leave his horse and car, and accompany us with my bundle, as far as the summit of the hill. To climb the steepest mountain side had become an amusement to me, and we ascended the one then before us, merrily, our host relating many anecdotes of sportsmanship, and detailing the startling incidents and wild rapture of badger-hunting. From the summit we commanded a view of the country for miles around. "Here we are," said our host, "higher than the proudest of your enemies." He then traced the route of the man with the bundle, through the open plain, and by the nearest way; and turning to me, he said: "You must not go in the same direction, for every yard of it is set. Follow my son," he said, and turning to the boy, he named several points in the path whereby he should conduct me. "Lead Mr. Doheny safely," he concluded, "and remember you are the son of—." In utter astonishment I inquired how he knew me, and he answered by waving his hand in the direction of the boy, who had bounded off and was scarcely perceptible above the tall heath. I soon overtook him, and as we went along, I learned that my two companions during the night were also evading the law's pursuit. One of them he described as having killed a man by accident, and ever after leading, the life of a "poor wild goose." I made no doubt but this was he whose spirit seemed so heavily laden. We had a couple of terriers of the truest breed, whose sudden discovery of a badger interrupted our conversation and impeded our journey. The young hunter became delirious with joy. His encouraging cries to the dogs were broken outbursts of wildest rapture; and when the game took shelter in his inaccessible den, he would dash himself against the rocks with the same reckless vehemence as his dogs, who, in their rage, attempted to bite away the hard mountain stones.

He left the spot with the utmost reluctance, after venting an oath of vengeance against the head of the poor badger, to which he promised sure destruction on the occasion of their next meeting. We quickly descended in the direction of Gougane Barra, where he parted from me, indignantly refusing a half-crown which I offered him.

Once more I found myself on the slopes of Shehigh, in sight of Lough Lua. My immediate object was to place myself in communication with my lady friend at Dunmanway. I was extremely anxious to see her. I wanted to procure through her some things to complete my costume as a disguised priest, and finally I expected to learn through her some news of my family. With the view of seeing her in the safest retreat, I determined to conceal myself in a wood belonging to a Mr. O'Leary, at a place called Coolmountain. I endeavoured to gain the friendship of a man in the neighbourhood, of whom I had learned the highest character for probity. It was necessary to confide in him fully; for his fidelity to his employer might induce him to betray me, if he suspected that my flight was occasioned by moral guilt. He did not disappoint me. At once he entered into all my plans, and immediately sent his wife with a message to Dunmanway. The distance was about six miles; and the utmost caution was necessary, for the police authorities, baffled in all their calculations, concerning my retreat, and deceived in every word of the information they were able to purchase, had determined on making simultaneous searches in all quarters of the country, so that scarcely a house remained in this vicinity that had not the honour of a domicilary visit. My friend, too, who during the past three weeks had made various attempts to see me, and had gone on to Kenmare for that purpose, was continually dogged, and arrested three or four times. On one occasion they stripped her nearly naked, searching for papers. She at once saw that to see me would be attended with danger; but she wrote a hurried note, and despatched it by another messenger, as well as a large packet of letters from home. In these letters I was adjured to continue the disguise of a peasant in whatever attempts I made. She, too, strongly objected to my proposed plan, and communicated to me a project of escaping which was suggested by a friend of hers at Cork, whither she had gone in her anxiety. His plan was that I should proceed to Cork, that very night, and take up my residence at some obscure lodging-house, until he could find means of stowing me in a coal vessel, which would take me as far as

Wales. If I agreed to this proposal, I was to be at Crookstown (already mentioned in this narrative) at six o'clock that evening, where I would meet three men who were to conduct me by a safe route to Cork.

When I received this information, it was four o'clock, and the distance to Crookstown was at least seventeen miles. The plan was one of which I could not approve; but it would be invaluable to me to have a safe asylum in Cork, for any project I might finally decide on. I accordingly communicated to my man of confidence the difficulty I found myself in, and requested he would procure a horse and car which I could drive along the high road, hoping to reach Crookstown before the promised guide would have left. He suggested the man at whose house I stopped on a former evening. Thither both of us repaired, after having completed my costume, such as is generally worn by the lowest Cork peasants— literally rags. We got the horse and car, but before the arrangements for our departure were made it was past the hour when I should be at Crookstown. A servant boy who led the horse was my companion. When we arrived at Crookstown it was eleven o'clock, and we found no trace of the messengers. Nothing remained but to try and get on to Cork. I proposed the journey to the boy; but he resolutely refused. I affected to acquiesce, and asked him to drink something in a publichouse, which was kept open for the accommodation of carriers, of whom there are large numbers at that season of the year. He soon yielded to the influence of milk punch, and allowed me to do as I pleased. We proceeded along the great thoroughfare, having an empty butter cask in the car. We passed several patrolling parties in the road, and at grey dawn we were entering the city of Cork; the boy sleeping in the car, and the horse led by me. I paid at the custom-gate for my butter, and passed on through the city unnoticed. A few gentle taps brought the gentleman, who undertook to have me conveyed out of the country, to the door. I introduced myself; was admitted, and conducted to a bedroom, where everything was prepared for my reception. Thus I found myself in the very heart of the city of Cork, while the strictest search was made for me in every cabin on the mountains of Kerry and the western shore.

I felt quite secure in my then retreat. During the day I learned that the men who were to conduct me safely to Cork were arrested three several times on their way back.

In my sojourn for two days and nights in the woods of Coolmountain, I received attentions for which it would be shameful not to express my gratitude. Although the crisis of my fate was so near at hand, I felt some hours of unalloyed pleasure in its shade. I had leisure to peruse my letters from home, so full of courage, hope and love; and to consider well the different proposals and means of escape, suggested by others and contemplated by myself. The weather had cleared up and there was a succession of brilliant harvest days. I employed my evenings in composing the following two pieces; and after nightfall I was visited by some friends, with whom I sipped delicious champagne, till a late hour, 'neath the calm watchfulness of a brilliant harvest moon.

EIBLIN A RUIN

I sang thee other lays,
          Eiblin a ruin,
But these were happy days,
          Eiblin a ruin,
When mount and vale and grove,
Where we were wont to rove,
Were beautified by love,
          Eiblin a ruin.

I said I loved thee well,
          Eiblin a ruin.
Too fondly far to tell,
          Eiblin a ruin.

I loved thee as the day,
Serener for the ray,
Thy smile shed o'er my way,
             Eiblin a ruin.

But day has turned to night,
             Eiblin a ruin.
With clouds and gloom and blight,
             Eiblin a ruin,
Yet here an outlaw lone,
My heart else, like a stone,
Is more and more thy own,
             Eiblin a ruin.

When in some rocky glen,
             Eiblin a ruin.
I share the wild dog's den,
             Eiblin a ruin,
Oppressed with woe and care,
As sleep comes o'er me there,
Methinks I hear thy prayer,
             Eiblin a ruin.

Throughout that troubled rest,
             Eiblin a ruin
Thy image fills my breast,
             Eiblin a ruin,
And ere the vision's fled,
My cold and flinty bed
Seems down unto my head,
             Eiblin a ruin.

As night's dark shadow flies,
                    Eiblin a ruin,
Along the opening skies,
                    Eiblin a ruin,
In the soft purpling ray,
That heralds early day,
I see thy fond smile play,
                    Eiblin a ruin.

When, dangers thick'ning fast,
                    Eiblin a ruin,
My fate seemed sealed at last,
                    Eiblin a ruin.
A low voice ever near,
Still whispers in mine ear—
"For her sake do not fear"—
                    Eiblin a ruin,

And oh, 'tis that lone hope,
                    Eiblin a ruin,
That nerves this heart to cope,
                    Eiblin a ruin.
With peril and with pain,
And surging of the brain,
More boisterous than the main,
                    Eiblin a ruin.

TO MY WIFE

And what was the world to me, love,
    Or why should its honours divide
The feelings that centred in thee, love,

As fondly you clung to my side;
Or why should ambition or glory,
    E'er tempt me to wander so far,
For sake of distinction in story,
    From thee, my heart's faithfulest star.

Or why should I call thee mine own, love,
    To sport with the life that was thine,
Or risk for a land overthrown, love,
    A stake that no longer was mine;
Or why should I pledge for the fallen
    What only belonged to the free;
For had I not gauged life and all on
    The faith that was plighted to thee?

And here, while I wander alone, love,
    Beneath the cold shadows of night,
Or lie with my head on a stone, love,
    Awaiting the dawning of light,
My spirit unthralled is returning,
    Where far from the coward and slave,
Her beacon of love is still burning,
    To light, to direct me and save.

And she, too, who watches beside thee,
    And loves as none other could love,
To counsel, to cherish and guide thee.
    To weep with, but never reprove—
Yes, she too, is lone and unguarded,
    The reed she had leant on in twain,
And though her trust thus be rewarded,
    She'd love that love over again.

COOLMOUNTAIN WOOD.

At Cork two families were compromised by my prolonged stay, one of them irretrievably, if I were arrested. However, they placed themselves entirely and unconditionally at my disposal. I stated my objections to the proposed conveyance of a coal boat to Wales, where I would be equally exposed as in Ireland, and have infinitely less sympathy or assistance. I suggested one of the London steamers instead, which they agreed to. After some preliminary negotiations, a person connected with one of those vessels promised to secrete me and have me landed at Southampton, where I could easily procure a passage to France. Just as this arrangement was concluded, news arrived that Tipperary was again in arms, under the command of my friend, O'Mahony. The report added that I was associated with him in command. Hour after hour brought some story stranger than that which preceded it; but in each and all I found myself figuring in some character or other, all, of course, contrary to the truth. This fact led at once to a suspicion of the accuracy of the whole. But I was aware that caution was a leading characteristic of O'Mahony's genius, and I felt assured he would not attempt any open movement without strong probabilities of success. The fabrications about myself I reconciled to the belief that he wished it to appear he had my sanction and support. The vessel was to sail next day, and I should determine at once, or risk the safety of the family who protected me. I endeavoured to find a middle course, and suggested the impossibility of leaving the country while even a vague report confirmed the belief that some at least of its people were prepared to vindicate her liberty, or die nobly in its assertion. They acquiesced, and the vessel was allowed to sail. I insisted, however, that after nightfall I should leave the house and take up my quarters in some obscure lodging house. Meantime it was arranged that if the next mail confirmed the accounts from Tipperary, I should be provided with a horse and car, and be able to leave Cork as I entered it. When night came, the lady of the house sternly and resolutely opposed

257

my leaving it. She would not consent to free herself from a risk she took so much honest pleasure in encountering. Another day and night left us in the same uncertainty. The reports were still more unsatisfactory and contradictory. But that there should be reports at all, satisfied my mind, and I finally prepared to start for Tipperary on the morning of the 29th of September.

Information at length reached me that the party under O'Mahony were dispersed and himself fled. The difficulty of my position, with respect to my protectors, left me no alternative. Any chance that presented itself should be embraced. The Bristol boat was in the river, panting to escape her anchorage; and following the horse, which was to bear me to Tipperary, to the quay, I walked on board the *Juverna*, just as she was loosing her cables. My baggage, made up in a small box, was put on board as a parcel addressed to a young friend of mine in London. The few moments that intervened were fraught with most intense suspense. I stood on the fore deck among cattle, covered with rags and dirt, my eyes fixed on two detectives who stood at the cabin entrance, scrutinising narrowly the figure and features of every cabin passenger. The bell rang, the detectives stepped on shore, one of my friends who watched my movements from a distance, waved a kind adieu, the *Juverna* slipped her cables, and by one bound was out in the river. The first motion of her paddles sounded to me like the assurance of fate, and I looked on the curling foam with measureless exultation. The *Juverna* made a momentary halt at Passage, and then glanced gaily through Cove harbour out into the sea. As she cleared the road I turned back to look for the last time upon my fatherland. Her prospects, her promise, her strength, her hopes, her failure and her fall rushed in burning memory through my brain. I endeavoured to embody in the following verses the feelings that agitated and almost paralysed my every faculty of body and mind. I wrote them on a piece of paper that had been wrapped round some cheese:—

Away, away, the good ship swings;
　　One heave, one bound, and off she's dashing,
Expanding wide her snowy wings,
　　The white foam round her paddles flashing.
Away, away, the land recedes,
　　Far into dim and dreary distance,
As gallantly our packet speeds.
　　Unconscious of the gale's resistance.
Away, away, how oft before,
　　With paling cheek and aching stomach,
I've trembled at the billow's roar.
　　And crouched me in my narrow hammock.
But now, I bless the wildest waves
That bear me from a land of slaves.

Away, away, yon crimson cloud,
　　Which, mounting the blue vault of Heaven,
Soars calmly o'er the murky shroud
　　That palls the close of boisterous even,
Is scarcely fairer than the form,
　　The light, the grace, from stem to stern—a
Fairy riding on the storm—
　　Of the fleet, trusty, dight Juverna,
Away, away, one last look more:
　　One blessing on the naked land—
Though the too glorious dream be o'er—
　　One blessing for her truthful hand,
Her proud old faith, though darkly grown,
Still lingering by each cold hearth-stone.

Away, away; poor fool of fate,
　　Couldst thou but dream this mournful end,

This midnight of a hope so great,
    Where shame and sorrow darkly blend—
Couldst thou divine that thus bedecked,
    With rags and dirt, thine eyes downturned:
Thou'dst flee, thy whole life's labour wrecked.
    Thy very heart within thee burned.
—Away, away, in all the past,
    There's not an act I would recall,
I bow me to the o'erwhelming blast,
    But 'tis the heart alone can fall,
And mine may once again defy.
The fate that mocks it scoffingly.

Away, away, if o'er the sea,
    My voice could reach the prison grate.
Where daylight creeping gloomily,
    Comes to deride the captives' fate;
Could I but prove by word or act,
    How firm my heart and purpose still,
Their life's worst pang to counteract,
    Before their proud young hearts were still—
To live but that the land they loved
    Should yet assert its native right,
That the immortal faith they proved,
    Should yet be robed in victory's light,
And, oh, to feel such promise high,
Were last to light their dying eye.

If apology were to be offered for the change of measure of the above,
and its somewhat conflicting sentiments, it would be found in the tumult
of passions, excitement, fear, hope, rage, disappointment and regret with
which, standing among cattle on the deck, and disguised in meanest rags, I

looked upon my country's shores for, it may be the last time, and thought of her hopes, her misery and fall. Both faults may be amended here, but I cannot help regarding it as irreligious toward thoughts suggested by the circumstances then around me to remodel even the structure into which they spontaneously shaped themselves.

Aheny Hill, showing the Constabulary Barrack
destroyed by the Insurgents. 1848

Night soon fell drearily upon the water. I engaged a berth from one of the sailors, and before half an hour, lost all consciousness of country and friends, of wind and tide, and hope, and shame, and peril, in tranquil repose. On ascending next morning, the shores of England were in view, and we sailed up the channel to the mouth of the Avon under a calm and mellow sky. I had some breakfast with one of the cowherds. We were delayed several hours waiting for the tide, which were spent for the most part in making difficult evolutions; and exhibiting to the cabin passengers the peculiar qualities of the *Juverna*. Night had fallen before we reached Bristol, and I slipped away from the boat, amid the confusion and bustle which checked the progress of the gay and rich, around whose footsteps avarice had gathered an eager and jostling crowd. Rude contact with, and unsavoury odours from, the unclean multitude shocked their nervous sensibility, as they made their way to their hotels amidst obtrusive obsequiousness, while the lone outlaw's pathway lay free through the open street and uncontaminated air. But a wretched exterior has its disadvantages also. I dared not present myself at a hotel, and many of the humbler hostelries refused me admittance, believing, no doubt, either that the seeds of pestilence were in my rags, or not a copper in my pocket. Indeed, to no brain but that of a very imaginative genius would the possibility of such a superfluity as a pocket suggest itself. All the beds were "full." At last I thought me of an expedient. I called for a glass of ale, for which payment in advance was duly demanded. I handed a sovereign, which at once emptied a bed, provided I slept in a room with another person which I refused, feeling that I had acquired a footing. I had something to eat, and finally found that there was a vacant room.

The next day was Sunday. No trains travelled to London except third class. This was rather unlucky, for I was aware that certain straitened gentlemen were often obliged, by stress of circumstances—the pressure of business which brooked not a moment's delay—reluctantly to avail themselves of this mode of conveyance. I felt, too, that the loyalty of these slender aristocrats, was on a par with the unhappy incidents which compelled them to consort with vulgar people, that is to say, so constrained, that however much against the impulses of their generous natures, they could not omit any opportunity of manifesting the sentiment in its full intensity, I selected my company on this occasion, being only anxious to exclude the "*arbiters elegantiarum*," Of my "*compagnons de voyage*," some were in gin, some in fumes and some in glee, and the journey passed off without an incident.

On arriving at the Paddington terminus, an unlooked-for difficulty presented itself. My costume attracted universal attention. It was, in fact, *outré* even in comparison with the most outlandish; for every article had been carefully selected for its singularity. My "caubeen" especially excited the risibility of the merry boys who thronged the streets. I was soon followed by an uproarious crowd of most incorrigible young rascals, who made lunges at my unfortunate head-gear. They peered at me round lamp-posts, and occasionally, "Teigue," and "Phelim," pronounced in a broad English accent, grated on my ear. Although not indisposed to be merry, I grasped one of my tormentors and handed him over to a policeman. The sentinel of city morals dismissed him with a harsh rebuke, and threatened to "haul up" whoever gave me further annoyance. We were then near Oxford street. I told him I wanted to go to Tottenham Court road; but after making several fruitless attempts to pronounce the name, his own fertile genius had to supply my deficiency. He walked with me until the last unruly boy had disappeared, and then he sent me on my way rejoicing, after having spent some minutes in teaching me to articulate distinctly "Tottenham Court Road." It was already nightfall. I felt as if all danger were passed. I could not anticipate the check I was about to receive.

I knew a man named Parker, who resided in Museum Street. I thought his house that to which I could easiest find access without exciting notice. I made my way to it unobserved, rapped, and to my great relief the door was opened by the man himself. He did not recognise me for some time, but as soon as he did, he fell into a paroxysm half hysterical, half frantic. I had completed his ruin, he exclaimed, and his unhappy family would have to curse me as the cause of his destruction. He was ready to sink on the floor in sheer terror, and with difficulty could he utter a request that I should instantly leave his house. This was a command, however harsh and heartless, which I dared not resist, for I was forced to admit to myself that under his terrified exterior might lurk a sentiment baser than fear.

I left the place in utter dismay. I could not venture into a house such as I had lodged in at Bristol, the night before, because my person was well known in London, and because those places are frequented by characters of all sorts. I could not venture, in my then guise, to the house of my young friend to whom I had addressed the parcel, because my appearance there would inevitably attract the notice of the policeman. I dare not, of course, venture to a respectable hotel. Thus perplexed, I bethought of a woman with whom I used formerly to lodge, and I repaired to her rooms (she had herself become a lodger). I met her on the stairs, where she nearly fainted. She hurried me into the street, and there told me that a person who lived in the house was actually watching to betray me. She suggested the house of an Irishwoman who lived in a court hard by. I had no alternative. The poor woman received me with tears. Such was her emotion that I could not hesitate to trust her with my life: Her son and daughter-in-law, who spent the day with her, were about returning home. They lived in the suburbs, at the Surrey side. They proposed to take me to their cottage, and I readily consented. We got a coach and drove home. The kindliest attentions were lavished on me by these people. As soon as I arrived, I shaved and cleansed myself; no small task, considering that I had on a fortnight's beard, and had rubbed my face over with soot and grease.

I had a shirt and clothes from my host, with whom, in my new trim, I sat down to a comfortable supper. Early next morning he informed my friend of my arrival, and I was at once surrounded by several who would risk their lives for my safety. I had by this time begun to regard many singular escapes of mine as preordained by Providence, and I ceased to feel much concern in my fate. I cherished a presentiment of safety until it grew into a conviction, and acting on its assurance, I gave way to an unconcern that was quite inexplicable to those around me. But one feeling of fear lingered with me: it was lest Parker should add treason to cowardice, which certain ominous expressions that were said to fall from him, confirmed. I otherwise felt so secure, and so thankful to my entertainers, that I would gratify their wishes to remain a day or two longer with them; but the tide answered so well—the whole journey to Boulogne being by night, that I determined to avail myself of the opportunity. I donned my clerical costume, got me a sleek wig, folded a stole round my breviary, and with Christian patience awaited the hour of departure. I was to be accompanied to Paris by my young friend, who spoke the French language perfectly, and was well acquainted with the etiquette of the journey. We entered the express train at London Bridge at half-past eight. When it was just starting, my host, who had accompanied us, clung to the panel of the door, and warned me, with provoking warmth, to "write, write, as soon as I was safe." As the train drove off and his boisterous adieus died on my ear, I lost the last feeling of anxiety on my own account. The carriage was full—a German with a toothache—two gossiping old bachelors—a jolly English resident of the sunny south—my friend and myself occupied the six seats. However fluttered may be the hearts of the passengers, whatever may be the pressure of guilt, or fear, or remorse upon their souls, the heart of the mighty engine, on its fiery course, throbs only with one passion, namely how to outspeed the flight of time. Our fellow-travellers conversed upon all subjects, and wished for my opinion upon each; but I was so reserved and pious, and my friend so ready and witty, and exuberant in his gaiety, that my obstinate silence was pardoned or forgotten. We were able to make our way on board Her Majesty's mail packet by the light of a clouded moon, then fast waning. I did not trouble myself to learn the name of the boat, but she appeared endued with more than the speed of fire. She flew over her allotted trip in one hour and three-quarters, and about two o'clock I set my foot on the free soil of the young Republic.

I had longed for such an event with an intensity of feeling not to be described; nay, I had often enjoyed anticipated exultation from indulging in a vague dream of its bare possibility, which absorbed all the gloom and horror of my situation. Yet when I stepped securely on what, to me, was hallowed ground, an adequate appreciation of the circumstance was far from realised in my feelings. New sights and sounds began to share my thoughts and engross my comprehension. In a moment the past vanished, with all its disquietude and alarm; and I entered on the new scene with a taste akin to the appetite of a convalescent. If I felt any deep emotion, it was only when my mind recurred to the fate of my comrades, or the feelings of joy with which my family would learn the tidings of my safety. We left our baggage at the Custom house—mine consisted of a pair of boots stowed away in a rather capacious valise—handed the keys, in due form, to the commissionaire of police, and directed them to be sent after us to our hotel. A commissionaire, so they call themselves, appeared in the morning with the keys, which he handed us bowing, adding that all was right.

There was a fete at Boulogne. Nothing was to be seen but glittering bayonets, and nothing to be heard but the harsh monotonous sound of the drum. Flags floated in the breeze, and cheers echoed from the distant hills, and everything proclaimed the festivity of liberty. It was a grand sight, and yet a sad one for me. I could not help contrasting with the scene before me the fate of my own unfortunate country. At ten o'clock we were on our way to Paris.

Such was the anxiety with which I gazed on the glad face of that sunny land during the entire of the journey that I could at this moment recognise every object that attracted my attention. But the scope of this narrative, now drawing rapidly to a close, does not embrace a description of France or Paris. Many pens have plied the task, and were mine more adequate than any, it were unfit to interweave so bright a theme with the gloomy details of this mournful history.

There remains to be told but one incident. On our arrival at the Paris terminus, we got into an English omnibus which brought us to an English hotel—the Hotel de Louvre in the Rue St. Thomas. There we dined together, some dozen or so of the passengers. After dinner my friend and I had champagne. While discussing its merits the conversation turned on Ireland. Opinions, of course, varied. Mine, it need scarcely be added, to an Englishman's ear sounded bloodily, and I urged them with the vehemence of baffled hope. An old English gentleman of that quiet school which affects liberality and moderation, but entertains deepest animosity, deprecated the violence of my language and sentiments, and expressed his painful astonishment at hearing such opinions from the mouth of a clergyman; "They would not be unbecoming," added he, with great bitterness of tone, "in that sanguinary brigand, Doheny." Involuntarily and simultaneously my friend and myself burst into an immoderate fit of laughter, The gentleman could not at all comprehend our mirth. He had, he thought, delivered himself of very sound and very gentlemanly philosophy, and he was really shocked to find it had made an impression so different from what he had expected. He had travelled much, he said, and met men of many lands, of whom Irishmen were ever the most polite and best bred gentlemen; a fact which rendered our laughing in his face rather inexplicable. The conversation was again resumed and again waxed warm. I expressed my opinion of English paupers in Ireland, and said they ought to be transported in a convict ship back to Liverpool, in the same fashion as Irish paupers of a different class are transmitted to Dublin by the Liverpool guardians. To this he replied by saying that there would be no peace in Ireland until the Mitchels and Dohenys were hanged, a fate which the latter was hastening to with irresistible impetus. At this self-satisfied prophecy we laughed louder than before, whereupon he waxed wrathful, and repeating his experience of the world in general, and of Irishmen in particular, demanded an explanation of the laugh. I said, "That is a straightforward question, and demands a direct answer. It shall be given, although you have refused to answer, as all Englishmen of your class invariably do, to several direct questions which I have put to you. I laughed because I am that same sanguinary Doheny": and pulling off my wig, I added, "Me *voila* at your service." The sudden appearance of him who answered the incantations of the weird sisters could not produce a greater panic. Chairs tumbled in every direction, and their occupiers fled the room, leaving myself and my friend ample space to enjoy the joke and the champagne in undisturbed quiet.

I have nothing further to relate in connection with myself. Paris appeared to me clothed with a grandeur, a glory, and a beauty, infinitely surpassing every description of them I had ever read or heard. Standing in any commanding spot surrounded by the monuments of her splendour and magnificence, upon each of which the genius of the land shed its immortal lustre, one feels coerced to the conviction that the high command and abiding destiny of France must be equally imperishable. But these considerations belong not to my story, and I renounce the idea of commemorating the sensations of gratified pride which that gorgeous capital awakened in my bosom. Her architecture and her art, her memorials of glory, and the triumphs of her progress, require to be scanned by the eye and portrayed by the ability of artistic genius. I must content myself with preserving a delighted recollection of the French metropolis which no scene or circumstance, possible in life can ever efface. The companion of all my hazards in Ireland, whom I again joined in Paris, more than shared my enthusiasm. He spent all his days wandering among the galleries of the Louvre or the statues of Versailles, forgetting in the sublime presence of their unmatched *chefs d'ouvres* all the shame and perils of the past. I hope he may be induced to give the result of his long examinations and fond reveries to the public.

FOOTNOTES:

12 "Alice and Uua."

13 This may be a harsh and unjust opinion; if so, no one could regret it more than myself. In any case I wish to disclaim the idea of making a charge against the body of the Roman Catholic clergy, to some of whose members it applies. I yet fully believe that the great majority of the priesthood would willingly die with the rest of their countrymen in struggling for the liberty of their common home. Even of those who acted against us with such deadly success,

I am sure some were influenced by pure and honourable motives: there were others, however, whose conduct the noblest motives would fail to justify, or even extenuate.

14 I hope my friend "Desmond" (a true poet and genuine Irishman, whom God long preserve) will allow me to borrow his "graceful spirit people" to elevate to poetical dignity the otherwise unattractive and straggling waters of Lough Lua. It is near the lone and lovely passes of Ceimeneagh, which his genius has invested with graceful immortality, and his

"Children of the earth and sea."

may be sometimes tempted to lave therein.

Lough Lua loses in the comparison suggested by the sublime scenery around it, of which the "green little island," and the pass are immeasurably the greatest. I saw it in no happy frame of mind, as I dragged my weary limbs along the rugged slopes of Shehigh. The only real feature of interest I could discover, was the solitary swan above alluded to, to which an intellect less fanciful than that of my friend could not refuse a claim to be recognised as the genius loci, or spirit of the spot.

15 Mr. Daniel MacCarthy

CONCLUSION

A word remains to be said in reference to the fate of those who were the special objects of the Government's attention. Of the six for whom a reward was offered, four escaped, namely, Mr. Dillon, Mr. O'Gorman, Mr. O'Mahony and myself. Mr. Dillon was the first who left Ireland. Late in August he sailed from Galway, and landed at New York after a voyage of seven weeks. In the same vessel sailed P.J. Smyth, who was despatched from Cashel to Dublin with directions from Mr. O'Brien. Richard O'Gorman, accompanied by John O'Donnell and Daniel Doyle, sailed from the mouth of the Shannon on board a vessel bound for Constantinople. After landing in the Turkish capital, they were obliged to lie concealed until able to procure passports for Algiers. Many foolish stories have been circulated in reference to Mr. O'Gorman's adventures and disguises in Ireland. Not one of them has the least truth in it. He or his companions never assumed any disguise, and though their adventures were more perilous, they were not so romantic as those that have been related. A more detailed account of their wanderings would no doubt be as interesting to my readers as it would be agreeable to myself. But both the time and the limits I have proposed to myself for this publication exclude it here. I could not, without too long a delay, acquire that minute and accurate knowledge of facts and dates, which would be indispensable to such a history.

But of succeeding events in Ireland, and the men who controlled them, it is imperative to speak more in detail. John O'Mahony was their chief, and John Savage his principal counsellor and comrade.

The former, although not compromised by any act previous to the arrest of Mr. O'Brien, evaded the vigilance of the detectives, and continued moving about from place to place, being generally guarded while he slept by a large number of faithful followers. No man was ever followed with truer devotion or served with more unwavering fidelity. He might have continued in the same district with perfect safety up to the present hour. But every moment of his time was engrossed by the endeavour to rouse the country to some becoming effort. John Savage, who had come to Carrick on a visit to a relation, partook of his enthusiasm and shared his toil. They spent many anxious nights in counsel together when it was supposed all spirit had left the country. The first ostensible object that brought the people together under their immediate guidance and control was the reaping of a field of wheat belonging to O'Mahony. A vast crowd amounting to several hundred stalwart men assembled. They had scarcely entered on their labour when the approach of a troop of horse was announced. O'Mahony and Savage were compelled to retire. The military cavalcade entered the field, and rode rudely among the men and ripe corn. Still the reapers desisted not. They proceeded with their labours sedulously and silently. But there was no pretext for arresting any of the men, and no pretext afforded for further outrage, and the business of the day went on without further outrage from the soldiers. This occurred on the 22nd of August. Some days later, sullen crowds were seen ascending Aheny Hill, about five miles to the north of Carrick-on-Suir. By what mysterious agency they were directed none could tell. About a similar distance from the town, in the opposite direction, near the village of Portlaw, another camp was formed with equal rapidity and mystery. With these men John Savage took his station. He was entirely unknown to the people; and owed his influence over them to his singular resolution. The understanding was that these two bodies, and a third consisting of an equal number of men which was promised from Kilkenny, should march simultaneously on the town of Carrick and the fort at Besborough where five hundred men were encamped. He who undertook to lead the Kilkenny men went on the execution of his mission, leaving O'Mahony at one side, and Savage on the other, to contend with the impetuosity of their respective followers who demanded with violence to be led on. As much perhaps from the precariousness of their situation as from a reckless daring, they could not brook the least delay. Their leaders, on the other hand, urged the necessity of steadiness and prudence. It was too late for such policy. The time between the first step in revolution and action is the most trying to the courage and faith of undisciplined men. In this instance it produced fatal results. The weakness of the timid increased, and the courage of the boldest was quelled. Suspicion was aroused, and desertion was the inevitable consequence. O'Mahony found it impossible to withstand the clamorous urgency of the men, and all his preparations were necessarily of a hasty and imperfect character. The arrival of the party from Kilkenny was the utmost limit of inaction that would be endured; and the leaders saw with regret that they had yielded too soon to the demands of those who precipitated the rising. The true guarantee of success would consist in perfect preparation under cover of secrecy, so as that the assembling could be followed by an immediate blow.

Scouring parties from each rendezvous, proceeded through the country in search of arms. Provisions were liberally supplied by the neighbouring farmers, and numbers were hourly arriving from distant parts of the country. But those who were engaged in the search for arms attacked police barracks and private houses. In general, these enterprises were rash, ill-advised and ill-arranged. In some instances they were successful, and in some they were repulsed with loss of life, while the police were able to effect a safe retreat. At the Tipperary side, two men were killed in the attack on the Glenbour barracks; and at the Waterford side, one man was shot at Portlaw in the assault on the police-barrack, and two in the attack on the Reverend Mr. Hill's house. These repulses checked the ardour of the boldest, and gave rise to disunion and distrust. Meantime, the promised reinforcements from Kilkenny failed to redeem the pledge that was given in their name. A whole day and night passed, and no tidings of them arrived. Several of those who were loudest and most urgent left the camp. A very large force, however, remained; but after delaying two days without hearing of the Kilkenny men, they determined to disperse. The party at Portlaw adopted the same resolution, and O'Mahony and Savage had to shift for themselves. A reward was offered for O'Mahony, but he eluded his pursuers, and in a few days was beyond their reach. He embarked at Bonmahon in the county of Waterford and crossed to Wales, where he was concealed for some time until he found an opportunity of escaping to France. Savage, whose person was not much known, made his way to Dublin, whence he sailed for America direct.

The Kilkenny men arrived at Aheny on the morning after those under O'Mahony had dispersed and finding the place deserted, they immediately returned. This accident once more baffled all hope of a struggle. From beginning to end, some mischance marred every propitious circumstance that presented itself. It seemed as if the failure had been predestined. But to yield to such a fate, to abjure the great and true faith which the attempt of the last unhappy year quickened in the hearts of all men, would be distrust of God's mercy and justice. In the struggle that preceded the outbreak a great victory was won. The most formidable power that ever fettered the consciences of men was struck to the earth. Truth, long lost sight of, was again restored as one of the great agencies of national deliverance and national elevation. The question between England and Ireland assumed its real character; and although huxtering politicians have since endeavoured to set up the honour of the island for sale, they have only been able to dispose of their own characters. The people have not debased themselves. In the lying homage to the Queen of England they took no part. They have preserved through the severest trials the old immortal yearning of their race, and the arms they had provided themselves with in '48 they have guarded religiously, in the hope of using them on some day of brighter auspices and loftier destiny.

John Savage (1848)

APPENDICES

I

THOMAS D'ARCY M'GEE'S NARRATIVE OF 1848

Early on Saturday the 22nd of July I left my pleasant home in Cullenswood, near Dublin, to which I was never to return. On reaching the city I found a telegraphic despatch from London had been just published, announcing the suspension of the Habeas Corpus Act, and that the "extraordinary powers" to be conferred on the Lord Lieutenant would be forwarded to Dublin on the following Monday. It was contended on all hands that the hour for action or submission or flight for the Confederates was now come. Of "The Council of Five,"[16] there were then in Dublin but three members. One is now in Van Diemen's Land; the others were Mr. Dillon and myself. We had a hasty meeting in the old Council Rooms of the Irish Confederation. They decided to proceed that evening to Enniscorthy to advise with Smith O'Brien, and, as I understood, to proceed with him to the district between the Suir and the Shannon, and to operate from that basis according to circumstances and their own best judgment.

A gentleman had arrived in Dublin that morning with a proposition which decided my movements and led me into some singular situations.

He was a professional man, by birth an Irishman who had resided a long time in Scotland. He had one only son, two rifles, and £120 in money, which he brought as his offering to the country. He informed us that several hundred Irishmen in Scotland had been all the year preparing for this event, that they had a good share of arms and ammunition, and that if any plan could be devised to bring them into Ireland, they could be relied on for courage and endurance. I do not mention this gentleman's name, because I do not know but he is still under the laws of England.

We perceived, on consultation, that if it were possible to land 400 or 500 staunch men in the north-west—say, at Sligo or Killala—where the Government were completely off their guard (all their anxieties being centred on the south), an important movement might follow in Sligo, Leitrim, Roscommon and Mayo. It would be like hitting the enemy in the back of the head. It would necessarily draw off some of the forces from Munster, through the valley of the Upper Shannon, which, with its continuous chain of lake, bog and mountain frontier, would be difficult ground for the movements of a regular army.

It was necessary, as our informant said, that "someone with a name" should go over and concert with the Irishmen in Scotland the mode and time of action, and I was the only person at hand willing for that service. For my encouragement, Meagher assured me I would be "as famous as Paul Jones" if I got the men out of the Clyde, and Mr. Dillon suggested as a landing-place "the old ground, Killala."

That afternoon I left Dublin, and on Tuesday morning I was in Scotland.

I cannot give the exact particulars of my movements while there. All who were in my confidence are still in Scotland, with the exception of Mr. Peter M'Cabe of Glasgow, now in the United States. I will only say that I visited and consulted our friends in four of the principal towns—Edinburgh included. I attended meetings of the clubs and in each instance instituted committees. I obtained in a few days a list of nearly 400 men, pretty well equipped, ready for the risk. A sub-committee surveyed the Broomielaw and the Clyde, and although their report was unfavourable to the attempt of getting out in one body, a gentleman, now in America, gained over the crew and officers of an Irish steamer to take us as passengers from Greenock where the tides in a few days would answer for departure about ten o'clock at night. The arms were to be previously shipped as merchandise or luggage, and the destination was to be Sligo.

These arrangements occupied from Tuesday till Friday of the last week of July. In the meanwhile, the London Journals arrived with news that O'Brien and his friends had been received with open arms in the south, and great excitement and suspicion of strangers arose in Scotland. In the Reading Room at Paisley I read myself in *The Hue and Cry*. One paper stated I was in Waterford, another said I was "revelling among the clubs in the Co. Dublin." The *Times* did me the honour to couple me with Meagher, calling us "the two most dangerous men now abroad." No one suspected my real locality.

On Friday I was in Edinburgh intending to return to Glasgow, when Mr.—, accompanied by a friend suddenly joined me. I saw they were a good deal agitated. They told me a Scotch mechanic who had been formerly in Dublin had seen me in the streets of Glasgow opposite Wellington statue, and that the news was "all round town." They added that the magistrates were in secret sitting, and as the writ of Habeas Corpus is unknown to the law of Scotland, I would be certainly arrested and summarily imprisoned if I returned. They were instructed to advise me to go to Ireland through the north of England, to prepare our friends in and about Sligo, and that they would complete the project which they had begun, and which was now in promising forwardness. I complied and Mr.—handed me a purse, as a personal gift from the Committee. This purse contained twelve or thirteen sovereigns, the only public money I received in this enterprise. After purposely driving to the West of Scotland depot [railway terminus] we returned to the North British, and my friends saw me off a station or two on the way to Newcastle-on-Tyne. I slept that night in Newcastle.

Between Newcastle and Carlisle the next day (Saturday) I had for a fellow passenger the Rev. Thresham Gregg[17] who was on a lecturing excursion against the Pope in the north of England. I had been introduced to him a year or two before and supposed he knew me. He certainly looked very hard at me from under his travelling-cap, with his half-shut cunning eyes. I had in my hand "Bradshaw's Railway Guide," which he asked to see. At the way stations he kept constantly inquiring the distance to Carlisle, and I sorely suspected he meant to "peach." He did not, however, though I still think he must have known me.

In Carlisle I met at dinner two Dublin priests (one from Westland Row chapel). They were bound on a pleasure-trip for Loch Katrine and the Trossachs. They informed me that I was "proclaimed," and seemed surprised at my returning. We parted very cordially and that night I went to Whitehaven where I had to wait over Sunday for the Belfast steamer.

In Whitehaven (by accident) I met with Mr. James Leach, the well-known Chartist, with whom I had some conversation unnecessary here to be repeated.

On Tuesday morning I arrived in Belfast. Two policemen entered the cabin as I was leaving it, and having been at the meeting which occasioned the Hercules Street riot,[18] I thought they would recognise me. They did not, however, and at 8 o'clock (after leaving a note for a dear and trusted friend of Mr. Duffy's, to mark my whereabouts) I was safely embarked on the Ulster railway for Armagh. At Aughnacloy a detective gave me a light, and before I went to bed (in Enniskillen) had read the proclamations against the leaders of the Southern movement, on the gates of the Barrack. The next morning I reached Sligo by the Leitrim road.

This was Wednesday morning, August 2nd.

At the Hibernia Hotel, where I stopped as Mr. Kelly (my travelling baptism), I saw for the first time in ten days the Irish papers. The Dublin *Freeman* and *Saunder's News Letter* were on the table. I read the list of the places where, and the clergymen by whom, the Southern movement had been "denounced," on Sunday, July 23rd and Sunday, July 30th. The same papers contained Lord Clarendon's wily letter to Archbishop Murray, offering to alter the statutes of the new colleges and to remodel the Bequests Bill so as to content the Catholic clergy, and artfully complimenting Pius IX. The game of the Government was clear—it was to separate the clergy from the people in the coming struggle.

The evening of my arrival in Sligo, I conferred with a few friends. The place chosen was "a shell house" in the demesne of Hazelwood on the shores of Lough Gill. Of those who formed that conference one at least, Mr. William M'Garahan, is now in America. We ascertained the garrison of Sligo to be but ninety men—the barrack to be surrounded by a common eight-foot wall, and the local authorities to be completely lulled to sleep. The circumstances were as favourable as could be expected.

But there never had been in Sligo or Leitrim any local Confederate or even "Repeal" organisation. The only local societies were secret—Molly Maguires and Ribbonmen. It was necessary to get into communication with them and late the next night Dr.——, a Confederate, introduced me to one of their leaders, on a road which crosses a hill to the south of the town. This gentleman I found wary, resolute, and intelligent. He said: "I have no doubt of what you say, but I must have certain facts to lay before our district chiefs. At present we don't know what to believe. One day we hear one thing—another, another. Bring us by this day week assurances that the South is going to rise or has risen, and we will raise two thousand before the week is out." I agreed to do so and he in the meantime went to prepare his friends.

I returned to my confidants of the first conference and "reported progress." It was rather difficult to find a trusty messenger. I volunteered to go myself, but they would not hear of it. At last a man who could be depended on was obtained, and, armed with certain passwords (unintelligible except to those for whom they were intended) he left to go through Roscommon and Westmeath into Tipperary by Borrisokane and Nenagh.

Simultaneously with this, agents went abroad in the country, and I, by the advice of the local leaders, went to lodge under Benbulben in the character of a Dublin student in search of health and exercise during the summer vacation. Within a week we expected to be openly arrayed against the authorities, and no man that I saw shrank from the prospect.

From my lodgings under Benbulben I made a visit to Bundoran to meet some friends from Donegal who were anxious to consult me as to the state of the county. By an odd chance I lodged in the same house with the stipendiary magistrate, Sir Thomas Blake, and had to go through his bedroom to my own. We met frequently but he was quite unsuspicious. He has, I find since, been dismissed from his office, after an ineffectual search for me through the county, a month from the time we had lived under the same roof.

While our messenger had gone south there arrived one from our friends in Scotland. Him I sent back the same night to expedite affairs there. In the meanwhile, on such maps as we had, my friends and I studied the roads and the formation of the country. There is in this part of Ireland a plateau of about twenty-five miles square of broken or mountainous ground. Of this district Ballinamore in Leitrim might be considered the centre; there are but three main roads leading through it—the Boyle road, the Red Lion road, and the Ballysodare road—which could all be easily rendered impassable, passing as they do over rapid streams, through narrow defiles or across extensive marshes. There is no great military depot within the district—Enniskillen, Athlone, and even Castlebar being within the spurs of the mountains. Sligo, its chief town was, as we saw, poorly garrisoned, and yet as a seaport of the second class it contained many things of the greatest use in a military movement—as lead, arms, canvas, tools, money, ships' stores, breadstuffs, types for proclamations and even some small cannon. From three to five thousand men it was calculated, could be well-equipped and could maintain themselves for three months within this district, with tolerable prudence and exertion. Before the time expired we hoped to receive help and officers from abroad, and afterwards to be able to undertake greater things.

We could not but remember that this was the district chosen by Owen O'Neill after his arrival from Spain in 1645 and that it was here he "nursed up" by slow degrees the army which fought at Benburb, and which in Napoleon's opinion, but for the premature death of Owen, would have checkmated Cromwell. The ground once chosen by a great general for its natural capabilities may safely be chosen again, and usually is, as in

Hungary for instance. The very posts and battlefields held and fought by Bem and Dembinski were the same whereon Huniad and Corvinus, four and five hundred years ago, fought against the Turks and Bosmens. Thus we had the sanction of a great example and the stimulus of an inspiriting tradition to point to for the choice of the ground.

We had not long to wait for news from the South—it came of itself. On Saturday the 5th of August Mr. O'Brien was arrested in Thurles. His companions, it was said, were fled hither and thither; but, at all events, his arrest had proved that, at that time, the South would not rise in arms against the Government.

This was the interpretation universally put upon it in the north-west. It was in vain I said, "There are other men as brave and as good who are still free and from whom we will hear better news." Those to whom I spoke were incredulous. Still I must do the people of the county the justice to say that in a meeting of their district-leaders at—it was discussed for two successive nights with great animation whether or not the district should rise even then. The parties for and against a rising were nearly balanced, but the latter prevailed on the argument that unless it was general it would be fruitless.

For ten dismal days I remained in this neighbourhood, hoping against hope and endeavouring to make others do the same. The proposals I then made, the result of desperation, I will not repeat, for now, even to myself, I confess they look wild and extravagant. But I felt the whole futurity of shame that awaited us for abandoning the country without a blow. It was well advanced in August before I could persuade myself that no hope remained. The Treasurer of our Scotch Committee came to Ireland expressly to urge me to consult my own safety in flight, in which he was joined by the whole of my local associates. Successively arrived the news of Meagher, Leyne and MacManus being taken. Then indeed I knew "all was up." Then, indeed, I felt the force of what I had long before prophesied—"What if we fail?" I resolved not to be taken if I could help it, and acted accordingly. After some personal adventures in

Donegal and Derry (with which I will not trouble the reader) I saw the last of the Irish shore early in September, and on the 10th of October reached Philadelphia.

I close here with this reflection: Had I been transported or hanged, I have no doubt full justice would be done me, because it would be nobody's interest to do me injustice. Had I kept silent, I might have lived an easy, prudent, reputable sort of life enough. But I established a journal on reaching America, and whereas my spine is not made of whalebone nor my conscience of indiarubber, I spoke the truth as I knew it in all things freely—thereby offending divers parties. This, I believe, could not be helped. After nearly a year of silence[19] I have at last (in self-defence) written this narrative, of which I assure the readers they never would have heard a word from me, but that misrepresentations not to be borne demanded its publicity. Those who from want of information misrepresented me hitherto can do so no more; and those who, knowing these facts, yet wilfully maligned me, I have now deprived of the power to do me further injury. Truth is powerful, and this is truth.

II
THE PROCLAMATION OF DOHENY AND HIS COLLEAGUES

By the Lord Lieutenant General and
General-Governor of Ireland
A PROCLAMATION

CLARENDON—

Whereas we have received information that THOMAS FRANCIS MEAGHER, JOHN B. DILLON and MICHAEL DOHENY have been guilty of treasonable practices, now we the Lord Lieutenant being determined to bring the said THOMAS FRANCIS MEAGHER, JOHN

B. DILLON and MICHAEL DOHENY to justice, do hereby offer a reward of

THREE HUNDRED POUNDS

to any person or persons who shall secure and deliver up to safe custody the person of any one of them, the said THOMAS FRANCIS MEAGHER, JOHN B. DILLON and MICHAEL DOHENY.

And we do hereby strictly charge and command all justices of the peace, mayors, sheriffs, bailiffs, constables and all other of her Majesty's loyal subjects to use their utmost-diligence in apprehending the said THOMAS FRANCIS MEAGHER, JOHN B. DILLON and MICHAEL DOHENY.

Given at her Majesty's Castle of Dublin, this 28th day of July, 1848.

By his Excellency's Command,

T.N. REDINGTON.

III
"THE HUE AND CRY"

The official description of himself read by Thomas Darcy M'Gee was more accurate and less intentionally insulting than the official descriptions of most of his colleagues compiled in Dublin Castle and published in the *Hue and Cry* of July 27th, 1848. Probably no other official document issued to the public in the last hundred years by Dublin Castle has equalled this stupid malignity. "Sketches of Doheny and some of the Confederate leaders, modelled upon the descriptions of burglars and murderers, that ordinarily adorn the *Hue and Cry* were," wrote Sir Charles Gavan Duffy, a generation later, "issued for the enjoyment of loyal persons." The *Freeman's Journal* of the day wrote that the public who were acquainted with the appearance of the gentlemen described will read with feelings of contempt the malignant effort to insult and wound the relatives of the men proscribed by the issue of a written caricature of their persons. This remarkable production of the genius and spirit of Dublin Castle, read as follows:—

DESCRIPTION OF PERSONS CHARGED WITH TREASONABLE PRACTICES

WILLIAM SMITH O'BRIEN.—No occupation; forty-six years of age; six feet in height; sandy hair; dark eyes; sallow, long face; has a sneering smile constantly on his face; full whiskers; sandy; a little grey; well-set man; walks erect; dresses well.

THOMAS FRANCIS MEAGHER.—No occupation; twenty-five years of age; five feet nine inches; dark, nearly black hair; light blue eyes; pale face; high cheekbones; peculiar expression about the eyes; cocked nose; no whiskers; well-dressed.

JOHN B. DILLON.—Barrister; thirty-two years of age; five feet eleven inches in height; dark hair; dark eyes; thin sallow face; rather thin black whiskers; dressed respectable; has bilious look.

MICHAEL DOHENY.—Barrister; forty years of age; five feet eight inches in height; fair or sandy hair; grey eyes; coarse red face like a man given to drink; high cheekbones; wants several of his teeth; very vulgar appearance; peculiar coarse unpleasant voice; dress respectable; small short red whiskers.

MICHAEL CREAN.—Shopman at a shoe-shop; thirty-five years of age; five feet eight inches; fair or sandy hair; grey eyes; full face; light whiskers; high fore-head; well-set person; dress, dark shooting frock or grey tweed, and grey tweed trousers.

FRANCIS MORGAN.[20]—Solicitor; forty-three years of age; five feet eight inches in height; very dark hair; dark eyes; sallow broad face;

nose a little cocked; the upper lip turns out when speaking; rather stout; smart gait; black whiskers.

PATRICK JAMES SMITH.[21]—Studying for the bar; twenty-nine years of age; five feet nine inches in height; fair hair; dark eyes; fair delicate face and of weak appearance; long back; weak in his walk; small whiskers; clothing indifferent.

JOHN HETHERINGTON DRUMM.[22]—Medical student; twenty years of age; five feet three inches in height; very black and curly hair; black eyes; pale delicate face; rather thin person; delicate appearance; no whiskers; small face and nose; dressed respectably; Methodist.

THOMAS D'ARCY M'GEE.—Connected with the *Nation* newspaper; twenty-three years of age; five feet three inches in height; black hair; dark face; delicate, pale, thin man; dresses generally black shooting coat, plaid trousers, light vest.

JOSEPH BRENNAN.—Sub-Editor of the *Felon* newspaper; five feet six inches in height; dark hair; dark eyes; pale, sallow face; very stout; round shoulders; Cork accent; no whiskers; hair on the upper lip; soft, sickly face; rather respectably dressed, a little reduced.

THOMAS DEVIN REILLY.—Sub-editor of the *Felon* newspaper; twenty-four years of age; five feet seven inches in height; sandy coarse hair; grey eyes; round freckled face; head remarkably broad at the top; broad shoulders; well-set; dresses well.

JOHN CANTWELL.—Shopman at a grocer's; thirty-five years of age; five feet ten inches in height; sandy hair; grey eyes; fair face; good looking; short whisker, light; rather slight person, dresses . . . Supposed a native of Dublin.

STEPHEN J. MEANY.—Sub-editor of *Irish Tribune*; twenty-six years of age; five feet eleven inches in height; dark hair; full blue eyes; dark face; small whiskers growing under the chin; smart appearance; was a constable of the C Division of Police, discharged for dirty habits; stout person; generally dressed in black.

RICHARD O'GORMAN, Junior.—Barrister; thirty years of age; five feet eleven inches in height; very dark hair; dark eyes; thin long face; large dark whiskers; well-made and active; walks upright; dresses black frock coat, tweed trousers.

FOOTNOTES:

16   After the merging of the Irish Confederation in the abortive Irish League, and the consequent dissolution of the Executive of the Confederation, a Council of Five was elected to direct the Confederate Clubs until the new organisation was perfected. The five elected were John Blake Dillon, Thomas Francis Meagher, Richard O'Gorman, Junior, Thomas D'Arcy M'Gee, and Thomas Devin Reilly. The five never met. O'Gorman was out of Dublin when the Habeas Corpus Act was suspended.

17   The Rev. Thresham Gregg was a notorious and blatant "anti-Popery" preacher of the period whom the wits of Young Ireland frequently made the butt of their jests. Apart from his bigoted sectarian obsession, he was, however, in several respects decidedly nationalistic, and steadily preached support of home trade and manufactures to his audiences. There can be no reasonable doubt that he recognised M'Gee. In this connection it may be stated that the Orangemen expelled from membership of their body Stephenson Dobbyn, an Orangeman who acted as a spy for Dublin Castle upon the Young Irelanders—drawing a clear and proper line between forcibly opposing their fellow countrymen and acting as spies for England upon them.

18   Hercules Street in Belfast, now swept away, was chiefly inhabited by butchers who were almost all Catholics and fervent O'Connellites. When the Young Irelanders attempted to hold a meeting in Belfast shortly after O'Connell's death, the butchers made a fierce attack upon them.

19   This narrative was written at the beginning of 1850

20   Law Agent to the Dublin Corporation.

21   Patrick Joseph Smyth

22   Sub-editor of the *Nation*; afterwards a clergyman.

CONTEMPORARIES MENTIONED IN "THE FELON'S TRACK"

ANGLESEY, LORD (1768-1854).—Henry William Paget, who lost a leg at Waterloo and erected a monument to its memory. Lord Lieutenant of Ireland, 1828-9, 1830-3.

ANTISELL, DR. THOMAS.—A Dublin surgeon and chemist of distinction, author of various pamphlets and addresses to the Royal Dublin Society on the geology of Ireland, reafforestation, and the sanitary conditions of Irish town-life. He supplied a large part of the capital to found the *Irish Tribune*. After the failure of the insurrection he went to the United States where he had a distinguished scientific career.

BANTRY, LORD.—(1801-1884) William Hare White, third earl, Lieut-Col, of the West Cork Artillery. The title became extinct in 1891.

BARRY, MICHAEL JOSEPH (1817-1889).—A Cork barrister, editor of "The Songs of Ireland" in the Library of Ireland, and author of several martial pieces, including "The Flag of Green." After the failure of the insurrection he renounced Nationalism and subsequently became a Dublin Police Magistrate.

BARRETT, RICHARD (17—-1855).—Brother of Eaton Stannard Barrett of Cork, the once famous author of "All the Talents." A journalist of fortune who changed sides with agility and enlisted under O'Connell in his latter years, having formerly vilified him.

BRENAN, JOSEPH (1828-1857).—The youngest of the Young Ireland leaders. Edited Fullam's *Irishman* in 1849 and unsuccessfully attempted to revive the insurrection in Waterford and Tipperary. On his failure he emigrated to the United States and died in New Orleans.

BRODERICK, CAPTAIN.—Inspector-General of Repeal Reading Rooms. He quitted Conciliation Hall after the death of O'Connell and died mentally afflicted.

BRYAN, MAJOR.—Of Raheny Lodge, Co. Dublin. Major Bryan acquired a moderate fortune in Tasmania and returned to Ireland where he joined the Repeal movement. He left Conciliation Hall with the Young Irelanders.

CAMPBELL, SIR JOHN (1779-1861).—Author of the "Lives of the Lord Chancellors." A Scots Tory politician, raised to the peerage subsequent to his connection with Ireland, and finally Lord Chancellor of England.

CANGLEY, DAVID (18—-1847).—A barrister and one of the hopes of Young Ireland. Ill-health pursued him through life and ended it prematurely.

CANTWELL, JAMES.—A Dublin mercantile assistant and, later, a restaurant-proprietor. One of the Council of the Confederation who supported Mitchel's policy.

CARLETON, WILLIAM (1794-1869).—Author of "Traits and Stories of the Irish Peasantry."

CAVAIGNAC, LOUIS EUGENE (1802-1857).—One of the most distinguished of the French Generals in the second quarter of the nineteenth century. On the establishment of the second Republic he was appointed Minister for War, and when the "Reds" threatened its stability he was invested with the dictatorship and speedily crushed the insurrection. In the contest for the Presidency the glamour of Louis Napoleon's name defeated Cavaignac. After Napoleon's *coup-d'etat* Cavaignac retired into private life. He had sympathies with Ireland, and in 1848 gave private assurances that in the event of an Irish insurrection winning initial successes, he would bring the influence of France to bear on England to force her to concede terms to Ireland.

CAVANAGH, JOHN.—President of the Fitzgerald Confederate Club, Harold's Cross, Dublin. Wounded at Ballingarry, he was brought to Kilkenny, where he was concealed and cured by Dr. Cane, and later smuggled to France, whence he proceeded to the United States, became an officer in the army and was slain in the Civil War.

"CHRISTABEL" (1815-1881).—Miss M'Carthy, of Kilfademore House, Kenmare, afterwards Mrs. Downing. A Popular poetess of the period, usually using the *nom-de-guerre* of "Christabel." Her best-known poem is "The Grave of MacCaura." She assisted Doheny and Stephens to escape.

CLARENDON, EARL OF (1804-1870).—George Villiers, the fourth earl, according to his English biographers, represented the highest type of English politician and English gentleman. Lord Lieutenant of Ireland, 1846-1852. He hired the editor of an obscene journal in Dublin to publish libels upon the moral character of the Young Irelanders, and conducted the affairs of the country from March to June, 1848, under this man's advice. He paid £3,400 for the services rendered and a demand for further payments led to a public disclosure of the facts. At the time Clarendon hired James Birch, Birch had completed a sentence of imprisonment for criminal libel.

CLEMENTS, EDWARD.—A barrister. One of O'Connell's "tail" in Conciliation Hall. The attempt of O'Connell to provide "poor Ned Clements" with a Government situation precipitated the rupture with Young Ireland.

CONWAY, M.G.—A journalist of ability and no principle who followed the path of fortune. He professed ultra-Catholic views while O'Connell was in the ascendant. After O'Connell's death he abjured Catholicism to ingratiate himself with the Ascendancy element.

CRAMPTON, JUDGE (17——1858).—Philip Crampton, called to the Bar 1810, Solicitor-General 1832, and raised to the Bench 1834. One of the judges at O'Connell's trial, a strong Tory but a clever lawyer.

CREAN, MICHAEL.—Like M.G. Conway, a Clare man, but of the opposite type. Crean worked in Dublin as a shopman and with Hollywood was one of the two trades-union leaders on the Council of the Confederation, where he opposed Mitchel's policy. After the failure of the insurrection he went to the United States.

CROLLY, DR. (1780-1849).—Archbishop of Armagh and Primate of All Ireland from 1835 until his death.

DAUNT, W.J. O'NEILL.—A Co. Cork gentleman, one of O'Connell's first Protestant supporters in the Repeal Movement. He was elected for Mallow, but unseated. He ceased to attend Conciliation Hall after the rupture with the Young Irelanders. Many years later he took a prominent part in the Home Rule movement.

DAVIS, THOMAS (1814-1845).—The founder and inspiration of the Young Ireland movement. Son of an English father of Welsh descent and an Irish mother. From the inception of *The Nation* newspaper until his death he was the chief writer of that journal.

DILLON, JOHN BLAKE (1816-1866).—The close personal friend of Thomas Davis and with him one of the founders of the *Nation*. On his return from exile he attempted to found an Irish Party in alliance with the British Radicals and sat in the British Parliament for Tipperary.

DOYLE, DANIEL.—A Limerick solicitor who acted with John O'Donnell and O'Gorman in inciting Limerick county to insurrection in July, 1848. After the failure he escaped across the water.

DUFFY, CHARLES GAVAN (1816-1903).—One of the three founders of the *Nation* and its editor from 1842 to 1854, when he left Ireland for Australia where he became Prime Minister of Victoria. In 1873 he received a knighthood.

"EVA" (1825-1910).—Miss Mary Kelly of Galway, afterwards Mrs. Kevin Izod O'Doherty. One of the chief poets of the *Nation*.

FERGUSON, SAMUEL (1810-1886).—A Belfast barrister and, save Edward Walsh, the most Gaelic of Irish poets in the English language. Ferguson took a leading part in the Protestant Repeal Association in

1848 and afterwards became one of the first of Irish archaeologists. In 1878 he was knighted.

FITZGERALD, JOHN LOYD.—Of Newcastle West, Limerick. A lawyer of high standing.

FITZSIMON, CHRISTOPHER.—Son-in-law of Daniel O'Connell, elected to the British Parliament for Co. Dublin. He deserted Repeal to support the Government and was rewarded with the post of Clerk of the Hanaper. His desertion caused the representation of the Co. Dublin to revert to the Unionists for half-a-century.

GRAY, SIR JOHN (1815-1875).—A medical doctor and owner of the *Freeman's Journal*, publicly supporting O'Connell, but personally in sympathy with Young Ireland. He sat in the British Parliament subsequently for Kilkenny and was an active member of the Dublin Corporation.

GRATTAN, HENRY, JUN.—Son of the great Grattan and member for Meath, 1831-52. An honest but weak politician.

GREY, EARL (1802-1894).—Third Earl. Colonial Secretary in the British Liberal Government, 1846 to 1852.

HALPIN, THOMAS M.—Secretary of the Confederation, and a Dublin working-man. According to Meagher he failed to transmit instructions to the Dublin Confederate Clubs to rise in insurrection in the streets of the capital when the fight opened in Tipperary. Halpin denied emphatically having received such orders. After the insurrection he made his way to the United States.

HEYTESBURY, LORD (1779-1860).—William A'Court, British Envoy in Spain and Naples, and Ambassador in Portugal and Russia. Lord Lieutenant of Ireland, 1844-6.

HOGAN, JOHN (1800-1858).—One of the greatest of modern sculptors. With MacManus and other artists he presented O'Connell with the "Repeal Cap," modelled on the Irish Crown.

HOLLYWOOD, EDWARD.—A silk-weaver and, with Michael Crean, an artisan leader. He acted as treasurer of the Davis Confederate

Club. Arrested in Wicklow with D'Arcy M'Gee for sedition, but the prosecution was abandoned. After the insurrection he escaped to France, and some years later returned to Dublin.

HOLMES, ROBERT (1765-1859).—Brother-in-law of Thomas Addis and Robert Emmet, and a vehement opponent of the Union in 1799-1800. He declined to accept promotion at the Bar while the Union endured.

HUDSON, WILLIAM ELIOT (1797-1853).—Described by Thomas Davis as the best man and the best Irishman he ever knew. A man of fortune and culture who devoted his leisure and his wealth to helping every movement for the betterment of Ireland.

HUME, JOSEPH (1777-1855).—An English politician who sat in the British Parliament for English, Irish, and Scotch constituencies as Tory and later as Radical. Chief author of the Radical shibboleth, "Peace, Retrenchment and Reform."

IRELAND, RICHARD.—A barrister, one of the founders of the Protestant Repeal Association in 1848. He emigrated to Australia afterwards and became Attorney-General of Victoria.

KENYON, FATHER (18—-1869).—Curate and afterwards Parish Priest of Templederry in Tipperary. A strong opponent of the "Old Irelanders" and the close political and personal friend of John Mitchel.

LALOR, JAMES FINTAN (1810-49).—Son of Patrick Lalor, M.P. of Queen's Co. A vigorous writer whose agrarian doctrine was converted by Henry George into Land Nationalisation—which it was not. He contributed to the *Nation* and the *Felon*, 1847-8, and attempted an insurrectionary conspiracy, 1849.

LAMARTINE, ALPHONSE DE (1790-1869).—Minister for Foreign Affairs in the French Republican Government. The British Ministry through Lord Normanby threatened him with the possible rupture of diplomatic relations if he gave an encouraging reply to the Young Ireland deputation. Politically Lamartine was more of the school of the British Whigs of his period than of any native French school. His high character and literary abilities were held in deserved esteem by his countrymen, but as a man of affairs he was never really successful.

LANE, DENNY (1818-95).—A Cork commercial man who identified himself prominently with the Young Ireland cause in Munster. Author of "Carrigdhoun" and some other popular ballads.

LAWLESS, HON. CECIL.—Son of Lord Cloncurry. An O'Connellite Repealer and somewhat virulent opponent of the Young Irelanders who nicknamed him "Artful Cecil."

LEDRU-ROLLIN, ALEXANDRE (1808-74).—Minister of the Interior in the French Republican Government of 1848. He was connected with Ireland by marriage and strongly sympathised with its people.

LEFROY, BARON (1776-1869).—One-time member for Trinity College in the British Parliament. Subsequent to 1848 promoted Lord Chief Justice of the Queen's Bench, and although he became incapable of discharging the office he refused to resign it until he had passed his ninetieth year.

LEYNE, MAURICE RICHARD (1820-1854).—The only member of the O'Connell family who identified himself with Young Ireland. He was an occasional contributor to the *Nation* from 1844 to 1848 and in June of that year, on the eve of the insurrection, formally joined Young Ireland. On the revival of the *Nation* in 1849 he joined Duffy in its editorship.

LOUIS NAPOLEON (1808-1873).—Son of the King of Holland, nephew of the great Napoleon, President of the second Republic and, after the *coup d'etat* and the plebescite, Emperor of France. Napoleon while in exile manifested some sympathy with Ireland, and as a member of the French Republic was, like Cavaignac, willing to intervene on this country's behalf with England if the Young Irelanders had succeeded in winning initial engagements against the British forces in the field.

Louis Napoleon (1848)

MACHALE, ARCHBISHOP (1791-1881).—"John of Tuam"—the greatest of the Irish prelates of his time. He was in partial sympathy with the Young Irelanders, but opposed to them on several educational questions.

MACNEVIN, THOMAS (1810-1848).—A leading Young Irelander and college friend of Davis. Author, in the Library of Ireland, of "The Confiscation of Ulster" and "The History of the Volunteers."

MACMANUS, TERENCE BELLEW (1823-60).—A prosperous Irish merchant in Liverpool who relinquished his prosperity to join in the insurrection. He escaped from the British penal colonies to the United States and died there in poor circumstances.

MACLISE, DANIEL (1806-1870).—One of the first painters of his time. He refused the presidency of the British Royal Academy.

M'CARTHY, DENIS FLORENCE (1817-1882).—One of the chief poets of the *Nation*, afterwards Professor of English Literature in the Catholic University.

M'GEE, THOMAS DARCY (1825-1868).—Son of a coast-guard at Carlingford, Louth. M'Gee between the ages of seventeen and twenty won a remarkable reputation as a journalist in the United States and came back to Ireland to take up the editorship of the *Freeman's Journal*, which he relinquished to join the *Nation* staff. After the failure in 1848 Bishop Maginn procured his escape to America disguised as a priest. M'Gee, Devin Reilly and Doheny quarrelled in the United States, and M'Gee's political views gradually modified. He proceeded to Canada, entered politics, and became one of the first statesmen of the dominion and a member of the Government. In that position he was continually attacked by a section of the Irish as a renegade, and the bitterness of his replies inflamed feeling. In April, 1868, he was assassinated by an alleged Fenian. Local and sectional political hatreds appear, however, to have had more to do with the murder of M'Gee than his virulent denunciations of the Fenians.

MAGINN, EDWARD, D.D. (1802-1849).—Son of a farmer at Fintona, Tyrone, Dr. Maginn entered the Church and speedily became noted for his vigour of intellect and strength of character. In 1845 he was appointed coadjutor-Bishop of Derry, and created Bishop of Ortosia in the Archbishopric of Tyre. A strong advocate of Repeal and tenant-right, he gradually attorned to the Young Irelanders when he discovered that the Whig Government had bought up Conciliation Hall. In 1848 he sent Sir John Gray to Gavan Duffy offering to take the field at the head of the priests of his diocese if the insurrection were held back until the harvest had been reaped. The sudden suspension of the

Habeas Corpus Act, however, forced the Young Irelanders' hands two months too soon.

MANGAN, JAMES CLARENCE (1803-49).—The first of the poets of the Young Ireland period. He declined to write for any but the Irish public, and died in poverty.

MARTIN, JOHN (1812-1875).—A landed proprietor of Co. Down. On his return from transportation, he re-entered Irish politics; was elected in 1870 to the British Parliament, for Meath, and played a leading part in founding the Home Rule movement.

"MARY" (1828-69).—With "Eva" and "Speranza" one of the triumvirate of the women-poets of the *Nation*: Miss Ellen Mary Downing of Cork—afterwards a nun, Sister Mary Alphonsus.

MEAGHER, THOMAS FRANCIS (1823-67).—Son of the O'Connellite member of the British Parliament for Waterford. He escaped from the British Penal colonies to the United States in 1852 and served as Brigadier-General on the Federal side during the civil war. When Acting-Governor of Montana he was drowned in the Mississippi.

MEANY, STEPHEN JOSEPH.—A journalist, imprisoned in 1848 under the Habeas Corpus Suspension Act. In the United States he became a leader of one of the wings of the Fenian Brotherhood and, returning to Ireland in 1866, he was arrested on the way in London and sentenced to a term of penal servitude.

MELBOURNE, LORD (1779-1848).—William Lamb, second Viscount, Chief Secretary of Ireland, 1827-8, and Premier of England with brief intervals from 1834 to 1841.

MILEY, JOHN, D.D. (1805-1861).—Curate at the Catholic Pro-Cathedral, Dublin, and private chaplain to O'Connell. He was the intermediary in arranging the reunion of the O'Connellites with the Young Irelanders in the stillborn Irish League. In 1849 he was made Rector of the Irish College at Paris. On his return to Ireland he was appointed parish priest of Bray. He was an eloquent preacher, and author of several works on the Papacy.

MITCHEL, JOHN (1818-75).—A solicitor of Banbridge, and one of the first Irish Protestants of note to join the Repeal Association. From the death of Davis until the end of 1847 he was the chief writer of the *Nation* newspaper. On his escape from the British penal colonies in 1853 he settled in the United States, and took an active part on the Confederate side in the civil war. He returned to Ireland a few months before his death, and was elected member of the British Parliament for Tipperary, as a demonstration of hostility to British Government in Ireland.

MOORE, JUDGE.—Richard Moore, called to the Bar in 1807, acted for the defence in the trial of O'Connell and the Traversers, Liberal Attorney-General in 1846 and "almost Lord Chancellor." He was raised to the Bench in 1847 and died in 1858.

MONAHAN, JAMES HENRY (1804-78).—Attorney-General in 1848, Chief-Justice of the Common Pleas, 1850.

NAGLE, DR.—"A Dublin doctor without patients," who acted as a handyman for John O'Connell. He was devoid of ability. Subsequently he received a small Government post.

O'CONNELL, DANIEL (1775-1847).—Successor to John Keogh in the leadership of the Irish Catholics, and although his actual achievements were not so much greater than those of Keogh and Sweetman, their brilliancy threw the fame of his predecessors into the shade, where it still rests.

O'CONNELL, MAURICE (1802-53).—Eldest son of Daniel O'Connell, and a member of the British Parliament. He was the cleverest and most national of O'Connell's children.

O'CONNELL, MORGAN JOHN (1804-85).—Second son to Daniel O'Connell. He served under General Devereux in South America, entered the British Parliament as a Repealer, deserted Repeal, and was appointed Assistant-Registrar of Deeds.

O'CONNELL, JOHN (1810-1858).—The chief political assistant of his father, Daniel O'Connell. After the collapse of the Repeal Association he received a place from the British Government.

O'CONNELL, DANIEL, JUN. (1815-1897).—The youngest of O'Connell's sons. He sat in the British Parliament until 1863, when he was appointed to a Government post.

O'CONOR DON, THE (1794-1847).—Repeal M.P. for Roscommon. He deserted to the Liberals, and was made a Lord of the Treasury.

O'DEA, PATRICK.—The Young Ireland leader in Rathkeale, Co. Limerick.

O'DOHERTY, KEVIN IZOD (1823-1895).—Son of a Dublin solicitor. After his release from transportation he settled in Australia and became prominent in its politics and medical science. In 1885 he returned temporarily to Ireland, and sat for a brief period in the British Parliament as Parnellite member for Meath.

O'DONNELL, JOHN.—A Limerick solicitor and an ardent Young Irelander. When Richard O'Gorman came to Limerick to urge the people to arms, O'Donnell travelled through the county with him as his aide-de-camp. On the news of the outbreak in Tipperary, O'Donnell, Doyle and Daniel Harnett raised the country around Abbeyfeale, cut off the mails and pitched an insurgent camp outside the town where the Abbeyfeale men waited for O'Gorman, who was elsewhere in the county, to take command. Before his arrival the news of the collapse at Ballingarry arrived and the Abbeyfeale Camp broke up. O'Donnell escaped from the country with O'Gorman.

O'DOWD, JAMES.—A Conciliation Hall lawyer. Afterwards appointed to a legal position in connection with the London Custom house.

O'DWYER, CAREW.—Repeal M.P. for Louth, 1832-5. He deserted Repeal and received a minor position in the Exchequer Court.

O'FLAHERTY, MARTIN.—A Galway solicitor and a member of the Irish Confederation.

O'GORMAN, RICHARD, JUN. (1826-1895).—Son of Richard O'Gorman of the Woollen Hall, one of the foremost Dublin merchants and Catholic leaders in the Emancipation struggle. O'Gorman settled in New York after his escape and became a judge of the Superior Court.

O'HEA, JAMES.—A lawyer described by Davis as of "vast abilities."

O'LOGHLEN, SIR COLMAN (1819-1877).—Second baronet, son of the Master of the Rolls. Afterwards M.P. for Clare, a Privy Councillor and Judge-Advocate-General.

O'MAHONY, JOHN (1816-1877).—A gentleman-farmer of ancient lineage and high scholarship. After the second attempt to kindle insurrection he fled to the Continent and later proceeded to the United States, where with Doheny and Stephens he founded Fenianism.

PEEL, SIR ROBERT (1788-1850).—Chief Secretary for Ireland and organiser of the "new police"—hence "peelers." In politics an opportunist, opposing and supporting Catholic Emancipation and Free Trade. Premier of England, 1834-5, 1841-6.

PENNEFATHER, BARON (1773-1859).—Chief Baron of the Irish Exchequer, 1821, and for thirty-eight years a judge.

PIGOT, CHIEF BARON (1797-1872).—Son of Dr. Pigot of Mallow and one of the founders of the attempted National Whig Party in the period 1820-30. He was a cultured man and an upright judge.

PIGOT, JOHN E. (1822-1871).—Eldest son of Chief Baron Pigot and the intimate comrade of Thomas Davis. Author of many ballads and articles in the *Nation* and other National journals, and an ardent collector of Irish music.

PLUNKET, LORD (1764-1854).—William Conyngham Plunket, member for Charlemont in the Irish Parliament and a bitter opponent of the Union. Lord Chancellor of Ireland from 1830 to 1841.

RAY, THOMAS MATTHEW (1801-1881).—A Dublin trades-union leader of great organising ability, appointed by O'Connell secretary of the Repeal Association. Subsequently Assistant-Registrar of Deeds.

REILLY, THOMAS DEVIN (1823-1854).—One of the *Nation* staff and one of the few leading Young Irelanders who supported Mitchel on the division in the Confederation in 1848. In the United States he won a foremost position as a political writer.

REYNOLDS, JOHN.—An Alderman of the Dublin Corporation and M.P. for Dublin City in the British Parliament, 1847-52. Subsequently Lord Mayor. He was utterly corrupt and a mob-leader.

ROEBUCK, J.A. (1801-79).—An English politician who professed Independent views, and from the violence of his denunciation of his opponents was nicknamed "Tear 'em."

RUSSELL, LORD JOHN (1792-1878).—Liberal Prime Minister of England, 1846-52, and again, 1865. He successfully opposed Lord George Bentinck's proposal to preserve the Irish from famine and pauperism by undertaking the construction of railways.

SAVAGE, JOHN (1828-1888).—One of the founders of the *Irish Tribune*. After the complete failure of the insurrection, he escaped to the United States where he became eminent in literature and for a time head of the Fenian movement.

SHEIL, RICHARD LALOR (1791-1851).—Dramatist, orator and politician. Deserted Repeal and was made British minister at Florence. Subsequently Master of the Mint.

SHIELDS, JAMES, GENERAL (1807-1879).—Born near Dungannon, Shields emigrated in early life to the United States, where he attained distinction in journalism and subsequently celebrity as a lawyer. On the outbreak of war with Mexico, he forsook the Bar for arms, and as a soldier acquired even higher renown. In 1848 he was chosen as governor of Oregon, and was considered one of the ablest of the United States Generals. His political views being in sympathy with the Young Irelanders, several of them looked towards Shields as another Eoghan Ruadh, who would accept the call of his country and return to lead the Irish once they had taken the field. Subsequently Shields engaged in the Civil War on the Northern side, and, although a comparatively old man, distinguished himself by defeating General Stonewall Jackson at the Battle of Winchester, although his army was inferior in numbers and he had been wounded at the opening of the fight.

SMYTH, P.J. (1826-1885).—One of the youngest of the Young Ireland leaders. He escaped from Ireland to the United States after the collapse of the insurrection, and carried out the rescue of Mitchel from Van Diemen's Land. On his return to Ireland he re-entered politics, and sat in the British Parliament successively for Westmeath and Tipperary.

STANLEY, LORD (1802-1869).—Secretary for Foreign Affairs in the British Liberal Government, 1846-52.

STAUNTON, MICHAEL.—Proprietor of the *Morning Register* newspaper and an alderman of the Dublin Corporation. His memory survives as the involuntary agent of bringing Duffy and Davis together—and thus leading to the foundation of *The Nation*.

STEPHENS, JAMES (1825-1901).—A Kilkenny railway employe. Afterwards chief organiser of the Fenian movement, of which, with O'Mahony and Doheny, he was one of the founders.

TORRENS, JUDGE.—Called to the Bar, 1798, raised to the Bench, 1823, where he sat for thirty-three years.

WILDE, SIR THOMAS (1782-1855).—Lord Truro, Attorney-General to the British Liberal Government in England, 1846; afterwards Chief Justice of the Common Pleas and Lord Chancellor of England, 1850-2.

WILLIAMS, RICHARD DALTON (1822-1862).—One of the most popular of the poets of the *Nation*. The Government prosecution failed in his case, and he emigrated to the United States where he became Professor of Belles Lettres in the University of Mobile.

WYSE, SIR THOMAS (1791-1862).—One of O'Connell's lieutenants in the Catholic Association, of which he wrote a history. He declined to support Repeal, but favoured what is now known as Federal Home Rule, served as a Lord of the Treasury in Melbourne's administration, and afterwards for many years as British minister at Athens. He was a man of superior character to the ordinary type of place-seekers, and his writings won him a temporary European reputation.

General Cavaignac (1848),

Ledru-Rollin (1848),

Lamartine (1848)

Ingram Content Group UK Ltd.
Milton Keynes UK
UKHW022301260623
424090UK00005B/235

9 781015 899988

.